SHAKESPEARE, THEORY, AND PERFORMANCE

Shakespeare, Theory, and Performance is a groundbreaking collection of essays which brings a full range of contemporary critical perspectives to bear upon the practical questions of performing Shakespeare.

Contributors from theatre and Shakespearean studies come together to offer a fascinating overview of the productive interplay between cultural materialism, theatre semiotics, feminism, deconstruction, and performance criticism.

Among the issues considered are:

- textual indeterminacy and the contingencies of performance
- implications of gender, race, and class for audience response
- reading the actor's body as a site of cultural inscription
- postcolonial strategies for performing the "hegemonic" Shakespeare
- the impact of technology on the study of performance as text.

Shakespeare, Theory, and Performance constitutes an exciting development within the expanding field of Shakespearean performance studies. It will be of particular interest to students and teachers of theatre, Renaissance literature, and literary theory.

James C. Bulman is Dean of the College and Professor of English at Allegheny College, Pennsylvania. He is general editor of Manchester's "Shakespeare in Performance" series and is currently preparing a new edition of *Henry IV, Part Two* for the Arden Shakespeare series.

SHAKESPEARE, THEORY, AND PERFORMANCE

Edited by
James C. Bulman

London and New York

First published 1996
by Routledge
11 New Fetter Lane, London EC4P 4EE

Simultaneously published in the USA and Canada
by Routledge
29 West 35th Street, New York, NY 10001

Typeset in Baskerville by LaserScript, Mitcham, Surrey
Printed and bound in Great Britain by
Biddles Ltd, Guildford and King's Lynn

British Library Cataloguing in Publication Data
A catalogue record for this book is available from the British Library

Library of Congress Cataloguing in Publication Data
A catalogue record for this book has been requested

ISBN 0–415–11625–2
0–415–11626–0 (pbk)

CONTENTS

1

INTRODUCTION

Shakespeare and performance theory

James C. Bulman

Ever since John Styan coined the phrase "the Shakespeare revolution" twenty years ago to characterize the emergence of stage-centered criticism from traditional literary study, critics have wrestled with the idea that Shakespeare wrote *playscripts* whose potentials are best realized in performance. For Styan, this revolution involved an attempt to recover the authenticity of the original "Shakespeare experience" (5) by a study of modern performance practices: it forged a link between theatre history and the imaginative recreation of dramatic texts.[1] Nevertheless, like others of his generation, Styan was a card-carrying essentialist. He subscribed to the notion that Shakespeare's texts are stable and authoritative, that meaning is immanent in them, and that actors and directors are therefore *interpreters* rather than *makers* of meaning. He believed, too, that audience responses to the plays are not historically particular, but universal. What *The Shakespeare Revolution* failed to take into account was the radical contingency of performance – the unpredictable, often playful intersection of history, material conditions, social contexts, and reception that destabilizes Shakespeare and makes theatrical meaning a participatory act. This volume marks how far we have come since the revolution.

In his opening essay, W. B. Worthen identifies in Styan's totalizing concept of Shakespeare – as author and text – a refusal to address the question of how our acts of representation are implicated in the dynamics of contemporary culture and in themselves acquire meaning. Drawing on Foucault and Barthes, Worthen argues that allegiance to the author-function blinds us to other determinants of performance that give us today's multiple "Shakespeares." In fact, recent work in theatre semiotics has altered our very notion of what constitutes a text. No longer simply a literary artifact, the *performance* text, in the words of Marco De Marinis, "is conceived of as a complex network of different types of signs, expressive means, or actions, coming back to the etymology of the word 'text' which implies the idea of texture, of something woven together" (100).[2] The literary or *dramatic* text, furthermore, which is but one element of the performance text, is itself subject to historical inscription, the result of a process Patrice Pavis calls its concretization, wherein "signifier (literary work as thing), signified (aesthetic object), and Social Context . . . are variables . . . which can be more or less reconstructed" (27). This idea of text as process, as an interweaving of variable elements, reflects a post-modern desire to replace the logocentric idea of theatre with one in which performance becomes the site of cultural and aesthetic contestation – not merely, as it was for critics of Styan's generation, "an incidental transcription, representation and explanation" of the literary text (Pavis 32).[3]

The relationship between a dramatic text and its performance, therefore, is neither simple nor oppositional. It has been further complicated by the work of textual bibliographers such as Michael Warren and Gary Taylor, who have demonstrated that Shakespeare's plays exist as multiple texts whose variations may be accounted for in part by alterations made for, or during, performance.[4] As Laurie E. Osborne suggests in her essay for this volume, Shakespeare left no originary text – no perfect, authorially sanctioned script – for performance. Even the Folio texts are, in a sense, copies, based on promptbooks or quartos or foul papers, and mediated by scribes and compositors. The much-maligned performance editions so popular in the eighteenth and nineteenth centuries are in many ways heir to the Folio, because they too record performance choices made in the theatre and, in so doing, inscribe the ideological pressures of their particular historical moment. By focusing attention on Shakespeare's plays as sites of ongoing reproduction, these editions reveal, in Osborne's words, "the global set of material practices which establish a particular play's currency as a work" (180).[5]

That a single play may have multiple material existences has been made abundantly clear by the access to performance afforded by the technologies of film and video. The ready availability of Shakespeare in these media has encouraged readers to become viewers, and thereby to recognize performative elements that would have been denied them in the study. In a sense, film and video have become today's performance texts. Film is a medium which has a peculiar power to subvert "authoritative" Shakespeare: especially as exemplified by Peter Greenaway in *Prospero's Books* or Derek Jarman in his *Tempest*, it can use visual and performance techniques to subvert theatrical tradition and deconstruct the dramatic text. But as Douglas Lanier observes in his concluding essay, technology has paradoxically revivified the idea of the author-function and the sway that Shakespeare's "book" – the monumental literary text – has held over performance studies. Because film and video allow us repeated viewings of a single performance, they encourage us to assimilate that performance to the condition of a literary text – a stable artifact rather than a contingent, ephemeral experience. Our challenge, therefore, is to discover how *not* to replace the old textuality with a new form of performance textuality which may be "read", Lanier warns, according to the interpretive protocols of close reading and with similar assumptions about textual monumentality (202). Such readings of video as text, increasingly common in the academy, risk an elision of the very historical and material contingencies which the return to performance has sought to recover.

* * *

This focus on "reading" a performance is indicative of how, in the past twenty years, Shakespearean performance criticism has emerged from literary theory. Long dismissed as old-fashioned and anecdotal, ancillary to "real" criticism and worthy of only a page or two in major editions of the plays, stage history (as it used to be called) has attached itself to new forms of theoretical discourse and as a result has tended to view productions through a literary lens – feminist, psychoanalytic, cultural materialist, deconstructive. For doing so, it has earned the disapproval of those who believe that stage-centered criticism unnecessarily limits the free play of imagination which readers of Shakespeare's plays as *literature* should enjoy. Harry Berger, Jr., for example, wryly labels performance critics "proponents of the New Histrionicism" who "argue that reading is irresponsible unless it imitates playgoing." Their argument, he suggests, "establishes the empirical experience and psychology of playgoing as the exemplar whose privileges and constraints are to be reproduced in armchair interpretation" – a prioritization he calls "inadequate and invidious" (xii, xiv).[6]

The empirical experience and psychology of playgoing, however, are precisely what performance critics in recent years have been interrogating. Wary of the unexamined response to performance that leads to totalizing discourses, they have begun to historicize the practices of performance criticism and to discover how their own literary and cultural conditioning have shaped the way they see, and write about, performance. In other words, they have begun to investigate the role of reception. Those concerned with recuperating historical performances now turn their attention to the ways in which reviewers – sources of supposedly reliable evidence – in fact construct narratives which foreground their own cultural perspectives, thereby creating fictions that pass, or once passed, for objective reporting.[7] In her essay for this volume, Juliet Dusinberre explores how performances of *Antony and Cleopatra* since Victorian times have inscribed cultural attitudes towards women in power, and how male reviewers have focused inquiry on the actress playing Cleopatra as "the principal signifier of the anxieties and obsessions, pleasurable and less pleasurable, which dominate the audience who watches her" (60).

In any criticism of performance, it must be recognized, we are bound by the perspectives of our own time and place. Indeed, as theorists are quick to point out, traditional assumptions about universality and continuity in the performance history of Shakespeare's plays are themselves cultural constructs. Yet this challenge to the universalizing impulse of traditional stage history – this insistence on seeing cultural pressures and material conditions as constitutive – is itself problematic, for those who issue the challenge are not of one mind about how performance criticism should be practiced. Some claim to be disinterestedly historical in their approach; others are avowedly ideological.[8] Historicists attempt to recreate authentic contexts for performances of a given play and thereby to gauge what the play has signified for its audiences at different times and in different cultures: in other words, they use performance history to discover what, and how, meanings are produced. Ideological critics, on the other hand, tend to delineate interpretive options independent of performance history: their "reading" of performance is thus less empirical and more politically invested than that of historicists.

The historicists' attempt to contextualize performance might at first seem to be a more disinterested critical activity; but in fact, their ideological perspectives are often visible behind the discursive practices that mask them. Dusinberre's findings about modern productions of *Antony and Cleopatra*, for instance, clearly are informed by a feminist interest in power relations and gender transference. Furthermore, any attempt to generalize about audience response to a given performance is suspect; for just as an author may envisage a community of readers but have no control over their individual responses, so, at a performance of a play, the cultural pressures that have helped to shape the production cannot guarantee that each member of the audience will experience the play in the same way.[9] Critics who rely on traditional research tools to reconstruct a performance – theatre reviews and programs, eye-witness accounts (their own or others'), promptbooks and directors' notes – frequently succumb to the temptation to generalize about its meaning for an audience.

The impulse to universalize audience response stands at odds with the insistence on contextual particularity which governs the poststructuralist approach to performance history. This is an understandable contradiction, for by such universalizing critics validate their own conclusions about a performance's cultural significance: they create the audience for whom the performance is said to have had a particular meaning and thereby bring a complex negotiation between performance and audience to closure when, in fact, it is as difficult to construct a stable community of interpreters as it is to generalize about their responses. In a recent book, Marvin Carlson complains that performance critics have largely ignored work by reception theorists – Iser, Jauss, Eco, Bennett – which could help to explain "the means and mechanisms whereby all texts . . . may be 'productively activated' during what is traditionally, and inadequately, thought of as the process of their consumption or reception" (Bennett 214). Very little attention has been paid to the contribution of the audience to this process, Carlson laments, and still less to the factors which contribute to the formation of their "reading" of performance (86).

Barbara Hodgdon is a notable exception. In various essays she has tested the applicability of reception theory to audience response, and especially how such response is informed, if not fully determined, by disparate conceptions of gender, ethnicity, race, and class. She considers the performance text as an event constituted by the concrete conditions of its spectators; for, she writes, "it is in the 'discursively saturated materiality' of the historical circumstances in which a performance is seen that it makes its demands for narrative intelligibility" (69). In her essay for this volume, she considers the problem of reception posed by an intercultural – and culturally confrontational – production of *A Midsummer Night's Dream* at the National Theatre in London. Alert to her own subject position as an historically mediated reader – as "other" in an audience characterized by significant cultural homogeneity, and as a woman in a field dominated by men – she interrogates the processes by which a performance achieves meaning(s) for spectators in a specific sociohistoric moment. Hodgdon recognizes the inevitable variability of reception, and that recognition releases performance from the grip of totalizing discourses.

The effort to contextualize the discourses we use to discuss performance has lately taken aim at the Shakespeare revolution itself. The "revolutionaries" of stage-centered criticism have become the new establishment, and their sacred cows are under fire: John Russell Brown's myth of a free access to Shakespeare, unencumbered by directorial intervention; Styan's belief that the modern stage has recovered Elizabethan performance practices. Cary M. Mazer, in his present essay, historicizes as "the great creation myth of its era" (151) the standard account of how twentieth-century directors, beginning with William Poel and culminating with Peter Brook, re-discovered the use of non-illusionistic acting space as the means to recuperate the authentic Shakespeare. Taking the highly regarded work of Alan Dessen as his test case, Mazer argues that the past generation's understanding of Elizabethan stage semiotics was not in fact historical, but grounded in the formalist assumptions of literary criticism in the 1960s and 1970s, when Shakespeare's plays were regarded as poems whose patterns of imagery, both verbal and theatrical, were woven into an organic whole by the "unitary artistic authority" of the playwright. The search for unifying patterns in action, staging, and gesture during this period strongly influenced productions by the Royal Shakespeare Company, which themselves helped to shape Dessen's conception of stage semiotics and his presumed discovery of a "neo-Elizabethan habit of mind" (Dessen 29). And so the wheel comes full circle: we reconfigure the Elizabethans as ourselves.

* * *

Poststructuralist theory, therefore, has liberated us to discover in performance contingencies more radically destabilizing than anything known to literary critics. The material conditions of performance, the dynamics of audience response, the possibility of error latent in live performance, and above all the physical presence of the actors themselves, all contribute to making performance criticism more tentative – and more precarious – than other forms of criticism. At the center of such precariousness is the actor's body. Long relegated to the margins of stage history, the body now occupies a dominant position, where indeed, in performance, it must. Literary critics read the body as a multivalent signifier; but when that body appears on a stage, its signification is made flesh. Feminist theorists, who have taught us to see the body as the object of the male gaze, have been particularly instrumental in defining ways in which actors bear cultural inscription.[10] On the Elizabethan stage, where boys played women's roles, audiences apparently were willing to construct the male body to signify something it wasn't: the biologically male body of the boy, according to Dusinberre, was erased by the performative energy of the theatrical experience (57). But when, after the Restoration, actresses began to play those roles that were not actually written for women, their bodies signified very different things to an audience, introducing a sexual dynamic and an intense focus on female physicality which would not have been available to Elizabethan audiences.

Performance critics often view the actor's body as a site of complex cultural negotiation. Such negotiation involves the actor's peculiar and historically marginalized role within bourgeois society, the character he or she impersonates, and the actor's age, gender, and race. Anthony B. Dawson, however, argues that an audience's experience of that body on the stage confounds critical claims about the actor's power of cultural signification. In an essay finely tuned to the rhetorical force of theatrical representation, he suggests that theorists fail to consider the affective power of the body, its present *bodiliness*, its capacity to arouse an audience's passions – the physical and emotive force of acting that resists inscription – which is part of the pleasure we derive from live performance. "The theatre," writes Dawson, "by concentrating on the body, may limit its power as a discursive practice – but this limitation may paradoxically free it, shifting the ground to focus on the power to move audiences and hence to incite who knows what kind of passionate participation" (42). The actor's body cannot be bound by the neat encodings of materialist theory; and this, perhaps, is the ultimate contingency of performance.

This focus on the actor raises the issue of representation, and in particular the tendency among critics and actors alike to *naturalize* assumptions about the relationship between actor and role. Actors, according to Worthen, essentialize the process of preparing for a role: in searching for the correct interpretation of a role, they cede authority to "Shakespeare." Their training conditions them to do so. Richard Paul Knowles likens training manuals of the past two decades – those that have gained legitimacy by recording the techniques employed by major British and North American theatre companies – to the work on neo-Elizabethan stage practices interrogated by Mazer. Such manuals, by teaching actors to "free" the "natural" voice so that Shakespeare may speak through it, reify the controlling agency of the playwright, much as performing his plays in an "empty space" is said to allow contemporary audiences a "direct access to Shakespeare's transcendental intentions that has been unavailable since the seventeenth century" (Knowles 120). The idea that an actor serves merely as a conduit for Shakespeare's voice – much like a ventriloquist's dummy – is analogous to the belief that there is immanent meaning in his texts which productions should try to discover, the belief that Shakespeare can "speak for himself" with transcultural authority. As Denis Salter points out, such beliefs are particularly problematic for actors in postcolonial societies. For them, "Shakespeare's texts often function as foreign objects that articulate imperialistic values of domination" (114). Unfamiliar, densely encoded, and authored elsewhere, these texts would seem to invite resistance in the form of "unnatural" – that is, unregulated and potentially dissident – modes of performance. Those postcolonial actors and directors who seek to replicate the hegemonic practices of British theatre, therefore, and especially of the Royal Shakespeare Company, do so at the expense of their own cultural identity. The sheer weight of tradition leaves them unable to make Shakespeare their own.

In recent years, however, theatre companies have challenged this hegemony by forcing the issue of "naturalized" representation. Multicultural casting, experimentation with non-Western styles of acting, and the introduction of alternative cultural values in *mises en scène* have begun to shake the imperial foundations of British theatrical tradition. Multicultural casting in particular has raised the problem of signification – and the audience's awareness of it – by drawing attention to the disparity between *what* is being represented and *who* represents it. As playfully as cross-gender casting did for the Elizabethans, multicultural casting disrupts our identification of the actor with the role. In her discussion of Robert Lepage's *Midsummer Night's Dream*, Hodgdon demonstrates how even on British soil, and in a state-subsidized theatre, a postcolonial director could use a troupe of racially and ethnically diverse actors to foreground cultural difference and to prioritize movement over language. Lepage's actors spoke Shakespeare's English as foreigners, in accents yet unknown – a heresy that undermined belief in an authorized, and therefore "natural," representational mode of performing Shakespeare.

The endpoint of this trend would be to deny Shakespeare his language altogether, to liberate performance from the text; and this is the topic Dennis Kennedy tackles in his essay on foreign – by which he means non-anglophonic – productions of Shakespeare.[11] The very act of translation subverts the authority of Shakespeare's text; and in the past twenty years, the option to translate Shakespeare afresh for each new production has enabled directors such as Mnouchkine, Ninagawa, and Zadek to explore the plays more freely, to focus more imaginatively on visual elements of performance – on physical over verbal expression – than their British and North American counterparts. The Shakespearean text continues to exert a tyranny over native speakers that non-English speakers do not feel; for unlike anglophonic playwrights who, in modernizing a Shakespeare text, are called (at best) adapters or (at worst) butchers, foreign translators, who of necessity produce a new text, are still said to be writing "Shakespeare." As Pavis observes, translators in effect adapt the classical text to the current situation of enunciation (140–1): translation does ideological, ethnological, and cultural work that can only be achieved extralinguistically in productions which remain "faithful" to the authorized text. In England and North America, this preoccupation with textual fidelity has inhibited theatrical experimentation and led to the preservation of old techniques, old methods, old effects – what Peter Brook ruefully calls "deadly" Shakespeare. Only slowly are directors in the English-speaking world learning to appropriate "foreign" theatrical styles which, though they may at first seem alien to the received inflections of Shakespeare's language, in fact revitalize the plays for contemporary audiences.

The freedom to translate Shakespeare into an intercultural idiom – to yoke "divergent cultural materials and identities into pastiche, collage, and bricolage" in opposition to "the grand literary and theatrical narratives that would draw national and cultural boundaries around 'Shakespeare'" (Hodgdon 81) – is resulting in more playfully eclectic productions in touch with a ludic sensibility which museum-like productions of Shakespeare have lost. Analogously, poststructuralist theory is liberating performance critics to act in a similar way: they delight in finding no fixed authority to which the theatre may appeal and revel in the *jouissance* of their own subjectivity. Insisting on the indeterminacy of meaning and on the radical contingencies which affect performance, critics themselves become performers who, in their acts of translation, play at constructing "Shakespeare." This critical self-consciousness sharply divides them from their forebears in the Shakespeare revolution.

The revolution Styan announced a generation ago is, in a sense, still in progress; for in the intervening years, a second and more fundamental revolution in critical theory occurred which caused critics to redraw the boundaries over which battles are fought. How has theory redrawn the boundaries of performance criticism? Above all, it has challenged traditional assumptions about textual authority and the production of meaning. It has interrogated the nature of the evidence we use to reconstruct performances and to assess audience response. It has raised questions about representation, made problematic the status of the actor's body, and alerted us to ways in which performances of Shakespeare may reproduce established aesthetic and political formations or serve as sites of cultural contestation. It has even forced us to come to terms with a "Shakespeare" who can exist without his language. By addressing such issues, the essays in this volume take arms against the theoretical presuppositions of the previous generation of performance critics. *The Shakespeare Revolution* – the document which twenty years ago proclaimed a new role for stage-centered criticism – has become today's orthodoxy, with which our heterodox theories now struggle for the right to speak.

NOTES

1 Roach, in a survey of theatre history and historiography, discusses how traditional theatre studies separated the study of historical documents – the "scientific" data from which conditions of historic performances could be reconstructed – from the study of dramatic literature, "the supposed domain of the subjective imagination" (Reinelt and Roach 294). Styan's work draws the two discourses closer together.

2 Rouse assesses the possibilities and limitations of semiotic analysis of performance texts by adopting Elam's distinction between *theatre* semiotics, which are concerned with "what takes place between and among performers and spectators," and the epithet *dramatic*, which signifies "the network of factors relating to the represented fiction" (Elam 2, quoted in Rouse 146).

3 Pavis acknowledges that though it is not simple to escape from the text, its authority – particularly that of the "classic" text – has been demystified in contemporary theatre (33). He quotes Jean-Marie Piemme:

> the text has indeed returned, but during its exile it lost any pretensions it had of being a fetish, a sacred or royal object. It questions us today without the burden of its old ghosts; our approach to the text is no longer dictated by that double-headed monster, faithfulness and betrayal. (42)

4 Orgel advances a theory that Shakespeare wrote anticipating that his scripts would be cut and altered in accordance with playhouse practice. By assuming that "the process of production was a collaborative one of selection" (7), this theory, as Lanier points out, reinvests Shakespeare with some authority over the performance text.

5 Osborne applies McGann's theory about the production of literary texts to the production of performance texts, with special regard to the historically contingent factors which enable and resist the production of the text as a physical, lexical object (McGann 31–2 and passim). In an essay which touches on the controversy surrounding contemporary Shakespearean editing, Worthen draws conclusions analogous to Osborne's:

> [I]n an important sense, textual and performance criticism share – or might come to share – an interest in determining how "the text" has been produced as a cultural artifact, and how the process of production inscribes itself into – and perhaps constitutes – the "text" it represents. (453)

6 In a controversial essay which records irreconcilable differences between theory and theatrical practice, Dawson dissects Berger's strategies for reinstating Shakespeare "as consummate poet who not only undoes any attempt to fix him theatrically but even undermines the primacy of the theatrical as a mode of representation." The material limitations of theatre, in Berger's view, always make it simpler than, and thus inferior to, literature: "Berger's procedure is to contrast playgoing and reading as if the two were analogous. . . .

But if we allow the analogy, then Berger's claim that reading provides a superior way to divine meaning is surely correct. For playgoers simply do not have the time to test and probe their thinking about any particular moment" (310, 317). Dawson questions the analogy.

7 A forthcoming volume of *McGill Studies in Shakespeare*, ed. Edward Pechter, is devoted entirely to the question of how evidence is used – and has been used historically – in performance criticism.

8 The relationship between performance and ideological practice is explored by Blau in his wide-ranging study of theatrical illusion as a manifestation of cultural power.

9 The idea of a community of readers who share common values and determine, collectively, the conventions by which texts are read and legitimated was, of course, first advanced by Stanley Fish.

10 Mulvey assesses the tension between the visual pleasure derived from watching film and the recognition that the spectator is constructed as primarily male. Her work has influenced feminist analyses of how we view Shakespeare, and particularly how Shakespeare's texts direct the male gaze and thereby attempt to co-opt female audiences. For a Lacanian reading of how Shakespeare's comedies "stage the gaze" and interrogate the cultural production of spectatorship, see Freedman.

11 For diverse theoretical approaches to contemporary productions of Shakespeare in the non-English-speaking world, see Kennedy's excellent anthology *Foreign Shakespeare.*

REFERENCES

Bennett, Tony. "Text, Readers, Reading Formations." *Literature and History* 9 (1983): 214–27.

Berger, Harry, Jr. *Imaginary Audition: Shakespeare on Stage and Page.* Berkeley and Los Angeles: University of California Press, 1989.

Blau, Herbert. *To All Appearances: Ideology and Performance.* New York: Routledge, 1992.

Brook, Peter. *The Empty Space.* New York: Atheneum, 1968.

Brown, John Russell. *Free Shakespeare.* London: Heinemann, 1974.

Carlson, Marvin. "Theatre Audiences and the Reading of Performance." *Interpreting the Theatrical Past: Essays in the Historiography of Performance.* Ed. Thomas Postlewait and Bruce A. McConachie. Iowa City: University of Iowa Press, 1989. 82–98.

Dawson, Anthony B. "The Impasse over the Stage." *English Literary Renaissance* 21:3 (1991): 309–27.

De Marinis, Marco. "Dramaturgy of the Spectator." Trans. Paul Dwyer. *The Drama Review* 31:2 (1987): 100–14.

Dessen, Alan C. *Elizabethan Drama and the Viewer's Eye.* Chapel Hill: University of North Carolina Press, 1977.

Elam, Keir. *The Semiotics of Theatre and Drama.* London: Methuen, 1980.

Fish, Stanley. *Is There a Text in This Class?* Cambridge, Mass.: Harvard University Press, 1980.

Freedman, Barbara. *Staging the Gaze: Postmodernism, Psychoanalysis, and Shakespearean Comedy.* Ithaca, NY: Cornell University Press, 1991.

Kennedy, Dennis, ed. *Foreign Shakespeare: Contemporary Performance.* Cambridge: Cambridge University Press, 1993.

McGann, Jerome. *The Textual Condition.* Princeton: Princeton University Press, 1991.

Mulvey, Laura. "Visual Pleasure and Narrative Cinema." *Film Theory and Criticism,* 4th edn. Ed. Gerald Mast, Marshall Cohen, and Leo Braudy. New York: Oxford University Press, 1992. 746–57.

Orgel, Stephen. "The Authentic Shakespeare." *Representations* 21 (1988): 5–25.

Pavis, Patrice. *Theatre at the Crossroads of Culture.* Trans. Loren Kruger. London: Routledge, 1992.

Piemme, Jean-Marie. "Le Souffleur inquiet." *Alternatives Théâtrales* 20/21 (1984).

Reinelt, Janelle G. and Joseph R. Roach, eds. *Critical Theory and Performance.* Ann Arbor: University of Michigan Press, 1992.

Rouse, John. "Textuality and Authority in Theater and Drama: Some Contemporary Possibilities." *Critical Theory and Performance.* Ed. Janelle G. Reinelt and Joseph R. Roach. Ann Arbor: University of Michigan Press, 1992. 146–57.

Styan, J. L. *The Shakespeare Revolution: Criticism and Performance in the Twentieth Century.* Cambridge: Cambridge University Press, 1977.

Taylor, Gary and Michael Warren, eds. *The Division of the Kingdom: Shakespeare's Two Versions of Lear.* New York: Oxford University Press, 1983.

Worthen, W. B. "Deeper Meanings and Theatrical Technique: The Rhetoric of Performance Criticism." *Shakespeare Quarterly* 40:4 (1989): 441–55.

2

STAGING "SHAKESPEARE"

Acting, authority, and the rhetoric of performance

W. B. Worthen

> What means are available to help us analyze performances so that we can properly understand and then judge the significance of the production? How can we know whether we are seeing Shakespeare performed or something that passes under the name of Shakespeare but is really something else, not Shakespeare at all?
>
> (Jay L. Halio, *Understanding Shakespeare's Plays in Performance* 3)

Despite Roland Barthes's announcement of "The Death of the Author" nearly thirty years ago, the Author remains alive and well in at least one corner of Shakespeare studies. We might expect this "Shakespeare" to inhabit modes of scholarship that have traditionally invoked the authorial origin of the literary work to challenge the ways that theatrical production rewrites the script. Yet when "Shakespeare" appears in contemporary literary studies, the name often summons a kind of critical ghost, a fiction, an openly rhetorical convenience labeling a network of discursive practices, legitimating strategies, and institutional pressures. "Shakespeare," that is, demarcates a zone of cultural transmission that includes various sixteenth- and seventeenth-century texts, their textual and performative history, and our own labor and conversation with them. It's odd, then, that Shakespeare-the-Author emerges in more conventional ways in stage-oriented studies, both in accounts of theatre practice and in the divergent forms of "performance criticism." I don't mean to suggest that this "author" emerges simply or unproblematically. After Artaud, reverence for masterpieces has been forever compromised, and the governing authority of the word has been similarly displaced as well. The theatre today produces a range of "Shakespeares": in stiffly "authentic" productions; in the vaguely "authorized" versions of the major British subsidy theatres; in the explicitly co-creative work of directors like Marowitz and Brook; in culturally confrontational productions around the globe. And "Shakespeare" is differently staged in other performance media – not only in recent films like *Hamlet, Henry V, The Tempest, Much Ado About Nothing, My Own Private*

Idaho, or *Prospero's Books*, but television incarnations as well, ranging from *The BBC-TV Shakespeare Plays* to *The Cosby Show* and reruns of *Gilligan's Island* – that fundamentally alter the performance relations of the theatre. On the wide horizon of contemporary performance, what can "fidelity" to "Shakespeare" mean?

Although Shakespearean production is perhaps peripheral to the most challenging and exploratory work in contemporary performance and performance theory, the questions posed by the production of classic texts onstage are both significant and distinctive. Given the literary and cultural status of Shakespearean drama, the production of a "Shakespeare" play generates intense and highly informed debate about the relationship between texts and theatrical production, a debate that centers on issues of legitimacy, power, tradition, and cultural hegemony. While these issues are implied in a variety of performance-writing – theatre reviews, actors' biographies, academic scholarship – they are the focus of an important, diffuse, and recalcitrant body of work: "performance criticism" of Shakespeare. Performance criticism – here I will consider only two versions, academic writing about text and performance, and actors' accounts of their work in transforming the text into meaningful behavior – enables an indirect yet incisive opening to the theoretical questions surrounding the production of "classic" texts onstage, by providing a sophisticated example of how we read performance today, and how that reading is complicit in other kinds of interpretation.[1] The function of "Shakespeare" in performance criticism points to what we are doing when we read performance, and so in a sense to what we think Shakespearean performance is and does.

We can take J. L. Styan's *The Shakespeare Revolution* as a paradigmatic text, one that has established many of the contours and assumptions of performance criticism.[2] Styan charts the ways that the modern theatre and modern scholarship have worked in tandem to discover the original performance environment of Shakespeare's plays; restoring that environment provides, Styan argues, a way of recovering an authentic "Shakespeare experience" (5). The phrase is a revealing one, correlating three moments where an author-effect is produced: in the author's original intention, in a mode of stage production understood to recover that authority, and in the response of the audience, whose "experience" of the stage reproduces that intention. The effort to synchronize these three moments sustains the argument of Styan's history.

As readers and as performers, we can approximate "Shakespearean" intentions by recovering the circumstances of the Elizabethan public theatre and asking how the plays of that period exploited them. Of course, Styan is not calling for more tights and rapiers in today's productions; rather than reproducing Shakespeare's medium, ersatz Elizabethan stagings impose a basically pictorial (Victorian, naturalistic) aesthetic between the Author and his audience. Instead, our ability to restore "what he intended" arises from a fortuitous constellation of otherwise disparate experiments in the modern theatre. Pioneers like William Poel worked to reproduce the circumstances of Shakespeare's stage, but Styan suggests that such antiquarian impulses only served as inspiration to the "new Shakespeare," who "did not, however, make his appearance on any make-shift Elizabethan stage." Instead, Styan argues that the widespread repudiation of the conventions of stage realism throughout early twentieth-century Europe forged a natural complicity between Shakespearean and modern performance practice. The modernist stage, as a result, could both recharge "the play's first meaning," and restore "the Shakespeare experience." By the second decade of the twentieth century, Styan suggests,

> the notion that theatre had to reproduce life by verisimilitude was already succumbing to the non-illusory assaults of the theatre men [Appia, Meyerhold, Craig, Fuchs, Reinhardt, and others]. Had they known, the students of Elizabethan dramatic convention might eventually have found themselves marching in step with such scandalous avant-gardists as Pirandello, Cocteau, Brecht, Genêt [*sic*] and others who have returned its former elasticity to the stage. (4–5)

In this history of modern theatre practice, "Shakespeare" serves a problematically neutralizing function: the historical particularity of the modern stage and of the various avant-gardes noted here is naturalized to a single "Shakespearean" essence – non-illusionistic representation. Yet the elasticities devised by the modern theatre are neither recuperative of Shakespeare's actual practice nor particularly similar to one another. Craig's largely unrealized impressions, Meyerhold's brilliant carnivalesques, and Reinhardt's secular rituals all oppose stage realism in different ways, and so necessarily construct Styan's key notions – "author," "audience," "experience," "intention," and "realism" – in different ways, and in ways different from how they might have been constructed in sixteenth-century London. Moreover, when modernist theatre practices are trained on Shakespeare, directors as diverse as Nigel Playfair, Barry Jackson, and Tyrone Guthrie turn out to be involved in a single effort:

> to give their audiences what they took to be the stuff of the Shakespeare experience. As far as it could be reclaimed three centuries later, they tried to capture and translate the temper of the original. Each man's search was for an authentic balance between the freedom a Shakespeare script grants the actor and the responsibility of recharging the play's first meaning. (5)

By essentializing the "elasticity" of non-realistic staging, Styan asserts a continuity between Shakespeare's mode of theatricality and our own, and a continuity between the audience's experience and the intention of the

Author. The flexible stage is our opening to authentic Shakespeare: "The secret of what he intended lies in how he worked" (4).

Styan is, of course, right to see the various practices of the modernist theatre as providing new ways to think through the process of Shakespearean drama onstage. But the claim that the modern stage restores an essentially "Shakespearean" meaning points out the extent to which this "revolution" is really a covert operation, a "restoration" in disguise. Seeing stage modernism as an accident of history that providentially makes Shakespeare once again legible, Styan brings a third term to bear: the work of modern scholars to recover the original performance circumstances of the Renaissance public theatre.[3]

> A surprising post-Second World War spurt in scholarship on the Elizabethan playhouse is associated with a much longer list of distinguished names: G. F. Reynolds, G. R. Kernodle, G. E. Bentley, Cranford Adams, Walter Hodges, Leslie Hotson, Glynne Wickham, Richard Southern, Bernard Beckerman and Richard Hosley. Although most of these would not claim to be dramatic critics, it is clear that each shares the idea of non-illusory Elizabethan performance, controlled by the medium of the playhouse. The flexible Elizabethan mode of performance, playing to the house, stepping in and out of character, generating a stage action allegorical and symbolic, making no pretence at the trappings of realism, encouraged a verbally acute, sensory and participatory, multi-levelled and fully aware mode of experience for an audience. (5)

The practices of the Elizabethan playhouse, and so the practices of the modern theatre are, by and large, not significantly inflected by history, social conditions, the composition of the audience, language, nationality, and so on: "flexibility" constructs a distinct mode of experience for any audience. This notion of a transcendent "flexibility" lends *The Shakespeare Revolution* its palpable teleology, in which "the new direction and focus of scholarly thinking about Shakespeare" and "the new freedom from the constrictions of realism and the proscenium arch" – and, presumably, the reinstallation of an authentic Shakespeare experience – "should culminate in Peter Brook's landmark production of *A Midsummer Night's Dream* at Stratford in England in 1970" (6).[4]

By laminating a uniform "Shakespearean" theatrical practice to a similarly homogenized "modern" stage tradition, *The Shakespeare Revolution* provides the modern theatre with a unique relation to Shakespearean authority, for the author-function that Styan finds in this "revolution" is in most ways eccentric to the history of the theatre.[5] As Stephen Orgel has suggested, modern notions of authorship have little relation to the production of dramatic texts in Shakespeare's theatre, in which plays were often written by several hands and revised by the company of performers who owned them.[6] Moreover, when stage practice has sought to recuperate the authority of "Shakespeare," it has more often than not had to resort to recomposing the play: rewriting the text in the case of Dryden, Tate, Cibber, Garrick, and Barton; reorganizing it in the case of Irving and Olivier; or editing and cutting it, the universal practice today. Styan's sense that Shakespeare emerges authentically on the stage only in the twentieth century necessarily defines the modern stage as a secondary or subordinate institution, working – as earlier theatres clearly did not – only to reproduce the constitutive "meanings" ascribed to "Shakespeare." The modern stage becomes a site of interpretation, rather than a place of production, a place where "meanings" are found rather than made. Described in this way, Styan's history of Shakespearean production is self-evidently at odds with the stated goals of the modern theatre's most influential practitioners – Brecht, Artaud, Brook – and works both to contain and to delegitimate the centrifugal and disruptive power of the stage. *The Shakespeare Revolution* in this sense seems no revolution at all: a revolution that invokes the past to erase it, and that finally denies the historical and material specificity of the present. Although the "students of Elizabethan dramatic convention" might be flattered to feel themselves "marching in step" with the avant-garde, it's hard to believe that the feeling would have been mutual. *Brecht?* Marching *in step?*

The Shakespeare Revolution is a deservedly celebrated and influential book, and in quarreling with Styan's situation of the Author in the action of history I have largely sidestepped his real achievement here: making stage production central to a critical history of Shakespeare in the twentieth century. And yet, the role performed by "Shakespeare" in this history finally represents modern performance almost exclusively as a mode of "interpretation," committed to recovering meanings already inscribed in the text (or – which is much the same thing – in the text's potential signification when performed in its original theatrical environment).[7] This work has been widely influential, and this "interpretive" sense that stage meanings are authorized by the text alone pervades much of the critical writing about Shakespearean performance today. Much as Styan's history forges an identity between the modern stage and the practices of the Globe – "flexibility" – so Shakespeare performance criticism tends to regard the theatre as a transparent vehicle for the Author's intention. As Robert Hapgood asks in a recent book. "What reliable guidance *does* Shakespeare give his interpreters?" (vii).[8]

Hapgood's *Shakespeare the Theatre-Poet* provides a useful example of how performance criticism uses the Author to regulate potential signification, and to cast the stage as an interpretive institution. Hapgood locates Shakespeare's "voice" or "presence" not in any of the characters or lines of the play, but as an effect of the "performance ensemble" itself, arising in the collaborative relationship between playwright, players, and playgoers in a theatre event (1). Hapgood's sense that "meaning" arises in the theatre through the interactive relationship of the ensemble of performers is sophisticated and rewarding, particularly if we consider the ensemble's players – author/text, actors, audience – to be constituted in and by the performance itself. Such a "performance ensemble" implies a creative collectivity among the theatre's participants, and locates the specifically *theatrical* nature of stage signification in their mutual performance. But the authority of Hapgood's performers is hedged in striking ways. For while Styan recognizes "Shakespeare" in the historical synchronicity of the modern and Renaissance theatres, Hapgood finds this "presence" in the perdurable economy of theatrical relations, the unchanging ensemble of interactions that shapes characters, actors, and audiences in performance. Passing over the fundamental discontinuities between what such terms – actor, character, spectator – might have meant in Shakespeare's era and what they might mean in our own, Hapgood defines the equilibrium of authority that animates the ensemble of Shakespearean performance:

> In these realms Shakespeare's presence is to be felt, and the players' function defined, by surveying the widest range of valid possibilities that the text leaves open to interpreting performers, by marking the outer limits of these possibilities, and by considering the pros and cons of the principal options within them (130).

The range of "possibilities" that the performance ensemble can engage is finally grounded in the already-authorized meanings left open by the text; the ensemble's freedom is the freedom to interpret and enact only what one of the players – "Shakespeare" – has already invented.

By mapping the Author into the design of performance, performance criticism hesitates to move in a direction charted by Roland Barthes some time ago, "from work to text." This is a surprising lapse, for although Barthes's notion of the Text refuses "to assign a 'secret', an ultimate meaning, to the text (and to the world as text)" ("Death" 147), it enables us to consider the text in terms that conform (or *should* conform) more closely to the working of the script in the theatre: "as play, activity, production, practice" ("Work to Text" 162). Although this sense of the text seems imperative for a truly performance-oriented criticism, it is a very different activity than Hapgood and others have in mind, "what may be called an anti-theological activity, an activity that is truly revolutionary since to refuse to fix meaning is, in the end, to refuse God and his hypostases – reason, science, law" – and, of course, *Shakespeare* ("Death" 147).

This interpretive sense of performance legitimates "readings" which mask the historical, social, and institutional particularity of the theatre at any given time, in order to privilege the "essential" operations of the stage, and so an "essential" vision of Shakespeare. This attitude enables us to locate "meaning" in the ineffable practices of ("Shakespeare's") drama, rather than seeing it as the consequence of the stage's place in contemporary culture, and of our own ways of acting in, and thinking about, theatre. Hapgood's reading of the performance ensemble at the opening of *Henry V* is typical of this tendency:

> Shakespeare challenges his spectators to a large-mindedness that can rise to his occasion. In the rest of the Prologue, the Chorus is very direct about the appeal he would make to our imaginary forces. First he confers upon us some of the nobility he had wished for in his ideal beholders: he dubs us "gentles all". Although in other places Shakespeare regularly refers to his spectators as "gentles," the Chorus's earlier wish for "monarchs to behold" the performance puts special emphasis on our implied ennoblement. He then proceeds to specify how (*noblesse oblige*) we can live up to our given title and grant his concluding appeal "gently to hear . . . our play". (20)

The Chorus can – and in many productions probably does – accomplish something of this kind, flattering the audience into a sympathetic engagement with the action to be seen, a gesture that perhaps still retains its original class inflections – we become "gentles all" if we see the scene in the way that the Chorus invites us to see it. And yet to say that this must happen in any legitimate performance today overlooks the extraordinary complexity of this scene in Shakespeare's theatre, where terms like "gentle" exerted a complex and *differentiating* function, rather than a blandly homogenizing one. In performance, of course, this speech would have been delivered by an actor who was anything but "gentle."[9] How might this have affected the meanings constructed by the performance ensemble, an ensemble much more evidently heterogeneous in demeanor, dress, behavior, and social privilege than audiences today? To those who *were* "gentle" in the audience, would the Chorus's invitation to the stinking crowd have been a kind of affront? Would it have been taken, as Meredith Anne Skura suggests, as part of the "tendentious formality" of the prologue convention, in which the player's "[a]bject flattery was taken to be a cover for self-serving greed, if not arrogance" (60, 61)? Might the invitation have been directed specifically toward some of the "gentles" in the house, reifying the class divisions already self-evident in the theatre audience, and between the audience and the performers as well? Although the "Chorus spells out precisely the faculties required for this particular play" (20), in 1600 those faculties emerged in their specificity within a densely particular milieu, one that is imaginable but not any longer recoverable in performance. Although other theatres may produce analogous effects – and so analogous ensembles – these are new vehicles for different kinds of meaning, and presumably require and produce different "faculties" in the performance ensemble. The performance ensemble of Shakespeare's era was differently related, differently constituted, and so differently *present* in the production than we are today; presumably a different "voice" and "presence" of "Shakespeare" – and so a different "Shakespeare" – emerged as well.[10]

To conceive the performance ensemble as interpreting the Author means that the ensemble is interpreting an Author it in fact creates: "Shakespeare" is a necessary fiction that organizes and stabilizes this interpretive community, working not to provide access to privileged meaning, but to legitimate a series of interpretive relationships – between actor and text, between spectator and stage, between critic and performance, for example (in Hapgood's reading, it masks the crucial [dis]continuities between the class effects of the Chorus's speech across history). By regarding the absent Author as the privileged origin of meaning in the ensemble's closed circle of interpretation, Hapgood finally removes the theatre from history itself. This sense of performance represses the material difference of the *past,* and – by repressing the differential character of theatre practice throughout history – it represses our specific, and specifically theatrical, ways of attending to the *present* as well.

As a genre of literary criticism, it is perhaps not surprising that performance criticism finally denies the authority of the stage, reserving it for an Author whose "presence" can be generated from a reading of the text. But what about actors? Surely actors have a clearer sense of their own creation, and would be unwilling to see themselves haunted by the ghostly presence of the Author, a ghost largely exhumed by professors of English. Modern theories of acting, and modern actor training and practice, tend to define a contestatory relation between Actor and Author, one that sits uneasily with the casual sense that actors "interpret" a text.[11] And yet when describing their work, actors often summon the Author to justify an "interpretation" of the play. In *Being an Actor,* for example, Simon Callow lists some of his notes for *Titus Andronicus*:

> *Revenge. No confidence in ability of law to settle righteous grudges: revenge regarded as legitimate (Cf. vigilantes).
> *Honour. Cf. Punk boy who killed a man who smiled at him. "'E was bringing me down in front of me mates."
> *Dismemberment. Cf. young Getty's ear from the kidnappers. (157)

Callow's account of his acting process locates his production of "character" firmly on the horizon of contemporary social life. Believing that until "ideas become translated into sensations, they're of no use whatever to acting" (156), Callow uses vigilantes, punks, and the news to generate the sensations that will substantiate his enactment of Titus, and so define his engagement with the character, and through the character with the audience. It is surprising, then, to find that Callow – who emphasizes the actor's creative experience of the role throughout his book – finally justifies the actor's labor in much the way that Hapgood and Styan validate the critic's and the spectator's activity. Indeed, Callow suggests that the actor no longer "interprets" the author, but communes more directly with the author's designs:

> The important thing is to restore the writer – whether dead or alive – and the actor to each other, without the self-elected intervention of the director, claiming a unique position interpreting the one to the other. We don't need an interpreter – we speak the same language: or at least we used to. (221)

Actors deploy a specialized regimen of technique and training to produce the dramatic text in the idiom of behavior; we might expect them to have a sharp sense of the aleatory play of performance, and of its constitutive authority over the script of the play. Yet when describing their work, actors also represent their activity onstage as a conversation with authority. How does this dialectic between production and interpretation inform how actors talk about their work, and so affect how we understand what Shakespearean performance is and does in contemporary culture?

It is perhaps easiest to raise these questions in relation to characterization, the production of a fictive "subject" as an effect of the signifying behavior of acting; the recent *Players of Shakespeare* volumes provide a convenient opening, in part because these "essays in Shakespearean performance by players with the Royal Shakespeare Company" deal almost exclusively with "character." What is remarkable here is that the process of characterization that the actors describe replicates the dialectic between Work and Text that sustains academic performance criticism. "Character" emerges both as a product, something latent in the play script, the Author's proxy, and (often simultaneously) as a process of production that arises only through the de-authorizing intertextuality of the actor's performance. Brenda Bruce, for example, describes the Nurse in *Romeo and Juliet* in this way:

> In my opinion, Nurse is no country bumpkin. She holds a very important position with an important family in Verona. She is the Italian equivalent of a bright Cockney with all the same energetic vulgarity and warmth, and the only interest in her life is Juliet and Juliet's happiness.
>
> (Brockbank 93)

Bruce's reading process – or the way she represents it here – is both typical and notable. Moving from the Nurse's social situation, Bruce begins immediately to particularize the role, in ways that imply not only an orientation to the character's psychology (compassionate, intimate with Juliet, maternal), but also an approach to playing, a feeling of sensory and physical embodiment ("bright Cockney," "energetic vulgarity and warmth"). Like acting, reading tends to obscure the "otherness" of characters, blurring the threshold between self and role, inside and outside. In this sense, we might suspect that Bruce's retrospective account of her preparation almost necessarily distorts her actual working process; Bruce's trained, affectual responses to the role's activities seem more immediate, and possibly to have produced the "textual" justification of the Nurse's class and social position. Does Bruce play the Nurse, or does the Nurse play Bruce?

This relationship between self and other, actor and "character" is typical, I think, of the way actors now talk about their work, about the necessity of self-exploration as part of the process of characterization. Describing Hamlet, for instance, Michael Pennington responds both to the extraordinary demands of the role, and to "the fact that finally to pull it off will take the actor further down into his psyche, memory and imagination, and further outwards to the limits of his technical knowledge and equipment, than he has probably been before" (Brockbank 117). Making "Hamlet" requires the actor to explore his "theatrical self" (122), a "self" that evidently combines features of both writer and text. The "theatrical self" is both inscribed by the role (which forces Pennington "further down into his psyche") and constitutes the role in performance ("Hamlet" is staged through Pennington's mastery of "technical knowledge and equipment"). Pennington describes his work as a complex engagement between identity and artifice, work that finally renders these categories problematic, inadequate. The journey to performance seems to require the negotiation of these boundaries, a mutual act of writing in which both "actor" and "character" become each other's author. The text inscribes itself in the person of the actor, textualizing his or her experience and identity; the actor represents the text, rewrites it in the dynamics of the theatrical self. In this sense, the Death of the Author is – in modern stage practice – accompanied by the Death of the Actor and the Death of the Character: neither actor nor character remains a self-present authority prior to their production in performance; both emerge as effects of representation. In *Being an Actor*, Simon Callow puts a finer point on it: "It's an incomparable feeling. Another person is coursing through your veins, is breathing through your lungs. But of course, it's not. It's only you – another arrangement of you" (166).

Even so, this deconstructive rearrangement of character and actor is finally accompanied by another gesture:

> It's not simply a question of seeing the character, knowing who he is. Nor is it a matter of impersonation (though that can help). What it needs is for you to locate him in you. Only then will the energy spring

> from within, instead of being externally applied; only then will you have renewed the umbilical connection between the character and the author.[12] (166)

Actor and character are both rearranged by the text of the other; yet this mutual rewriting is finally referred to the Author, who appears *ex nihilo,* mysteriously present in the flesh of the actor/character. The appearance of the Author in Callow's remarks is arresting not least for the way in which the Author makes his (or her) presence known: coursing through the veins, breathing through the lungs, something is materialized in the actor's body, transforming the body into an "umbilical connection" where two fictive beings, two sites of ideological activity, are collapsed into one: Character and Author. We might expect the actor's body – so local, so immediate – to provide a final point of resistance, the zero degree of the Author. And yet the Author is frequently summoned to substantiate not only a conception of "character," but its bodily enactment as well.

Geoffrey Hutchings's account of playing Lavatch in *All's Well That Ends Well* is a case in point. At the outset of the acting process, "the work of an actor on a text is like that of a detective":

> You have to look for clues to the character's behaviour in what he says, to a certain extent in what others say about him, in what he does and the way others react to him. You then have to interpret those clues and bits of information and create in your mind an "identikit" picture, which is then processed through your senses. Using your experience, talent and ability, you hope to arrive at a comprehensible and recognizable human being as near as possible to the dramatist's original intentions.
>
> (Brockbank 80)

Having sleuthed his "character" back to "the dramatist's original intentions," Hutchings runs into difficulty finding "a modern function for the character that would allow him to behave in the way that he does" (48). First, Hutchings decides to speak the role in his own South Dorset dialect, bringing Lavatch more into line with his own class affinities. Then, deploying the rhetorical instruments of New Criticism, Hutchings notices that Lavatch makes "more than a dozen references to the Bible and the clergy," a texture of imagery that enables him to define a moral and psychological perspective on the character: "There seems to be within him a continual battle between the forces of good and evil" (84). Yet this preparation still fails to animate the body; the life of the role eludes Hutchings until he hits on the idea of using a physical deformity to isolate Lavatch, to motivate his aggressiveness, and to explain why others allow him the license of speaking the way he does. Hutchings's seamless binding of past and present here is striking:

> I began, though, to think about other ways of setting him apart, and wondered if he should be in some degree physically abnormal. The history of professional fools is full of references to dwarfs and hunchbacks being used as a butt, a figure of fun and, in time, they developed a reputation and skill in providing their patrons with a constant and ready source of wit and invective. When confronted by some physical deformity it is natural for most people who believe themselves to be normal to extend towards that person an element of generosity and license that would not be granted to a so called equal. This would allow Lavatch the freedom to express himself without fear of censure. (85)

Hutchings necessarily thinks of the role in the present tense as a way of particularizing it; yet he authorizes his enactment by inserting "Lavatch" into a vision of human nature and "normal" social interaction that identifies Shakespearean society with an idealized version of our own. As Harry Berger, Jr. has suggested, the "author-function is a principle of closure, of semiotic inhibition, employed in the conflict of interpretations to privilege certain readings and control 'unruly meanings'" (153). Here, the body is used to naturalize a distinctly political vision of social process to a particular conception of character, a conception assigned finally to "the dramatist's original intentions." The "organic growth of the character" that Hutchings describes is, in other words, a powerfully rhetorical process in which the actor's body reciprocates the principle of closure initiated by the Author; "Shakespeare" naturalizes the cultural work of acting. Characterization represents fictive individuals through a variety of shared codes – movement, language, behavior, dress, acting style, mise-en-scène, disposition of the audience – that render performance an act of ideological production, much as Hutchings's conception of Lavatch is traced by a kinder, gentler view of interpersonal and social relations. The Author grounds characterization by effacing its rhetorical agency, its rhetorical complicity in our specifically contemporary modes of ideological production. The Author inscribes our dominant ideologies in the body of the actor, where our own modes of corporeality make them at once powerful and unquestionable.[13]

It is hard to imagine that we can inhabit the body in ways even approximating those of Shakespeare's era; although sight, pain, cold have probably not changed, our ways both of understanding the body and of mapping it into the signifying web of our culture are radically altered, and so the experience of the body has been altered as well. It is also difficult to denaturalize the working of our own bodies, in part because our modes of corporeality provide the first, most internalized, and so most fully ideological means of structuring our being in the world. Yet the body's implication in the naturalized codes of modern social interaction ought to make it a vehicle for decentering the Author, provided of course we could bring the dialectic between body and Author into view. We can, perhaps, get a sense of one way in which such questions might be raised from Antony Sher's account of working on the Fool in *King Lear*:

> The first breakthrough came in a rehearsal of the heath scenes when Adrian [Noble] asked each of the actors involved to find an animal to play, in order to release the savagery and wildness of the situation. I chose a chimpanzee, chattering and clapping hands, hurling myself around in forward rolls, and found this very liberating for the role. That weekend I hurried to London Zoo to watch the chimps and became even more convinced that they had all the requisite qualities for the Fool – manic comic energy when in action, a disturbing sadness when in repose.
>
> (Jackson and Smallwood 154–5)

In the chimps' behavior, Sher finds a useful model for the Fool's movement and gestures, but what is more arresting is that the strange likeness/otherness of animals seems to concentrate his attention to the role in a new register. Describing the chimps, Sher seems lightly to "characterize" them and to internalize their attitudes as well; the chimps become, in a sense, the authors of Sher's Fool. Sher inhabits himself and the Fool differently, not through the umbilical connection to the Author, but by acting against the grain – of the self, of the text, of "Shakespeare." As Francis Barker has remarked, the body's meanings arise "in a system of liaisons which are material, discursive, psychic, sexual, but without stop or centre" (12). I don't want to place too much weight on Sher's visit to the zoo, but attempting to discover the "character's" humanity in the gaze of a near-human other images a distinctly postmodern liaison/rupture between the body and the social world, and between the actor's work and the legitimation of the Author. Moreover, Sher was not alone at the zoo. He discovered his Lear, Michael Gambon, "presumably also in search of his character, leaning against the plate-glass of the gorillas' cage, man and beast locked in solemn contemplation of one another" (155). What's striking about this scene is not only its brilliant approach to the "savagery" of *King Lear* – in which, after all, man's life is cheap as beast's – but the image of acting it provides: contemplating himself in the other, and the other in himself, the actor's economy of production finally excludes "Shakespeare" altogether.

Drama, in the theatre, is a means of "textualizing" the body, making the body and its actions – gesture, movement, speech – readable in specific ways. This "textualization" does not, however, take place in isolation from other forms of social signification, as though the textual formalities – conceptions of character, action, language, behavior – were somehow already complete and immanent in the text of the play. Instead, textual formalities of the drama collide with the practices of the theatre, forcing a negotiation between the organization of the written text and the discursive materiality of the mise-en-scène. In actors' descriptions of their work, as in the wider scope of performance criticism, the Author works to legitimate "meanings" that are in fact constructed as the effect of our own ways of reading, thinking, acting, *producing* texts as plays. Perhaps the fiction of the Author is just a way of gaining some leverage as spectators, critics, and performers, a way of speaking that enables us to act. Possibly so; but it seems to me that recourse to "Shakespeare" is also a way of turning away from the question of how our acts of representation are implicated in the dynamics of contemporary culture, a way of passing the responsibility for our theatrical and critical activities on to a higher authority.

The complex invocation and subversion of the Author confirms, I think, the volatile place where "Shakespeare" lives in the institutions (university classrooms, books, theatres) of cultural production today. This "Shakespeare" points not so much to an Eliotic "tradition," but to the function that such traditions fulfill: effacing the dynamic of cultural change behind the mask of permanence. Performance, as Clifford Geertz recognizes, is a way of interpreting ourselves to ourselves; performance of the "classics" necessarily threatens to become an act of transgression, in which the cultural tradition embodied by the text is forced to tell a new story. Of course, this act is transgressive only if we believe that there are other alternatives, if we think that both the text and the tradition it metonymically represents can be known apart from their performance, if we think that the past is not constantly being remade by – and remaking – the present. Legitimating the Author *is* a way of authorizing ourselves, which perhaps explains the anxious acts of filiation that, surprisingly, continue to animate accounts of stage performance. But by allowing "Shakespeare" such authority, we reify Shakespearean drama – and the past, the tradition it represents – as sacred text, as silent hieroglyphics we can only scan, interpret, struggle to decode; we impoverish, in other words, the work of our own performances, and the work of the plays in our making of the world.[14]

NOTES

1 For an overview of contemporary performance criticism of Shakespeare, see Marvin and Ruth Thompson.

2 I have developed some of these assumptions in an earlier article, which also provides an overview of the range of performance criticism; see Worthen.

3 It is important to note that Styan represents modernist innovation as resisting and more or less displacing a realist aesthetic. In practice, though, many of these innovators worked with several modes of theatre, suggesting that realism and modernist experimentation were – and are – both contemporaneous, and in some fundamental ways involved in similar strategies of representation.

4 Styan's narrative of modern stage production and how it approximates the flexibility of the Elizabethan stage has been unusually influential. In his Introduction to *Players of Shakespeare*, Philip Brockbank also argues that "It may well be that our present experience of Shakespeare's plays is closer to that of the audiences of his time than it has been for many generations," a proximity enabled by a "keener respect for Shakespeare's text than was usual on the stages of the eighteenth and nineteenth centuries" (2). And like Styan, Brockbank tends to essentialize the functioning of the empty stage, arguing that "Bertolt Brecht did much to return European traditions of theatre to public and social modes of thought and feeling, but in England the communal styles have not, from present evidence, displaced those techniques of empathy and illusion practised, for example, by the player of Priam in the court of Elsinore" (9). Much as Brecht's massive effort to reconceptualize the ideological functioning of the theatre is assimilated to (pre-capitalist) modes of popular theatre, so the notions of empathy and illusion represented within *Hamlet* are continuous with, even identical with, those common in the theatre today (this despite the fact that the Player's Priam speech, and "The Mousetrap," already seem dated in the context of the play, part of a residual dramatic and theatrical style).

5 It should be noted that Styan, like others, tends to regard the circumstances of the Globe as normative, taking little account of the different performance environment at other public theatres, at the private theatres, and at various court performances.

6

> The company commissioned the play, usually stipulated the subject, often provided the plot, often parcelled it out, scene by scene, to several playwrights. The text thus produced was a working model, which the company then revised as seemed appropriate. The author had little or no say in these revisions: the text belonged to the company, and the authority represented by the text – I am talking now about the *performing* text – is that of the company, the owners, not that of the playwright, the author.
>
> (quoted in Stallybrass and White 75)

7 It might be useful briefly to recall Michel Foucault's "What Is an Author?" here. Foucault redirects our attention from the author as a material individual to the author as a function in discourse: "The author's name manifests the appearance of a certain discursive set and indicates the status of this discourse within a society and a culture. It has no legal status, nor is it located in the fiction of the work; rather, it is located in the break that founds a certain discursive construct and its very particular mode of being" (147–8). Although it "does not affect all discourses in a universal and constant way" (149), the author-function has several typical characteristics: it denominates ownership and the limits of appropriation, it valorizes the cultural position or significance of works, and, most importantly, it becomes a principle of unification, justifying and to some extent instituting the kinds of critical practice that can legitimately, authoritatively claim to represent the truth, value, content, meaning of a work. That is, the author-function serves to place critical activity in the mode of recovery or interpretation, as Barthes suggests: "Such a conception suits criticism very well, the latter then allotting itself the important task of discovering the Author (or its hypostases: society, history, psyche, liberty) beneath the work: when the Author has been found, the text is 'explained' – victory to the critic" ("Death" 147). The author-function, in this sense, serves finally both to sponsor and to regularize interpretation as our main attitude toward reading.

8 Hapgood is straightforward about his own intentions and critical practice: "This book was in part prompted by my neo-conservative desire – in a time of deconstruction – to reassert the primacy of the writer's creative presence," a presence that can be located in the writing, and that serves – or ought to serve – a particular function for readers and producers (vii).

9 At best, an actor like Shakespeare, Burbage, or Alleyn – that is, a successful sharer in the company – might have been seen in economic and class terms as a member of the bourgeoisie, though the theatre's identification with the court might have interfered with this perception. In most cases, though, actors were identified economically with the artisan classes, but socially and legally with servants or with vagrant "rogues and vagabonds." In the popular imagination, of course, actors were routinely associated with prostitution, gambling, vice, "effeminacy," and even with Satan.

10 On the different ways that stage and film versions of the Kenneth Branagh *Henry V* constructed the performance ensemble, see Collier.

11 Despite decades of impugning Stanislavski and the techniques he developed or inspired, several Stanislavskian principles – continuous characterization, an organic connection between scenes, the need to develop an inner life for the role, a consistent through-line of action – suffuse thinking about acting today, and particularly suffuse actors' descriptions of their work. This is hardly surprising. As the theorist of modern realistic enactment, as much so as Ibsen, Chekhov, or O'Neill, Stanislavski is involved in the production of the bourgeois subject at the heart of modern realism: an individual, delimited, organic, non-commodified, spontaneous psyche. And, Stanislavski or no, it would be difficult to expect actors any more than the rest of us to stand outside this dominant mode of ideological transmission, producing the world by producing us as its subjects invested in particular notions of what such subjectivity entails.

In "The Bard Goes to Univers(al)ity," a paper discussed at the 1992 Shakespeare Association of America meetings in Kansas City, Anthony Dawson undertakes a brilliant reading of the relationship between materialist criticism of Shakespearean drama and the "universalist assumptions" implicit in theatre training and production today, assumptions fully formed in the "utterly pervasive force" of notions of "character" in actors' accounts of their work: "It stands as an unquestioned truth that what the actor does is create character."

12 The difficulties of this dialogue where living writers are concerned, though, points to the extent to which the Author is (perhaps) a necessary fiction of the actor's work. Callow has an arresting account of working with Edward Bond on *Restoration*, in which Bond's inability to communicate a more lively sense of Lord Are's character to Callow forces him into an anxious inspection of Bond's intentions (134–5).

13 On "modes of corporeality," see Barker.

14 For an interesting, interested, and insider account of how "Shakespeare" is produced by various contemporary institutions (theatres, the academy, publishing), see Taylor chs. 6 and 7.

REFERENCES

Barker, Francis. *The Tremulous Private Body: Essays on Subjection*. London and New York: Methuen, 1984.

Barthes, Roland. "The Death of the Author." *Image–Music–Text*. Ed. and trans. Stephen Heath. New York: Farrar, Straus & Giroux, 1988. 142–8.

—— "From Work to Text." *Image–Music–Text*. 155–64.

Berger, Harry, Jr. "Bodies and Texts." *Representations* 17 (Winter 1987): 144–66.

Brockbank, Philip, ed. *Players of Shakespeare: Essays in Shakespearean performance by twelve players with the Royal Shakespeare Company*. Cambridge, London, and New York: Cambridge University Press, 1985.

Callow, Simon. *Being an Actor.* [1984.] New York: Grove, 1988.

Collier, Susanne. "Post-Falklands, Post-Colonial: Contextualizing Branagh as Henry V on Stage and Film." *Études Théâtrales/Essays in Theatre* 10 (1992): 143–54.

Dawson, Anthony. "The Bard Goes to Univers(al)ity." Unpublished paper. Shakespeare Association Annual Convention, April 1992, Kansas City, Missouri.

Foucault, Michel. "What Is an Author?" *Textual Strategies.* Ed. Josué V. Harari. Ithaca, NY: Cornell University Press, 1979. 141–60.

Geertz, Clifford. *The Interpretation of Cultures.* New York: Basic Books, 1973.

Halio, Jay L. *Understanding Shakespeare's Plays in Performance.* Manchester: Manchester University Press, 1988.

Hapgood, Robert. *Shakespeare the Theatre-Poet.* Oxford: Clarendon, 1988.

Jackson, Russell and Robert Smallwood, eds. *Players of Shakespeare 2: Further essays in Shakespearean performance by players with the Royal Shakespeare Company.* Cambridge and New York: Cambridge University Press, 1988.

Skura, Meredith Anne. *Shakespeare the Actor and the Purposes of Playing.* Chicago and London: University of Chicago Press, 1993.

Stallybrass, Peter and Allon White. *The Politics and Poetics of Transgression.* Ithaca, NY: Cornell University Press, 1986.

Styan, J. L. *The Shakespeare Revolution: Criticism and Performance in the Twentieth Century.* Cambridge, London and New York: Cambridge University Press, 1977.

Taylor, Gary. *Reinventing Shakespeare: A Cultural History from the Restoration to the Present.* New York: Weidenfeld & Nicolson, 1989.

Thompson, Marvin and Ruth Thompson, eds. *Shakespeare and the Sense of Performance: Essays in the Tradition of Performance Criticism in Honor of Bernard Beckerman.* Newark: University of Delaware Press; London and Toronto: Associated University Presses, 1989.

Worthen, W. B. "Deeper Meanings and Theatrical Technique: The Rhetoric of Performance Criticism." *Shakespeare Quarterly* 40 (1989): 440–55.

3

PERFORMANCE AND PARTICIPATION

Desdemona, Foucault, and the actor's body

Anthony B. Dawson

I

This essay has a history relevant to the position it takes and the ground it seeks to occupy. It began as a contribution to a seminar at the 1991 World Shakespeare Congress in Tokyo on "The Body as Site of Gender and Class Hierarchy and Differentiation," chaired by Peter Stallybrass and Steven Mullaney, and was designed to pose a number of questions. The seminar clearly assumed that the body *was* such a site, but I wanted to approach the topic interrogatively, refusing the implicit assumptions. One of the questions I had, and still have, concerns the relation between what I call here "discourse theory" and theatrical performance. I wanted to raise the matter of performance in the discussion of Shakespearean texts and the body, since cultural materialist criticism has frequently failed to take the measure of the stage, and yet the stage is one place where the body is clearly on the line. The term "discourse theory" is a catch-all, but what I mean generally by it is that complex of ideas, put into circulation by new historicist appropriations of Foucault and cultural anthropology, that insists on the primacy of discourse, that views culture as an interweaving of texts, and that regards as a critical responsibility the task of unraveling discursive networks and exposing their ideological weft and warp. What is meant to emerge from such analysis is a description of culture that historicises texts by linking them to each other and to "social texts" (modes of social negotiation such as courtship or courtiership, for example, or various types of ritual), and by establishing analogous social and textual patterns. There is of course a whole politics associated with this kind of analysis, but it is a troubled and uneasy politics at the moment, having emerged somewhat scathed from the critiques of new historicism and cultural materialism that were widely circulated in the late 1980s, not to mention the assault on "political correctness" from a number of quarters. It is notable now that a dissatisfaction with the restrictiveness of discourse theory is making itself felt, and there is a resurgence of interest in subjectivity and a broadening insistence on heterogeneity of response to cultural phenomena. There is by now a strong sense of *déja entendu* in the very sound of words like "gender" and "class," and the ideologically pure concepts such terms represent tend to incite resistance, even when one shares the leftish assumptions of those who utter them. So my Tokyo intervention was part of a broader movement of sceptical detachment. My suspicion of the hold on contemporary theory exerted by a particular reading of Foucault is clearly shared, as are my concerns about some of the narrowing implications of that particular version of materialism. There are other versions – didn't Nietzsche (Foucault's great precursor), reflecting on the corporeality of thought, make a remark about what happens to idealism when the philosopher has a bad cold?

One reason discourse theory has had little to say about performance is that what happens onstage and the effects generated in theatres are unpredictable and mixed. Theatrical practice, whether in the present or in Shakespeare's theatre, is inescapably concrete and material–dependent not only upon bodies but upon ordinary physical objects such as hats and tables. As such it tends to be resistant to theory since theory of any kind (and cultural materialism is no exception) is uncomfortable with the ungoverned and heterogeneous. One of the prime impulses behind recent theoretical criticism has been the call to historicize. But historicization in such a context has not generally meant paying delighted attention to the particular and concrete. Of course there are the famous new historicist anecdotes, and the frequent recourse to social history and documentation, to ancillary texts rescued from obscurity, and to specific historical conjunctures; but all these are invoked in the interest of producing an abstract, usually political, meaning, one that rewrites subjectivity as subjection.

The place of the body in this scheme is vexed. As a site of "differentiation," the body functions as a cipher, a sign of subjection; but as a real historical object its meanings are considerably less clear. Pleasure, for one thing, theatrical pleasure included, is rooted in the body. Actors use their bodies both to represent and to affect. Audiences respond with their bodies as well as their minds. Unwilling to let go of that dimension, but cognizant too of the need to historicize, to understand Elizabethan performance in Elizabethan terms, I want to explore ways to bring the unruly ambience of the Shakespearean playhouse into consideration without sacrificing the gains made by ideological criticism. I am not interested in reinstating claims about a "universal" Shakespeare whose meanings or effects are somehow unchanging and trans-historical. Such essentialism has played a part in the development of "performance criticism," which has until recently ignored the call to historicize,[1] and it is evident as well in the way modern-day theatre producers talk about their work. While materialist critics are committed to seeing the Shakespearean text historically, theatre practitioners generally are not. Like their Elizabethan counterparts, they are interested in *effect*. They want to speak to today's audiences by finding in the text those elements they assume to have affected Elizabethan audiences, and transferring them into modern terms without disturbing their "essential" nature. But there is no necessary connection between powerful effect and universality.

And so, taking a cue from theatrical as well as critical practice, I want to understand the actor's body and its effects historically, though outside the confines of specifically materialist analysis, resisting both universalist temptations and ideological purity. My title therefore proposes an encounter, one in which the performing body, represented by the embodied person of Desdemona, is linked by that most flexible of punctuation marks, the comma, to discourse theory, represented (unfairly I know) by the name "Foucault."

II

There are a lot of things we already know about the body. Mary Douglas has become *de rigueur* for Renaissance scholars, so we now know about the body as a natural symbol, a site of circulating, intersecting, clashing meanings. Foucault too has shown, vividly, unforgettably, how power and discourse make themselves felt in relation to the body of the criminal, the madman, the lover. We are familiar with gendered bodies (Laqueur), scattered bodies (Vickers), enclosed bodies (Stallybrass), tremulous bodies (Barker), even leaky bodies (Paster). What might we make of all this discursive embracing? Is it a sign merely of a kind of nostalgia, a wishful retreat to the physical on the part of an intellectual class with clean hands and electronic tongues, a class that grows increasingly uncertain of itself or suspicious of the values that have traditionally given it credibility? Is the "new bodyism" a move to carnivalize the academy (happy, if vain, thought)? Should the rush to the body be regarded as an attempt to break through the tyranny of a rigid dualism? Or is it in fact a subtle reinstatement of that tyranny?

The cultural materialist claim that the body is a site or discursive nexus assumes that differences of power are *written* on the body. That this is in some ways true it would be pointless to deny. The body does carry messages, no question. But those messages are so heterogeneous and dispersed that they are difficult to trace. To smooth them out in ideologically inflected ways tends to turn the body into one term in a polarity, rendering it newly invisible in that it comes to stand for something else, for a culture's way of defining gender hierarchy, for example. So, even in the particular cluster of critical practices included in a term like "cultural materialism," dualism is reimposed and with it we get the reproduction of a hierarchical position of mastery. Body/mind is replaced by body/abstract meaning, with meaning given the position of dominance. The body in this view is important only for what it says, for how it is transformed from sentience into discourse.

But can we find a way of talking about the Renaissance body in itself, apart from the constructions twentieth-century materialists place on it? And if we could gain access to the body of the Shakespearean actor, what would that tell us? What, for example, did Burbage *feel* during the storm scenes of *King Lear*, or Robert Armin singing the circling song at the end of *Twelfth Night*? In the first case, an expanding chest, a vertigo brought on by the sheer excess of the rhetoric, a rhythmic syncopation in the pulse of the neck? In the second, a subsidence, an exhalation, together with the pitch of contracting muscles below and around the rib-cage? Obviously, we'll never know, although there are plenty of places in Shakespeare where we could come fairly close to naming the exact bodily experience demanded of the actor – Romeo's breathlessness in the "balcony" scene, for example, or the staccato tension in the gut required by some of Macbeth's punctuated speeches. The actor's body fits the character, the voice the text. Shakespeare's language is first of all a physical fact. But even if we could answer all such questions with some certainty, what would that tell us? Why, nothing at all. Questions about physical specificity are, at least from the point of view of critical thought, *meaningless*, although they are the actor's stock and trade. The institutional requirements and categories that govern criticism ensure that access to meaning involves a move away from the fundamentally physical. What I want to do in what follows is to rethink the performing body so as to open up the category of meaning, to suggest a distinction between "meaning" and "meaningfulness" whereby the heterogeneous, particular and concrete, insofar as they are a part of living experience in the theatre, are included in what counts as significant – they may not *have* meaning, but they are meaningful.

Even if what actors actually felt is mostly inaccessible, there are scattered bits of evidence about what they did, and what effect they had. Let me take up two of those for a start. First, Thomas Nashe's well-known comment from *Pierce Penilesse* about (presumably) Burbage in *Henry VI*:

> How would it have ioyed brave Talbot [asks Nashe] to thinke that after he had lyne two hundred yeares in his Tombe, he should triumphe againe on the Stage, and haue his bones newe embalmed with the teares of ten thousand spectators at least, (at seuerall times) who in the Tragedian that represents his person, imagine they behold him fresh bleeding. (87)

The "Tragedian that represents his person" – there is a nicely ambiguous phrase. Where can we locate the body in that word "person," leaving aside for a moment the problem of representation focussed by the verb? "Person" has a complex history, since it means, among other things, both *body* and *dramatic character*, the latter sense being, apparently, prior, deriving from the Latin *persona*, an actor's mask (*OED*). "Person," for the Elizabethans, is primarily an embodied character, a real fiction, and bespeaks the impossibility of splitting body from self or self from role. The body, the person, is something *seen.* Think of Cleopatra, whose "person . . . beggar'd all description," her bedecked body identified with the role she is playing on the river of Cydnus. So the body itself is tied up with person and personage and, in the example from Nashe, points to what "Talbot" was. The actor, in bodying forth the person of "Talbot," is thus a representation of a representation (the fictional "Talbot" being a stand-in for the real historical Talbot). The body of the actor both represents and is what it impersonates, since it is that body, as identified with the character's, that generates emotions, or "passions" to use the favored Renaissance word. The person, the body, is bleeding, at least in the imagination of the spectators who behold not Talbot, but Burbage (who of course is *not* bleeding), but who believe in Talbot and weep at his (or is it the actor's?) "triumphe." Whose body is it, we may want to ask, and how does it excite tears? Such is the age-old question of acting – how can the represented body not only stand in for the actual one but stir up passions in those who are but mutes or audience to its act, passions akin to but even stronger than those conjured by the "real" Talbot? What the linkage of body and persona in the word "person" makes clear is that such strong effects arise from the fact that the body is always already involved in representation; it is marked that way by what Diderot calls the paradox of acting – the fact that in order to make the audience recognize and respond to what the impersonated person feels, the actor must suppress those feelings in himself.[2]

Quintilian, in his Institutes, takes up the question of representing passion rhetorically, and enacts it by speaking poignantly of the death of his son and then coolly analysing how one goes about creating feeling in one's audiences. For him and for the many Renaissance theorists who followed in his wake, there was a link between rhetoric and its effects and the functioning of the body. Physiology, as Joseph Roach shows, underlay theories of acting. Cultural ideas about how passions generate bodily effects colored theories about how such passions were to be represented or what happened in the course of such representation. In the Renaissance, the body was, so to speak, a mixed bag. On the one hand it was regarded as a sludgy mass of humours. On the other hand it was dangerously malleable and volatile, instantly and capriciously capable of passion; this view depended on the notion of vital "spirits" and the protean capability of the imagination to transform the very shape of the body. Passions could deflect and trans-shape the person (as with Othello falling into a fit), the various "humours" seeping around inside being liable to percolate wildly, repelled or attracted by various organs. In the Renaissance medical body, says Roach, there is a kind of "class hierarchy of corporeal substances," in which the "plebeian humours," potentially dangerous in revolt, are kept in check by the vital spirits, imaged as "Tories"

(40). But "passions cut across class lines"; they are of both the body and the mind and complicate the dualism that we have inherited from Descartes and that we might assume was in play in the Renaissance. The rhetoric of the passions suggests a less rigid definition of the relation between matter and spirit. This kind of theory affected the actor, since the body's protean volatility was regarded as dangerous. The actor thus had to work against the tendency to tear a passion to tatters; he had to moderate the fierce force of the imagination.

Renaissance acting theory therefore tended to instruct the actor not to free inhibitions but to foster them, to exert control over a far too easily stirred body. On this question, Hamlet is an exemplary critic. In admonishing the actor to "acquire and beget a temperance" that may "give [a] smoothness" to the "torrent, tempest, and, as I may say, whirlwind" of his "passion," Hamlet insists on the mastery of art over the body, just in order to ensure that the kind of mimetic impersonation invoked by Nashe actually will occur and have the desired effect. The actor must *feel*, but he must also practice his art, play on his body as on a pipe. The potential contradiction here is plainly discernible in Thomas Wright's *Passions of the Minde* (1604), when he argues that orators, in order to make their audiences feel, must experience the same passions at the moment of delivery that they want to convey. But then he goes on to describe in great detail how an orator must conduct himself: "he ought to endevour, that every part of action immitate as lively as may be the nature of the passion." How? "Looke upon other men appasionat," observe their motions and "then leave the excesse and exorbitant levitie or other defects, and keepe the manner corrected with prudent mediocritie" (179).

Effective oratory thus depends on intense feeling and at the same time a prudent detachment from such feeling. Wright goes on to praise stage players for the "perfection of their exercise" which "consisteth in imitation of others," though he blames them for their lack of seriousness (what they do is "fained"). In praising orators and denigrating actors, Wright ignores the parallel between them – that the business of acting, like that of rhetoric, is a double one. In both arenas, the body is instrumental in delivering a sense of interiority, one that is constructed in and through the separation between inner and outer, self and body. In that sense, Renaissance acting theory looks ahead to the split characterized by Descartes; the insistence on mastery over the body's motions as a route to interiorized personhood becomes an agent of dualism. Diderot, almost two centuries later, based his *Paradoxe sur le Comedien* precisely on the denial in the actor's body of the affective power that it is thereby enabled to wield, the player substituting for deep feeling the mastery of the instrument on which he plays – his own person. So Diderot, although he overstated his case, finally articulated what actors must always have known and what Hamlet and Wright clearly imply, that a disjunction between passion and technique is crucial to effective representation. In Nashe's evocation of Burbage's Talbot, we note that the fruit of imitation is precisely to affect the audience's bodies, to effect a rhetorical and physiological exchange (real tears for impersonated bleeding, however fresh); this is the mark par excellence of the Tragedian.

I shift now to my second bit of evidence. From Oxford in 1610 comes another early instance of Shakespearean dramatic criticism: "Desdemona, killed in front of us by her husband, although she acted her part excellently throughout, in her death moved us especially when, as she lay in her bed, with her face alone she implored the pity of the audience."[3] Here again, though less overtly, the person of the actor moves the spectators, if not to tears, to a lively and productive passion; in fact in the passage immediately before that quoted, the King's Players have been commended for exciting tears not only by their words but by their actions as well. The writer, Henry Jackson, is clearly responding to the person of Desdemona – it is *she* who moves the audience – ignoring, for example, the actual gender of the actor, while at the same time praising the actor for his impersonation and its power to generate passion. Note too that the actor's vitality is invoked even though the represented character is dead. This kind of response may help to qualify the sort of reading to be found in recent materialist criticism, where, for example, Desdemona and her "desire" are frequently objectified and her agency ignored or denied.[4] Jackson, by contrast, sees Desdemona as an advocate,[5] not a mere exemplum, and the fact that he sympathizes with the female Desdemona as she lies dead and also admires the boy actor's skill suggests that for him the character/actor "Desdemona" is not a mere object. On the contrary, Desdemona's body, because it is also the boy actor's, will always remain a performing body. We have, in Jackson's response, an example of that dual consciousness that William Archer finally gave a name to in 1888 (184ff.), but which Diderot explores in the *Paradoxe*: the ability of the actor to be both *in* the emotion and outside it, and the concomitant effect in the audience of being utterly absorbed by, and at the same time critically aware of, the performance. Taken all in all, I would argue, Jackson's account of the reception of the play in performance puts into question the reading of the victimized, subjected Desdemona that some recent critics have seen as central to the cultural work the play is said to have performed.

III

A crucial effect of attending to the present, performing body is to allow for the evocation onstage of interiorized personhood. The very disjunction between the actor's body and what it represents, or means, drives this process. The theatre depends on the body, on personation, and yet it tends paradoxically to make the body untrustworthy, taking away from the body's power as the locus of passion, shifting attention toward mind and meaning, toward discourse. Or that's one way of reading the force of the Shakespearean theatre. We have heard, let us say accepted, the view that Shakespeare's texts helped to create for Western culture the notion of the interiorized subject (see Fineman), giving us the illusion of depth, a paradigm for what we mean by "character," even by "self." Hamlet: the fictional being with an internal life, fully realized, rendered to us through the body's voice. But does this personation happen at the *expense* of the body? The actor puts his body on the line – this is demanded by theatrical presentation. The body trembles, vibrates with the sheer resonance of the Shakespearean text. The ear vibrates in response. The audience *sounds* the performance.[6] But as all this rough magic is taking place, in its stead, even because of it, arises the illusion of the (represented) person who speaks, the person not the actor, distinct from the actor. The actor, that is, uses his body to falsify his body, or better, to break away from it. All those bodily reactions belong to the performance. In the theatre, the truthful body always lies. The blushes, the tears, the stretched tendons, the quickened heartbeat, are signs, not symptoms, moments of representation whose point is to establish a set of meanings or, more often, a rush of feeling, that exists aside from the actor's body, in the minds (or "hearts," to use a favorite Elizabethan term) of the spectators.

A paradox emerges similar to that named by Diderot: the body exists under erasure, and yet that elision of the body, that move toward discourse, is a direct result of the body's presence. Further, this process of denying the body while at the same time mounting it as a scaffold is precisely what allows the text, the performance, to produce interiorization. The audience, that is, is encouraged to read past the body, to recognize the literal falsification, on the part of the actor, of his own person, its transferral to some-body else. This means that the audience must put aside its sense of what the actor's body seems to be telling it (e.g. that this person, say Burbage, is in pain, angry, erotically aroused) in order to read meaning, i.e. what is represented – the *person* of the character. But at the same time it cannot forget the actor. There is, then, a further paradox. While the audience members are encouraged to construct meaning through the elision of the physical, their bodies are engaged in physical responses: tears, shudders, held breath, or whatever. At the same time, as is clear from the Renaissance dramatic criticism cited above, we are capable of admiring actorly technique, aware always of the power of performance, engaged in turning the body into a sign.

What we might want to call the "personation process" tends to produce interiorization in two distinct ways – first for the character who leaves the actor behind but retains his (her) body as a sign of an internal life, and second for the *audience*, who are encouraged into double consciousness by being led to respond to the represented person (being *possessed* by him/her we might say) and simultaneously being made aware of the very process by which the player constructs the fictional character. As audience members, we shed real tears on account of what we recognize as unreal feelings; that is, we separate out the actor's body from what it represents and the character's "body" from what it means – what it says about mind, or "soul" or "self" – on the basis of our *meta-theatrical* experience, our sense of a complex set of parallels and distinctions between actor and character, fictional and actual situation.

IV

The body signifies in the theatre as a crucial part of the performance; it establishes *person.* In that capacity it may, of course, speak of gender or class differentiation, if only provisionally. My point, however, is that it exists in tension, as a site less of differentiation than of "presencing," of "participation." I have drawn this latter term from theological discourse concerning the Eucharist. In its ordinary meaning, participation implies either a kind of sharing, or simply taking part in some joint activity – one participates *in* a ritual or a game. But the term has a more specialized, transitive use in accounts of the Eucharist, and the debate surrounding the question of the "real presence" of Christ in the sacrament. Originating in Paul's description of the Lord's Supper as an act of "participating" the body and blood of Christ (Corinthians 1.10), the term is central to various understandings of the meaning of Eucharistic representation. Richard Hooker's defense of the Anglican position is particularly germane here, and I want to use it to steer between two untenable positions on the question of what is actually involved in theatrical representation: the essentialist view that acting is "pure presence" (noticeable in some performance criticism) and the meta-theatrical and/or materialist notion that the body is *mere* representation – a site of contestation or field of representational struggle – and hence emptied of its meaningfulness as physical presence.

In an important article, Joel Altman reads the idea of "participation" in relation to the theatre in a double sense: playing a part and being a part that is shared by others in mutual partaking. For Altman, the "royal presence" in *Henry IV* and *Henry V* is "a form of physical and spiritual nourishment" akin to Hooker's description of the Eucharist (5), which involves being both taken apart and taken in (ingested), a process that makes for a mutual partaking and hence a fellowship. "The fruit of the Eucharist," says Hooker in a passage cited by Altman, "is the participation of the body and blood of Christ." All this may sound vaguely mystical, if not mystified, but Altman's analysis is resolutely historical. In his account, the players and the text construct a secular, self-legitimating, ritual: at a time when English soldiers were actually losing their lives in Ireland, in a campaign about which the London population was decidedly ambivalent, "ritualizing the occasion [of playgoing] legitimates actor and auditor, relieving the potential shame attendant upon performing war and enjoying the performance" (17). And ultimately, the violence of the play is turned outward, on to a foreign enemy, so that the ambivalences about the king and his requirements are displaced and "participated fellowship" (32) is thereby constituted.

This may lead us to speculate that Hooker's reading of the specifically Anglican form of participation (which he carefully distinguishes from both the Reformed Protestant and the "popish") is homologous to the forms of participation invented by the secular theatre. (I here follow C. L. Barber and Louis Montrose, among others, in suggesting that the Elizabethan theatre absorbed and recast the rituals of pre-Reformation England, and the social desires that those rituals codified and enacted.) Hooker's "via media" neatly fudges the issue of "real presence," reading the Eucharist as "instrumentally a cause of that mystical participation" (294) which binds Christ to his people. Hooker makes "participation" a matter of *reception*, of audience response and transformation: "The real presence of Christ's . . . body and blood is not therefore to be sought for in the sacrament, but in the worthy receiver of the sacrament" (291). By concentrating on inner efficacy and turning away from the question of where the body is, he skirts the problem of representation both raised and occluded by the Catholic doctrine of transubstantiation whereby body and blood "really" replace bread and wine, or indeed by Luther's own very similar notion whereby the "substance" of Christ's body *co-exists* with the sanctified bread (see *Works*, vol. 37). The Anglican view is rifted – it insists on both presence and representation. Unlike for the Reformed Protestants (the "left wing" in the controversy with Luther), the sacrament is not simply representation. At the same time, "presence" is no longer absolute and unquestioned, behind the appearances of bread and wine, but rather is itself troubled or mediated – unreal but also efficacious.

Such debates may seem arcane to our sceptical ears, but they reflect what Deborah Shuger calls "habits of thought," ways of thinking that infuse the culture and give it a recognizable coloration. What I want to suggest is that, in the Shakespearean theatre, analogous habits of thought are in play, transferred to a secular realm. As in Hooker's reading of Anglican ritual, the theatrical presence of the *person* is virtual, dependent on reception and negotiation. The actor's body is obviously present, but the "presence" of the *character's* body is more ambiguous because it depends on representation in the person of the actor. Such virtual (real and unreal) presence is sanctioned by, or figured by, meta-theatrical mediations: audience awareness of "personation" is always in play, while at the same time there is a forceful insistence on the value and meaning of theatrical experience itself, its physical power to *move*, despite its mediated quality. There seems, that is, to be a constant oscillation between two different and opposing constructions of the theatre (and the theatrical body), on the one hand as mediated, self-conscious, meta-theatrical, and on the other as immediate and present. Participation, involving presence and representation in the ritualized act of reception, is a notion that links the two conceptions.

The actor, by participating his body, creates his part, constructs the person he represents; the audience participates the actor, exchanging its hold on ordinary reality for an embodied, but also, of course, impersonated, passion. In this process the body of the actor is primarily a *rhetorical* instrument, and the exchange in which he is engaged can best be construed as a kind of socially efficacious ritual enabled by the act of participation. Thus, even though Shakespeare's texts make us continually aware of how untrustworthy the body is, they ground every effect they have on the body's pulse and nerves.

V

Conceiving of the actor's body as a rhetorical instrument means investing it first with agency, linking it with will, and hence with subjectivity. It is expressive of character and interiority and, in the actor's hands, it is instrumental. As I said above, this involves a kind of displacement, occasioned by the personation, whereby one kind of interiority (the character's) supersedes another (the character displaces the person of the actor). Most of the time in Shakespeare, despite his fondness for the meta-theatrical, we are not alerted to this paradoxical interplay, even though we are, cannot help but be, aware of it. Let us take the example of Lady Macbeth, sleepwalking, carrying a taper, rubbing her hands. The moment is a richly textured one, not only in its verbal resonances but in the way in which it displays the body. The scene is framed by Doctor and Gentlewoman, setting up the potential for meta-theatre that Shakespearean crises so often flirt with; but the intensity of the moment, its "presencing," stands against the faintly deconstructive possibilities suggested by the multiple watching. In fact, the scene offers an object lesson in how theatrical presence can be wrested from the dazzling abyss of absences and erasures that the meta-theatrical gesture opens up. We move, as it were, from *mise en abime* to *mise en scène.*

For what happens when she enters? "She advances rapidly to the table, sets down the light and rubs her hand, making the action of lifting up water in one hand at intervals." Thus G. J. Bell describing the greatest English actress in one of her greatest parts. When Sarah Siddons took on the role she broke with theatrical tradition by actually setting the candle down, a move that provoked a protest from Sheridan, who visited her in her dressing room to try to dissuade her from such iconoclasm. But upon seeing the performance, he recanted. As for contemporary reaction to the performance of the scene, nothing is more vivid that Sheridan Knowles's remark to an actor friend: "Well, sir, I smelt blood. I swear I smelt blood" (Sprague 65, 67; Dawson, *Watching* 203). Bell's detailed description ends with a comment on Siddons's reading of the great open "O's" following "Here's the smell of blood still – all the perfumes of Arabia will not sweeten this little hand": "This not a sigh. A convulsive shudder – very horrible. A tone of imbecility audible in the sigh" (Bell, quoted in Matthews 95–6). The actor's body is thus deeply implicated throughout (as is its effect on the audience's nerves), and seems always to express, or represent, something akin to an ongoing inner life.

Let me now try to meet the question head-on. Is the body here a *site*, a point of transaction and intersection of discourses? That the discursive formation that goes under the name "Lady Macbeth" *is* a cultural construction we may readily allow (see, for example, Stallybrass or Adelman). But this in a sense begs the question. If we deploy discourse theory in posing the question, our answer will necessarily fall into formation. If, however, we shift the ground, our conclusions may be different. We are, after all, talking about bodies (plural) – or at least I choose to avert my gaze from the nakedly abstract body that figures *meaning*, and focus on the person. And that person forms before me as a curious amalgam of the physical body of the actor, say Sarah Siddons, invested paradoxically with the interior life, however constructed and culturally determined, of the character. And that *person* has a powerful physical effect in the theatre, on an audience – "I swear I *smelt* blood."

Further, Shakespeare's text actually puts in play the complex effects we have been discussing – that is, it raises the issue of ideological inscription and, so to speak, *engages* it (and here I invoke images of betrothal as well as combat, models of attraction as well as negotiation). To explore this terrain, I want to turn to the vexed question of the boy actor. Sarah Siddons in 1800 is one thing, a boy actor in 1610 quite another. Whenever Shakespeare creates an intense scene for a female character, the issue of course comes up – how aware is the audience of the "boy" and how does that affect response? The simple answer and certainly that supported by what eyewitness accounts exist is that the audience by convention simply ignored the gender of the actor, reading him as her.[7] This is borne out by the lengths to which Shakespeare and others have to go when they want, as in *As You Like It* or *Twelfth Night* or *Antony and Cleopatra*, to bring audience attention to the boy actor as part of the total scheme. Similarly, the often-noticed satirical exaggerations of the boys' companies, in performing the texts of a writer like Marston for example, suggest an effort to bring to the forefront of audience consciousness what was usually, we may legitimately infer, more or less unconscious – the discrepancy between actor and character, whether that be boy actor and female part, or boy actor and adult male part, or indeed adult actor and adult male part. A common-sense approach to the problem thus leads to the view put forward by Michael Shapiro that a "dual consciousness" (to cite Archer's term once again) was undoubtedly in play, by which awareness of the actorly, while potentially present throughout the performance, is only activated at certain moments as part of the effort to achieve certain specific effects. So we can safely assume, I think, that where there is no clear dramatic reason for the raising of such interruptive consciousness, and no textual hook on which to hang it, then for most audience members it simply did not exist. This is borne out by the testimony concerning Desdemona quoted earlier, where Henry Jackson, even in praising the quality of the acting, speaks of "Desdemona" and uses feminine forms ("illa," "occisa," and "interfecta" in the original Latin).

But the Shakespearean boy actor still has to play the sleepwalking scene and has to use his body, to rub his hands despairingly together to make the effect – and what effect? Here we get into ideological questions. For one way of looking at the scene would be to see it as an instance of recuperation, a move to establish an essentialist notion of the "good woman" underneath the monster. In such a reading, the production of interiorization, of conscience, becomes an instrument of ideology, female nature reconstituted as non-monstrous, and hence the female threat to male power is neutralized by referral to a benevolent nature according to which order and patriarchy are maintained. Even this threatening, dominant, *monstrous* woman, the text might be made to say, must rub the stain of blood from her guilty hands and therefore be gathered back into the hierarchical system which she has so outrageously challenged earlier in the play.

What I am arguing, however, is that by setting the scene metatheatrically as it does (with Doctor and Gentlewoman watching and commenting), by allowing the boy actor full scope and demanding, implicitly, audience belief – by, that is, offering us and then withdrawing the deconstructive pleasures to be derived from the special knowing or ironic consciousness that such staging potentiates – the text puts the ideological reading into play and at the same time engages it with a theatrical one. The space between the two kinds of reading is both contested and negotiated; forced upon us is an awareness of a feeling, personating body that contends against the discursive one, not thereby knocking the latter out of commission but perhaps allowing for a ritual of participation. What is staged is a contest between alternative ways of making meaning, of turning theatrical experience into meaning.[8]

The boy actor figures in this because of the relationship he bears to the part he plays. There is an implicit conflict between the person he is and the woman he impersonates, which at key moments exerts enormous pressure on the order of representation itself. To put it another way, the boy actor is a possible site of the abyss – a marker of the idea that representation is all there is, that there is no *hors-texte*; and the discrepancy which he can be made to enact invites a range of ideological readings, new historicist or feminist/materialist, which depend on the notion of the primacy of discourse. Further, in the particular instance of Lady Macbeth's last scene, the actor faces the problem of having to represent a character who at this point is curiously pared down, refined, without that histrionic element so visible in most of what Lady Macbeth does in the play, whether calling on the spirits to unsex her or encouraging her husband to screw his courage to the sticking place. At those moments she is "acting," and the actor enacts her acting and her own self-conscious complacency about the roles she plays. In her final scene, the histrionic element is entirely missing: she is asleep. But for the actor, of course, the acting continues, more than ever a matter of the body. (The same can be said even more obviously for the impersonation of the dead Desdemona.) Now, however, its object is to deny the histrionic (paradoxically through a display of pure personation), even though the scene is weightily *theatrical* in every sense. The actor both utterly effaces him/her/self and doubly makes his presence felt by having to realize the passions of someone who is absent.

We may now read the scene doubly: in reducing Lady Macbeth to a dreaming essence, an inner reality of imbecility and guilt, and hence recuperating her as a woman within patriarchy, the scene holds out the possibility of an ideological reading. But by limiting the scope of the character, by de-theatricalizing her and at the same time cranking up her force, her effect on the senses of the spectator, Shakespeare paradoxically re-theatricalizes the person he has exposed – i.e. he reduces the histrionic nature of the character, but he invests the body with more power to convince (nowhere in the play is Lady Macbeth more ineluctably *present* – she is now *herself*). The effect of this is to bracket any ideological question about Lady Macbeth as a discursive site, though not exactly to disqualify it – rather to bring it into dialectical play with the affective. Ideological questions are thereby negotiated; they don't disappear but are temporarily finessed. Thus the Shakespearean theatre may be said to seek the primacy of its art *over* criticism, and, in the present instance, the medium it uses is the (boy) actor's body. This raises complex questions about the scope and power of the theatre, too knotty to go into here; but it seems possible to say that the theatre among other things is interested in defining a space of mastery for itself, in speaking, that is, of the power of its own representations.[9] The theatre, by concentrating on the body, may indeed limit its power as a discursive practice – but this limitation may paradoxically free it, shifting the ground to focus on the power to move audiences and hence to incite who knows what kind of passionate participation.

Recently, Lacanian readings of cinema and theatre have tried to locate and displace the fixed and settled gaze of the spectator, undermining the metaphysics of presence that springs from the fact that, in the theatre, actor and body are present to the spectator. From that point of view, the meta-theatrical as I have been discussing it might be seen as contributing to such a disturbance of presence. Barbara Freedman, for example, identifies the "fractured gaze" as the essence of a postmodern redefinition of theatre which takes its cue from a psychoanalysis presumably freed of the explanatory mastery often associated with it and liberated into a Derridean space of free play. "Theater," Freedman argues, "offers a perspective glass by means of which our look is revealed as always already reflected, defined by the exchange of signifiers that displace as they place us in the symbolic" (72). That Shakespeare allows for such a displaced awareness is unquestionable, as we have seen in the case of Lady Macbeth's sleepwalking (an even more telling example might be Iachimo's gazing at and noting the prone body of Imogen in *Cymbeline*). However, such effects in the Shakespearean theatre seem to me not to exist only for themselves but to weld the gaze to the other major source of visual, and personal, delight – the body of the actor and the effects he can generate with it. In my view, it is precisely the engagement of free play and self-reflexive awareness with the "real" presence of actor and spectator that produces participation. And so I opt for a conception of theatre that distinguishes between theatrical and meta-theatrical effects, and see the Shakespearean performance-text as shifting from one realm to the other in the pursuit, partly, of representational power. Engaging in *watching* is for Shakespeare the most potent way of releasing that power, so he points to it not simply to subvert it, but to embody it. What seems most to be at stake is the process of activating participation, whereby the spectator participates the present body of the actor, sometimes in a displaced but nonetheless deeply engaged and meaningful way – as the testimony of Nashe, Jackson, and others makes clear. Participation finally requires a way of thinking about the actor's body that invests it with the rhetorical power to move, to affect the physical bodies of the spectators and to signify as the *person* who both represents and is represented.

NOTES

1 For further analysis of the theoretical assumptions of performance criticism, see my essay "Impasse over the Stage" and W. B. Worthen's "Deeper Meanings and Theatrical Technique."

2 That paradox, we may note, is peculiarly marked when acting is construed, as it is in the Renaissance, as mimetic, since it is the actor's job to convince the audience of the truth of the represented person. Acting then becomes a focus for what has been called the "crisis of representation."

3 The letter from which this excerpt is taken, originally written in Latin, is quoted in Tillotson. The translation here is my own. The Latin text which, together with a somewhat different translation, is available in Salgado (30), runs as follows: "At vero Desdemona illa apud nos a marito occisa, quanquam optime semper causam egit, interfecta tamen magis movebat; cum in lecto decumbens spectantium misericordiam ipso vultu imploraret."

4 See, for example, Karen Newman 87.

5 The phrase "causam egit" could be translated "pleaded her case" as well as "acted her part."

6 John Webster's Character of "An Excellent Actor" is apposite: "by a full and significant action of the body, he charms our attention: sit in a full theatre and you will think you see so many lines drawn from the circumference of so many ears, while the actor is the centre" (quoted in Chambers IV: 257–8).

7 This even includes the comments of Lady Mary Wroth which Michael Shapiro has recently discussed. Since she is speaking not about theatrical performance at all, but rather about the hypocrisy of a certain type of false woman, her use of the trope of the actor behind the mask actually reveals very little about audience response in the theatre – beyond of course the fact that it was possible to see the "delicate play-boy" behind the "louing womans part." It could even be argued that Wroth's simile confirms the idea that the ordinary response to the "play-boy" was to believe in his "action," since she is describing a situation where an auditor, by intentionally focusing on technique alone, is refusing the emotional sympathy normally demanded in the theatre.

8 In a sense what I am saying is the dead opposite of what Harry Berger has been saying off and on for several years now (though he has modified his views somewhat in his book, *Imaginary Audition*). His argument is that Shakespeare stages the inadequacy and relative superficiality of theatrical meanings, providing a critique of performance as a "flight from text," and making manifest how theatrical embodiment and concern with character limit the *text's* free-ranging analysis of, say, the effects of discursive inscription. My own point is that Shakespeare, rather, stages the conflict between body and meaning in a way that locates fundamental, though of course not exclusive, signifying power in the theatrical body. My argument about participation should also be distinguished from what Stephen Greenblatt suggests about the Shakespearean theatre eliciting not belief but *complicity* (118–19); I would say in contrast that complicity and belief are inextricably entwined and involve each other.

9 There are several ways in which what I am saying here intersects with the work of my colleague Paul Yachnin (see References), to whom I am indebted not only for sharing his work with me but for offering many fruitful observations about the present paper.

REFERENCES

Adelman, Janet. "'Born of Woman': Fantasies of Maternal Power in *Macbeth*." *Cannibals, Witches and Divorce: Estranging the Renaissance.* Ed. Marjorie Garber. Baltimore: Johns Hopkins, 1987. 90–121.

Altman, Joel B. "'Vile Participation': The Amplification of Violence in the Theatre of *Henry V*". *Shakespeare Quarterly* 42:1 (1991): 1–32.

Archer, William. *Masks or Faces* (1888), in *The Paradox of Acting and Masks or Faces.* Ed. Lee Strasberg. New York: Hill & Wang, 1957.

Barber, C. L. and Richard Wheeler. *The Whole Journey: Shakespeare's Power of Development.* Berkeley and Los Angeles: University of California Press, 1986.

Barker, Francis. *The Tremulous Private Body.* London: Methuen, 1984.

Berger, Harry, Jr. *Imaginary Audition.* Berkeley and Los Angeles: University of California Press, 1989.

—— "Text against Performance in Shakespeare: The Example of *Macbeth*." *The Power of Forms.* Ed. Stephen Greenblatt. Norman, Okla.: Pilgrim Books, 1982. 49–81.

Chambers, E. K. *The Elizabethan Stage.* 4 vols. Oxford: Clarendon, 1923.

Dawson, Anthony. "The Impasse over the Stage." *English Literary Renaissance* 21:3 (Autumn, 1991): 309–27.

—— *Watching Shakespeare.* London: Macmillan, 1988.

Diderot, Denis. *The Paradox of Acting.* Trans. W. H. Pollock, in *The Paradox of Acting and Masks or Faces.* Ed. Lee Strasberg. New York: Hill & Wang, 1957.

Douglas, Mary. *Natural Symbols.* London: Barrie & Rockcliff, 1970.

Fineman, Joel. *Shakespeare's Perjured Eye: The Structure of Poetic Subjectivity in the Sonnets.* Berkeley and Los Angeles: University of California Press, 1986.

Freedman, Barbara. *Staging the Gaze.* Ithaca, NY: Cornell University Press, 1990.

Greenblatt, Stephen. *Shakespearean Negotiations.* Berkeley and Los Angeles: University of California Press, 1988.

Hooker, Richard. *Of the Laws of Ecclesiastical Polity.* Ed. A. S. McGrade and Brian Vickers. London: Sidgwick & Jackson, 1975.

Laqueur, Thomas. *Making Sex: Body and Gender from the Greeks to Freud.* Cambridge, Mass.: Harvard University Press, 1990.

Luther, Martin. *Works.* 55 vols. Ed. Jaroslav Pelikan (vols. 1–30) and Helmut J. Lehmann (vols. 31–55). St Louis: Concordia Publishing House, 1955–76.

Matthews, Brander, ed. *Papers on Acting.* New York: Hill & Wang, 1958.

Montrose, Louis. "The Purpose of Playing: Reflections on a Shakespearean Anthropology." *Helios* 7 (1980): 51–74.

Nashe, Thomas. *Pierce Penilesse, His Supplication to the Divell* (1592). Ed. G. B. Harrison. London: Bodley Head, 1924.

Newman, Karen. *Fashioning Femininity and English Renaissance Drama.* Chicago: University of Chicago Press, 1991.

Paster, Gail Kern. "Leaky Vessels: The Incontinent Women of City Comedy." *Renaissance Drama* ns 18 (1987): 43–65.

Roach, Joseph. *The Player's Passion: Studies in the Science of Acting.* Newark: University of Delaware Press, 1985.

Salgado, Gamini, ed. *Eyewitnesses of Shakespeare.* London: Sussex University Press, 1975.

Shapiro, Michael. "Lady Mary Wroth Describes a 'Boy Actress'." *Medieval and Renaissance Drama in England* 4 (1987): 187–94.

Shuger, Deborah. *Habits of Thought in the English Renaissance.* Berkeley and Los Angeles: University of California Press, 1990.

Sprague, A. C. *Shakespearian Players and Performances.* Cambridge, Mass.: Harvard University Press, 1953.

Stallybrass, Peter. "*Macbeth* and Witchcraft." *Focus on Macbeth.* Ed. J. R. Brown. London: Routledge, 1982. 189–209.

Strasberg, Lee, ed. *The Paradox of Acting and Masks or Faces.* New York: Hill & Wang, 1957.

Tillotson, Geoffrey. "*Othello* and *The Alchemist* at Oxford." *TLS* (20 July 1933): 494.

Vickers, Nancy. "Diana Described: Scattered Woman and Scattered Rhyme." *Writing and Sexual Difference.* Ed. Elizabeth Abel. Chicago: University of Chicago Press, 1982. 95–110.

Worthen, W. B. "Deeper Meanings and Theatrical Technique: The Rhetoric of Performance Criticism." *Shakespeare Quarterly* 40:4 (Winter, 1989): 441–55.

Wright, Thomas. *The Passions of the Minde.* London, 1604.

Yachnin, Paul. "The Politics of Theatrical Mirth." *Shakespeare Quarterly* 43:1 (Spring, 1992): 51–66.

—— "The Powerless Theatre." *English Literary Renaissance* 21:1 (Winter, 1991): 49–74.

4

SQUEAKING CLEOPATRAS

Gender and performance in *Antony and Cleopatra*

Juliet Dusinberre

With a curious irony of fate, Ladbroke's, the betting and casino magnates, became the chief sponsors of Peter Hall's 1987 production of *Antony and Cleopatra* at the National Theatre with Anthony Hopkins and Judi Dench in the title roles (Lowen 99). Shakespeare would perhaps have been the first to appreciate the appropriateness of such backing for a drama in which hero and heroine compete ceaselessly for prowess in the world of the play, in the theatre, and in the consciousness of the audience. The heart of that competition lies in the oscillating constructions of the masculine and the feminine which dominate not only the play, but the conditions of its reception in the consciousness of the audience. The play's theatrical history amply demonstrates the curious interplay between cultural assumptions – in both audience and actors – and a text which was conceived for an all-male cast in which Cleopatra would have been played by a boy.

Antony and Cleopatra is the only one of Shakespeare's tragedies in which the figure of the boy actor arrests the audience's attention. Moreover, no tragedian among Shakespeare's contemporaries experiments with the theatrical possibilities of putting the boy player into dialogue with the woman he plays. *The Duchess of Malfi* constructs the role of the woman ruler unmediated by any textual recognition that she is acted by a boy. Shakespeare's highlighting of the boy's part in *Antony and Cleopatra* creates a drama which constantly comments on its own status as theatrical performance. The part played by that boy in the creation of Shakespeare's most sensual and least boyish heroine has always seemed the biggest gamble of all in a play in which metaphors of gambling and of competitive games interlace the entire text. Cleopatra herself fears the boy actor as the medium through which Octavius would expose his winning of herself:

> The quick comedians
> Extemporally will stage us and present
> Our Alexandrian revels; Antony
> Shall be brought drunken forth, and I shall see

Some squeaking Cleopatra boy my greatness
I'th'posture of a whore.[1]

In *Antony and Cleopatra* Shakespeare pushed the boy actor to his limits, and possibly beyond them. There is no contemporary account of performance in his own time, although the Lord Chamberlain's records state that it "was formerly acted at the Blackfriars" (Bevington 44). Did the dramatist perhaps imagine and long for a theatre in which his heroine might by played by a woman?

Modern audiences, who enjoy the luxury of seeing Cleopatra acted by a woman, bring to this play their own conceptions of sensuality and attach them to the bodies of the players, as they must have done also in Shakespeare's theatre when the male body of the actor had to be fictionalized into a female form. The role of the audience is more pervasive in the action of *Antony and Cleopatra* than in any other Shakespearean tragedy. *The Times*'s review of Trevor Nunn's 1972 production at the RSC with Richard Johnson and Janet Suzman pointed to the incorporation into the play itself of a dynamic of audience appeal: "As the lovers' fortunes decline, their audiences dwindle. In Antony's case it seems that the loss of an applauding public helps to sap his virility."[2] Once the part of Cleopatra was played by a woman, the sapping of Antony's virility became inseparable from the audience's own assumptions about the relations of men and women in the world to which they must return when the play is done.

The actress and the part she plays thus coalesce in the audience's imagination. That confusion of actress and role has formed a central part of reactions to the play in performance from the Restoration onwards (Maus 599). A woman acting Cleopatra can never be simply a medium, as the boy in Shakespeare's theatre arguably was. She is always a representative of her society's views on sensuality, and these views color her own interpretation of the part and the reactions of the audience. As soon as the boy actor ceased to perform, the idea of a physically based seductiveness became associated, in the consciousness of male critics and commentators, with the woman playing the part. Yet the attraction of the actual biological body could not form part of Shakespeare's theatrical realization of Cleopatra. Nor did it need to. Plutarch's *Life of Antonius* makes it plain that Cleopatra's attraction, unlike that of other women, came from her lightning quickness and unpredictability (Bullough V: 275). Granville Barker declared that the presence of the actress was a disadvantage in parts written for boys:

> Let the usurping actress remember that her sex is a liability, not an asset. The dramatist of today may refuse to exploit its allurements, but may legitimately allow for the sympathetic effect of it; though the less he does so, perhaps, the better for his play and the more gratitude the

> better sort of actress will show him. But Shakespeare makes no such demands, has left no blank spaces for her to fill with her charm.
>
> (Granville Barker 15–16)

The better sort of actress – a speaking phrase – is one who ignores the advantage given to her by her body.

Or, doesn't play the part at all. It has been alleged that the great Sarah Siddons refused to act Shakespeare's Cleopatra because she would "hate herself" if she did it as it was meant to be done. This presumably means that she felt Cleopatra's sensuality to be beyond the reach of a chaste woman actress. However, this speech of Siddons's seems to have been an invention of the late nineteenth century, appearing first in direct quotation (source unacknowledged) in an essay in the New York *Cosmopolitan* in 1897 (Wingate 10). It has since found its way into numerous accounts, including Herschel Baker's biography of John Kemble, which footnotes Campbell's eighteenth-century biography, in which I have not found any authority for Siddons's demur.[3] Campbell gives a more professional reason for Siddons's reluctance, namely, that Shakespeare's Cleopatra would not have suited her powers: "The energy of the heroine, though neither vulgar nor comic, has a meteoric playfulness and a subtle lubricity in the transition of feelings, that accords with no impression which can be recollected from Mrs. Siddons's acting." Campbell does not even think Siddons particularly suited to Dryden's Cleopatra in *All for Love* – a part she played many times – averring that if Dryden had not written the tasteless slanging match, she would have been well cast as Octavia (Campbell II: 126–7). Boaden also emphasized in *Memoirs of Mrs. Siddons* the professional reason for Siddons's reluctance to play Shakespeare's Empress. The skittishness and caprice of Shakespeare's Cleopatra was ill-suited to her talents. The more prudish and amateurish reason for non-performance, involving personal rather than professional considerations, appealed to nineteenth-century notions of female propriety.

A different kind of propriety is challenged in the play by the blatant competitiveness of the lovers. From the beginning of his infatuation with Cleopatra Antony has had to see her steal his audience: the very air went to gaze on her in her barge while he was left whistling in the market-place. Quoting the two parallel barge speeches, Shakespeare's uttered by Enobarbus and Dryden's by Antony, Boaden declares:

> Dryden's convinces us of the *dotage* only of Antony, Shakespeare's of the perfect attraction of Cleopatra. In the first, *his fondness* seems to have embellished her voyage; in the second HE is rendered a nullity by it, and, but that he is named by the poet, would have been forgotten by us, as he was by the people.
>
> (Boaden I: 243, 245)

The assessment of a balance of power between hero and heroine in *Antony and Cleopatra* spills over into a notion of theatrical power which is also implicit in the play itself (Singh 116). Whoever is perceived as winning dominion in the romance, is also perceived as theatrically dominant. The sense of taking sides, on which the dramatic action of the play is structured, has continued to dominate not only the experience of directors and actors, but also of critics and audiences.

The question of who, in *Antony and Cleopatra*, is *winning*, whether in love or politics or war, is canvassed from the opening speech of the play. According to the Roman verdict, Antony has kissed away kingdoms. He has changed clothes with Cleopatra and sold his manhood to her. At every turn Cleopatra has the measure of him, laughing when he is sad, melancholy when he is merry, turning in flight in the sea-battle in the sure knowledge that he will follow her like a doting mallard. Even in the monument, she interrupts his death speech: "I am dying, Egypt, dying./ Give me some wine, and let me speak a little." "No," cries Cleopatra, "Let *me* speak" (4.15.43–5, my emphasis). Antony is dispatched at the end of the fourth act, leaving the stage to Cleopatra, ready and possibly willing to catch another Antony in her strong toil of grace. The dramatist ousts from his play a hero who in the eyes of the heroine often seems as much rival as lover.

Antony's competition with Cleopatra is inseparable from his military and political rivalry with Octavius. At a key moment the Soothsayer warns him that Octavius's star is in the ascendant: Antony's guardian angel fears Caesar's, and Antony, whether from belief, or from policy, recalls that in the kind of sports now supported by Ladbroke's, Octavius always wins: "The very dice obey him" (2.3.33). The competition between the two men is not just for military command, nor for moral supremacy – Antony's inglorious present against his heroic past – but for manhood itself, Octavius's youth and virility against Antony's middle age: "He wears the rose/ Of youth upon him" (3.13.20). The boy Octavius who has worn his sword but as a dancer gambles in the end on displaying Cleopatra as his prize to the stinking multitude. When Octavius calls Antony his "great competitor" (1.4.3) in the Elizabethan meaning of the word as "partner," he might just as well be using the modern word, for in this play partners are competitors, whether in love or in war.

Competition, whether for sexual or military power, is from the first implicit in the idea of performance in the play. In the scene where Cleopatra allows Thidias to kiss her hand Antony demands what Thidias is, and he retorts:

> One that but performs
> The bidding of the fullest man, and worthiest
> To have command obeyed.
>
> (3.13.88–90)

The lines contain a deliberate sexual taunt, of the performance of the fullest man, implying the sexual nature of the command which such a man utters. The tone and frame of reference of the taunt are prompted by Cleopatra's own lines, which immediately precede the speech, about the greater Caesar's (sexual) performance. Thidias implies that not only may Octavius claim a right to Cleopatra, but even his messenger plays a part in the performance of the fullest man. At this point the boy actor seems to emerge from the shadows, protesting against the erasure of his biological identity. The threat that Cleopatra has stolen Antony's manhood would have carried a particular piquancy when the part was played by a boy, an up-and-coming youth whose sexual vitality could provide its own menace to the middle-aged hero.

As if subconsciously aware of such complications, Dryden in *All for Love* (1678), writing for a theatre in which both Cleopatra and Octavia were played by women actors, altered the terms of *Antony and Cleopatra*'s dramatic confrontations. Octavia is restored to domestic power, playing a vital part in the play's renewed competition between respectability and trollophood, the virtuous wife and the "other," the Egyptian whore. In this, Dryden is truer to Plutarch than Shakespeare was. Intriguingly, even in Shakespeare's time when the female parts were played by boys, the characters of Cleopatra and Octavia seem sometimes to have entered male consciousness as role models, desirable or undesirable, for real women. When Samuel Daniel dedicated his "Letter from Octavia to Marcus Antonius" to his patron, Margaret, Countess of Cumberland, he made it plain that he considered Octavia's sufferings to have a real-life counterpart in the distress caused to the Countess by her husband's life-long philandering (Rees 76). The letter was written in the 1590s at about the same time as the earliest versions of his own play of *Cleopatra*. Daniel, in half of his mind, thought Octavia the real heroine of the piece, as Dryden was later to do.

Elizabethan audiences would also have been aware of a real-life situation in which gender issues were constantly canvassed: around the person of their own woman ruler. Elizabeth I fictionalized her own body relentlessly, so that its manifest ageing and incapacity for child-bearing bore no relation to the narratives she continued to spin around her putative future as a marriageable woman capable of producing an heir even beyond the age of fifty. Charmian's remark to the Soothsayer, "Let me have a child at fifty, to whom Herod of Jewry may do homage" (1.2.26–7), with its almost blasphemous allusion to the Virgin birth, must have awakened ambivalent memories of a different Virgin and a peculiarly Elizabethan dilemma. Elizabeth's godson, Sir John Harington, wrote in an (unpublished) *Tract on the Succession* in 1602: "To make the world thinke she should have children of hir owne, she entertained till she was fiftye yeares of age mentions of marriage" (Harington 40). *Antony and Cleopatra* recalls the activities of a woman ruler whose play with gender roles and with the manipulations of her own femininity for political purposes kept her male courtiers in thrall for the best part of half a century (Jankowski *passim*). Elizabeth is renowned for having told Essex that she would be mistress in her own kingdom (Montrose 78), and for having bought her power over him at the price of his head. But such domination is, as the Queen herself was the first to appreciate, at war with traditional notions of sexuality in which mastery of the woman is the badge of manhood.

Some scholars have been reluctant to accept that Elizabeth I had any part in the creation of Cleopatra. Initially some tenuous arguments were advanced to demonstrate that the competition between Cleopatra and Octavia drew some inspiration from Elizabeth's enquiries to Sir James Melville about her rival (Bevington 12, n. 4). But although this particular instance is now discounted, renewed interest in the plays as performed within their own historical contexts has led to a conviction that the image-making capacities of both Elizabeth I and her successor, James I, form part of the play's subsoil. Indeed, just as a competition is enacted within the play between Antony and Octavius, and between Egypt and Rome, so is that competition played out in our own times between scholars who see the play as a Jacobean statement about the rise of the new Augustus, James I – an iconography adopted by that monarch which would make Octavius a subtle compliment to the king – or as nostalgia for the glorious past of the Elizabethan age, in which Antony acquires some characteristics in common with the disgraced Earl of Essex (Yachin 9). The cultural associations which Shakespeare's Cleopatra calls into being, however, reach beyond the gender disruptions of Elizabethan and Jacobean politics.

Shakespeare's Cleopatra has recently been inserted into the tradition of feminizing culture associated with the advent of Christianity, as part of a tradition of holy prostitutes originating in the figure of Mary Magdalene and the iconography of the Song of Solomon. The final tableau of Cleopatra's suckling of the asp resonates on images of Madonna and child (King 445, 449; Rackin 206). Elizabeth's deliberate annexing of the cult of the Virgin, a phenomenon exemplified in Book III of Spenser's *The Faerie Queene*, creates further links between Elizabeth and the Egyptian queen. Against Elizabeth's cult of the Virgin Queen, with its associations with the Song of Solomon and the Bride of Christ, James I constructed his own cultural myth of the new Augustus (Yachin 10). Herod of Jewry is mentioned three times in Shakespeare's play, as if to blur the historical distance between the pagan Egyptian world and the mystery plays which had made Herod a familiar figure to Shakespeare's own audiences. Cleopatra's Egypt is dramatized as on the brink, historically, of a new Christian sensibility. The competition in Shakespeare's play between the Roman Octavius and the Egyptian Queen can in this context be read as a truly Renaissance confrontation between Christian and Pagan cultures, between the new feminized Christianity – Cleopatra's fluid water imagery with its Christian associations of baptism and repentance – and the hard dry masculine culture of Rome.

Obliged to carry such a wealth of suggestiveness, the male body of the boy actor playing Shakespeare's Cleopatra in the theatre becomes as insignificant as the biological maleness of the adult players who performed in the mystery cycles (Rastall *passim*). The boy provides a medium for these immensely varied and resonant images of gender. That sense of connecting with multiple sources of myth and symbol, and of a dimension which stretches beyond the theatre into the world of the audience, has remained vital in both the reading and the acting of *Antony and Cleopatra* in later periods. The obsession with real-life parallels is evident in Anna Jameson's remarkable analysis of Cleopatra, first published in 1832, where the author maintains that "Shakespeare's Cleopatra is the real historical Cleopatra" (Jameson 218–19). But in the modern theatre the play is always in danger of attrition from the sheer inability of the players and audience to reimagine the powerful cultural cross-currents from which it sprang, and which contribute so vitally to its complex negotiations of gender and performance.

As masculinity and femininity, the roles of gender, are themselves performed in the play, the male body of the boy actor becomes a fiction invented by Cleopatra. Her scorn of being played by a boy illuminates Judith Butler's analysis in *Gender Trouble* (1990) of the fictionalization of the biological body, which ceases to be a "given," outside the concepts of gender, but becomes instead a part of those gender constructions.[4] This is certainly true of the boy actor in Shakespeare's practice of writing; one of the misunderstandings which modern criticism tends to perpetrate is a belief in the original audience's firm conviction of the boy as biological male.[5] Both Stephen Orgel and Laura Levine have argued that the audience entered the theatre with an already destabilized sense of the actor's body (Orgel 13; Levine 131; Sprengnether 202). Reviewing Michael Langham's production in Stratford, Ontario in 1967, Walter Kerr exhorted his readers to

> recall, just for one moment, that the performer who read these lines [about the squeaking boy Cleopatra] in Shakespeare's time was actually a squeaking boy and your eyes are apt to begin double somersaults. We are – now – looking at the very play that Cleopatra is killing herself to avoid seeing. She is already an actress playing herself, expressing the hope that she will never see herself played.
>
> (Kerr 1; Williamson 45)

Langham's production aimed, through Tanya Moisewitch's modified Elizabethan stage design, at some idea of authenticity, which may have prompted Kerr's remarks about the boy actor. The critic identifies gender as performable. However, Kerr's account misses an important point. Cleopatra killed herself to avoid seeing a *boy* perform. Would she have felt equally threatened by the concept of a woman performer?

If the boy actor was a part of Shakespeare's Cleopatra not only because he had to act, but because Cleopatra herself *imagined* him, his presence has dominated the imaginations of later actresses, who echo Cleopatra's incredulity at the idea of a boy's being able to play the part. They often manifest an awareness of the boy behind the woman which never occurs in their discussions of other tragic heroines. Barbara Jefford said of her performance at the Old Vic in 1978: "I can't imagine what kind of boy played it at the time it was written – perhaps no one ever did and perhaps that is why it was hardly ever played." Janet Suzman (RSC, 1972) also doubted the capacity of the boy actor and proposed an older man in the role:

> I find it hard to think he wrote it for a boy. I think he must have written it for a man, perhaps a kind of Shakespearean Danny La Rue – there must have been some kind of prima donna in his company playing women's parts and men are notoriously good at it. It could never have been acted by a boy – Portia, Rosalind, Viola, yes – they could be breathtaking played by a stripling, a clear young spirit, but not Cleopatra.
>
> (Cook 139, 137)

A reviewer in *The Times* declared that "Janet Suzman, in a role created for a male actor, creates a woman who is only incidentally voluptuous." The *Financial Times* went further, claiming that of the two lovers "Cleopatra seems the stronger. Janet Suzman has given her a touch of masculinity: she is an Egyptian Elizabeth I." The *Gloucester Citizen* thought Miss Suzman "a tempestuous, gypsy tomboy Cleopatra. . . . This was scarcely the highly intelligent politically shrewd Queen who ruled a vast empire with skill and cunning."[6] Both actress and reviewers cannot rid themselves of preconceptions about how a boy could transform himself into a woman. The word "tomboy" is a staple of Cleopatra criticism: the woman usurping the boy's cultural role is somehow the equivalent to the Elizabethan boy actor's usurping the woman's part.

If anything, the recollection of the boy confuses, for both actresses and reviewers, the issue of how Cleopatra might be played by a woman. The idea of the boy stands in the way of an appreciation of the woman. When George Rylands described Vivien Leigh as Cleopatra (with Olivier in 1951) he asked: "How are we to assess Vivien Leigh's performance in the part – which is not playable by mortal woman, and was written for a boy?" Rylands, like Redgrave, had played some of Shakespeare's women and had a keen sense of their origins in the boy actor. He lamented that in modern productions "the Cleopatra of Gautier and Flaubert still exerts her spell and Shakespeare's boy player is suppressed" (Rylands 140, 142). The actress who came nearest to an understanding of the various elements which make up Shakespeare's Cleopatra was probably Peggy Ashcroft, who ignored the boy in favor of the *Greek* Cleopatra, a being who might be the female equivalent in cunning of Ulysses in *Troilus and Cressida.* Instead of trying to perform the part with the boy haunting her imagination, Ashcroft declared: "What a relief to act Cleopatra and *cause* suffering for a change. For years in plays I have been the woman who has suffered through other men on stage."[7] Would this perception of reversed power structures within the theatrical fiction have had any parallel in the relation between Cleopatra and the men on stage when the part was played by a boy?

Part of the answer to that question might lie in comments made by Judi Dench on Peter Hall's 1987 production for the National Theatre, in which she played opposite Anthony Hopkins. Michael Billington asserts that all later Cleopatras owed something of their success to Ashcroft, who "finally proved that Cleopatra was not the unattainable K2 it had seemed but a role that could be conquered through forethought, planning and the support of a first-rate team" (Billington 150). Judi Dench consulted Ashcroft about the part, and the concept of a "team" may have come from the idea of the earlier Ashcroft–Redgrave partnership. Redgrave suggested that the collaborative principle was a reason for his own success as Antony, pointing to the paramount importance of Enobarbus: "'for Enobarbus creates Antony's nobility and Cleopatra's fascination as much as the protagonists can hope to do'" (Findlater, *Michael Redgrave* 129). Peter Hall had required all his actors to read Granville Barker, who observes of Cleopatra: "Shakespeare's Cleopatra had to be acted by a boy, and this did everything to determine, not his view of the character, but his presenting of it. He does not shirk her sensuality, he stresses it time and again; but he has to find other ways than the one impracticable way of bringing it home to us" (Granville Barker 435). If the boy's presence was not palpable in the deliberately mature and middle-aged passion of Dench's and Hopkins's lovers, the idea of a team of players and of the vital importance of other players, particularly in helping to realize the sensuality of Cleopatra, recaptured the dynamic of the original theatrical conditions under which both the dramatist and his boy actors worked. Shakespeare offered the boy playing Cleopatra maximum support not only from the other apprentices who play the parts of Iras and Charmian, but from adult players – Enobarbus, Alexas, the Soothsayer, the Messenger. A review of Hall's production noted with approval that Hopkins and Dench "play the title roles as if they were not star actors" (12 April 1987, Williamson 77–8).

Antony and Cleopatra both represents within the play itself, and exemplifies in its theatre history, a curious battle for supremacy between two concepts of theatre: the theatre of stars and repertory theatre. Paradoxically, the stage history of the play suggests that in performance it works the least well in the theatre of stars. This was presumably the case in

Shakespeare's time. If Antony was played by Burbage, by 1609 a recognized star, his Cleopatra must have been the most accomplished of the boy actors, but he was not a star. Part of the dramatic tension of the play comes, however, from a latent drive, within the creation of Cleopatra, for a supremacy which resurrects the social condition of the apprenticed boy actor, playing the part of an Empress, possibly to his own master, Burbage himself, whom he is allowed, in theatrical terms, to supersede. Like Ashcroft, Judi Dench saw Cleopatra in terms of cunning and a will to survive: "Although Peter says that after Antony dies, the audience are longing for Cleopatra to join him, I keep finding moments when she seems to want to live" (Lowen 93). Beneath that perception lies not Peter Hall's romantic Cleopatra, but the theatrical reality of a boy apprentice revelling in the theatrical power bestowed on him in the final act of the play. Why should he die? This is the moment which, as an actor, he has been eagerly awaiting.

This awareness of subordination, and what it means in terms of performance, surfaces in scenes which manifest a surprising sense of the significance of supporting parts, so liberally provided in the play. In 3.1 Ventidius, successful against the Parthians in Antony's name, points out that great commanders are always feeding off the successes of the unnamed men who do the real work for them. "Caesar and Antony have ever won/ More in their officer than person" (3.1.16–17). But those people must be careful. They need to stifle the wish to take the credit for an action which can be registered only in the master's name. Ventidius explains the careful limits which must be set on his own performance:

> I could do more to do Antonius good,
> But 'twould offend him, and in his offence
> Should my performance perish.
>
> (3.1.25–7)

The ostensible context is military performance, but Ventidius's language conjures up theatrical performance just as strongly. In the play the two are constantly linked, as they are both also linked with concepts of sexual performance. Ventidius, apart from this one scene and this one speech, is a walk-on part. Yet in fact he controls the action of the play not just through the winning of the battle, but through a manipulation of the public perception of the origins of power. The theatre audience's apprehension of Antony's mythology is momentarily destabilized by Ventidius's claim that where the General appears powerful, it is only because his inferior has allowed him to seem so.

The boy playing Cleopatra in Shakespeare's theatre intervenes, as Ventidius here intervenes in a military context, in the authority structures which surround him. The competition for ascendancy between the boy and the adult actors has been in evidence throughout *Antony and Cleopatra.*

From the opening scene the boy actor who plays Cleopatra has danced circles not only around Antony but also around Octavius, persistently upstaging both men. When Cleopatra first enters, it is not her voluptuousness which the text evokes, but her capacity to perform. The word "perform" is used sparingly by Shakespeare in this play, but at every point it carries a startling multiplicity of meaning. When Cleopatra urges Antony to hear Caesar's messengers, she declares:

> [W]ho knows
> If the scarce-bearded Caesar have not sent
> His powerful mandate to you, 'Do this, or this;
> Take in that kingdom and enfranchise that;
> Perform't, or else we damn thee.'
>
> (1.1.21–5)

"Perform" here means "act," and thus immediately invokes the playhouse: the false peremptoriness of Caesar is mocked by Cleopatra's aping of his speech and manner. The concept of Roman control is queried through imitation. As Cleopatra enacts Caesar's control of Antony she undermines it with mimicry, in a manner which might have been applauded by the French feminist Hélène Cixous, with her exhortation to explode male control with laughter (Cixous 258). Through an act of ventriloquy Cleopatra creates a female subversion of Caesar's master-text of control. Caesar's imperiousness is *made up*, a speech written for him by another performer, Cleopatra herself. The impact of the mimicry is possibly even more subversive if spoken by a woman than by a boy actor. But as he plays not only the Empress, commanding her world, but also himself, the boy actor – an apprentice – momentarily steals the language of the master, just as the woman herself takes it. Ellen Terry wrote: "To act, you must make the thing written your own. You must steal the words, steal the thought, and convey the stolen treasure with great art" (Terry 15).

The whole of the first act of *Antony and Cleopatra* elaborates on notions of performance set up in this speech: of imitation, of the undermining of what is serious, of role-playing and manipulation. The compeer of the acting, the action of the play, and political action in Act 1 is Cleopatra herself, a virtuoso performer who criticizes the performances of other people, urging Antony to simulate grief for his dead wife Fulvia:

> play one scene
> Of excellent dissembling, and let it look
> Like perfect honour.
>
> (1.3.78–80)

She talks of playing the fool, but implies that behind the role is the wisdom of the serpent of Old Nile:

Why did he marry Fulvia, and not love her?
I'll seem the fool I am not.
(1.1.43–4)

Contrasted with Antony's poor acting is Cleopatra's sense of her own fine performance, underwritten by her audience on stage as well as by the theatre audience who observes her exposing the amateurishness of her Roman lover. Enobarbus's tributes to her wonderful "celerity in dying" and her sighs and tears which make "greater storms and tempests than almanacs can report" (1.2.140, 144–5) salute a professional. The audience is reminded of the figure of the actor behind the mask of the Egyptian Queen: "Pray you, stand farther from me" (1.3.18), she commands Antony, a command which the great late-nineteenth-century Shakespearean actor Henry Irving used to make to the lesser mortals acting on stage with him. Give me space to breathe, Cleopatra insists to Antony, at the same time that the actor playing her demands: Give me stage space in which to upstage *you*. The question of upstaging – in theatrical terms, in military terms, and ultimately in sexual terms – dominates this play.[8] The boy, just an apprentice in Shakespeare's company, is given a role in the play which constantly upstages those more powerful than he in theatrical terms.

This dynamic becomes an enormous focus of energy in the play, the *event* which has been compared to the scientific perception that "energy, not matter, is the basic datum" (Schmitt 231–4), a dictum which can be applied to the situation of the boy actor. The energy of the performance is the "given" of the Elizabethan theatre, where matter itself – the male body of the boy – is subjugated to the energy released by the fiction of gender transference. The actual biological male body of the boy is erased by the performative energy of the theatrical experience. Once women were acting on the Restoration stage, that "given" reverted to matter: the physical body that performs.

The circulation of energy in the Elizabethan theatre is better understood in our contemporary period, with its theoretical interest in performance, than it perhaps was in the earlier star theatre, where so many Antonys felt thwarted by the role which seemed to deny them star status. Richard Findlater observes:

> Although Cleopatra's Antony is one of Shakespeare's most magnificent creations, he has been an infrequent visitor to the English stage; the role of "strumpet's fool" and "plated Mars" baffles some actors and repels many more. Garrick and Phelps failed in the part; Irving and Kean avoided it; Macready noted it, after consulting Plutarch, as "long, and I fear not effective", and found his own performance "hasty, unprepared, unfinished".

Findlater is unimpressed by the Antonys of Gielgud, Olivier, Wolfit, and Godfrey Tearle: "It is a curious record of defeat, much more surprising than the similar roll-call of routed Cleopatras. As Herbert Farjeon said, Shakespeare 'might almost have written the part of the two lovers for the express purpose of ruining histrionic reputations'" (Findlater, *Michael Redgrave* 129). Shakespeare has set up a dialectic in *Antony and Cleopatra* between the protagonists who compete relentlessly with each other under the charade of partnership, and the myriad supporting characters who purvey them to the audience, as Ventidius purveys Antony's success in battle. Without both elements – the ruthless competition, and the support from the other members of the cast – the play cannot ignite.

The dynamics of this competition are complicated by the presence of women actresses, because the competition becomes inseparable from extra-theatrical notions of the proper relation between men and women. The twentieth-century performance history of the play suggests that an originally ludic theatrical creation has as a consequence become *serious.* When Glenda Jackson acted Cleopatra in 1978 the production "did not forget that Cleopatra was first created for a boy actor. The Queen's sensuality was private in her relationship with Antony, although renowned throughout the world. She was an Elizabeth I in a very different and much hotter climate: powerful, but wary of her own feelings and emotions" (Scott 54). Nevertheless Jackson's performance of Cleopatra – perhaps remembering her earlier role as Elizabeth in the 1971 television drama – stressed authority at the expense of sensuality, underplaying the Cleopatra for whom sensuality and power are both part of a theatrical performance and an entertainment, for both performer and audience. Jackson's display of power was not a game, but a cool distancing of private emotion. But Cleopatra is a constant player of games,[9] as Elizabeth herself was. One of the reasons for the chequered fortunes of the play in the theatre is that game-playing is considered the stuff of comedy rather than of tragedy.

When Shaw decided to "improve" on Shakespeare by writing his comedy of *Caesar and Cleopatra,* he declared a Johnsonian distaste for making "sexual infatuation a tragic theme," where it can only be a comic one. Shaw's dislike of English theatre audiences centered on the inability of the English male to *play.* "The well-fed Englishman," he remarks, "cannot play. . . . When he wants sensuality, he practises it: he does not play with voluptuous or romantic ideas. From the play of ideas – and the drama can never be anything more – he demands edification, and will not pay for anything else in that arena" (Shaw 30, 8, 9–10). In an essay written more than fifty years later in 1954, entitled "Some Notes on Stage Sexuality," Kenneth Tynan shows that the terms of Shaw's argument about play could still dominate discussion of sensuality in the English theatre: "The English, as their drama represents them, are a nation endlessly communicative about love without ever enjoying it. Full-blooded physical relationships engaged in with mutual delight are theatrically tabu" (Tynan 61). His own trenchant criticism of both Olivier and Leigh in 1951 and of Redgrave and Ashcroft in Glen Byam Shaw's Stratford production of the play two years later in 1953 reveals the preconceptions which created the taboo he identifies.

In the double bill – of Shakespeare's play and Shaw's – Olivier was widely accused of playing down to allow his wife to shine (Findlater, *Player King* 224). Tynan declares of Leigh's performance in *Caesar and Cleopatra*: "She keeps a firm grip on the narrow ledge which is indisputably hers; the level on which she can be pert, sly, and spankable, and fill out a small personality." On Shakespeare's play he remarks:

> "You were a boggler ever," says Antony at one point to his idle doxy; and one can feel Miss Leigh's imagination boggling at the thought of playing Cleopatra. Taking a deep breath and resolutely focusing her periwinkle charm, she launches another of her careful readings; ably and passionlessly she picks her way among its great challenges, presenting a glibly mown lawn where her author had imagined a jungle. . . . Yet one feeling rode over these in my mind; the feeling Mr. Bennet in *Pride and Prejudice* was experiencing when he dissuaded his daughter from further pianoforte recital by murmuring that she had "delighted us long enough."
>
> (Tynan 9–10)

Tynan wanted Antony to be more of a hero; in the theatrical competition between the two stars he believed that Antony must win. But Olivier's own comments are revealing. He thought Vivien Leigh the finest Cleopatra he had ever seen, and he declared of his own performance as Antony:

> I'd never really thought a lot about Antony – as a person, that is. I mean, really, he's an absolute twerp, isn't he? A stupid man. But thank God Shakespeare didn't try to rectify that; if he had, there would have been no play. Not a lot between the ears has Antony. Now Cleopatra, she's the one. She has wit, style and sophistication, and if she's played well, no Antony, however brilliant, can touch her.

Olivier rightly believed that the play presents a competition in which Cleopatra vanquishes Antony. Of its sensuality he declared: "There is nothing cerebral about their love: it is pure passion, lust and enjoyment. And why not? How would you feel alone in a chamber with that lady? I don't think you'd want to discuss the *Times* crossword" (Williamson 17, 28). How swiftly the reference to the "*Times* crossword" identifies the world described by Shaw as that of the average English playgoer, a world from which Tynan in spirit still comes.

Would Tynan's criticisms of Leigh as Cleopatra have been so scathing if he had seen Shakespeare's boy actor in the part? When he wrote about Vivien Leigh it is evident that the real body and the real actress had become inseparable in his mind from the fiction of Cleopatra and her subjection of Antony. When Tynan sees Vivien Leigh, all he can think of is, first, that

British girls can't act sensuality – the point he proceeds to when he reviews Ashcroft two years later; second, that Leigh has been corrupted by Hollywood; third, that a great male actor, Olivier, has (i) made a terrible mistake in his marriage to such a pert little miss, and (ii) is allowing his marriage to ruin his career. These judgements show just as odd a confusion between life and art, the real body and the fictional body, the woman who is, and the woman who plays, as anything written of actresses from their first appearance on the Restoration stage to the present.[10] The heart of Tynan's objection is that he doesn't want Cleopatra to win the competition with Antony, any more than he wants Leigh to win the competition with Olivier, or for Olivier, worse still, to let her do so. Olivier himself is in no doubt on the matter, saying of Antony: "It's a wonderful part. But just remember, all you future Antonys, one little word of advice: Cleopatra's got you firmly by the balls" (Williamson 28). Linda Charnes has pointed out that "in this play he [Antony] occupies a subject position almost always culturally reserved for women, and in relation to a Cleopatra who occupies a position almost always reserved for men" (Charnes 9). Would Tynan have minded Leigh's dominance as Cleopatra over Olivier as Antony, if a boy who looked like Leigh had been playing the part?

The question about the boy actor might be answered by turning to the review Tynan wrote of Redgrave and Ashcroft, which begins with some general reflections on English actresses and sensuality:

> There is only one role in *Antony and Cleopatra* that English actresses are naturally equipped to play. This is Octavia, Caesar's docile sister. . . . The great sluts of world drama, from Clytemnestra to Anna Christie, have always puzzled our girls; and an English Cleopatra is a contradiction in terms.

Ashcroft's Cleopatra became for him a version of Lady Chatterley: "A nice intense woman, you nearly murmured; such a pity she took up with the head gamekeeper." Somewhat inconsistently, he urged Redgrave to "let up a little on lust" (Tynan 49–50). Antony's lust didn't fit his notion of Roman (for which read English?) manhood any more than Cleopatra fitted his idea of the English actress. Sensuality was not a fiction of sensuality, but the real thing. Wasn't Redgrave pawing Ashcroft rather more than was tasteful? Had the part been played by a boy, none of the cultural anxieties aroused by the presence on stage of a woman's body would have been set in motion.

Both these productions demonstrate the way in which the woman playing Cleopatra in the modern theatre has become the medium through which the audience produces meaning.[11] Since the re-establishment of Shakespeare's play in preference to Dryden's – with Samuel Phelps's revival at Sadler's Wells in 1847 – the actress has become the principal signifier of the anxieties and obsessions, pleasurable and less pleasurable, which dominate the audience who watches her.

In the first successful revival of Shakespeare's play since Elizabethan times, staged just ten years after Victoria came to the throne, Isabella Glyn as Cleopatra bears – to twentieth-century eyes – an uncanny likeness to later photographs of Queen Victoria. The same actress's 1867 performance was considered "ripe in animal desire" (*Examiner*, 8 June 1867, Lamb 75), a desire whose prohibited nature perhaps fascinated audiences the more because of the actress's curious physical resemblance to their own impeccably proper queen. The sensuality of Shakespeare's heroine blatantly contradicted notions of social respectability, thus making the theatre a site for the unleashing in the audience of repressed fantasies. From its mid-Victorian revival onwards, Shakespeare's play became a witness not only to sensuality, but to that other great symbol of male power, conspicuous consumption, linked in Herbert Tree's 1906 revival with unmistakable images of empire. Cleopatra was displayed as the goddess Isis in a curiously titillating mixture of representing "the other" to the great British public, and reminding it of past glories where another exotic title – Empress of India – represented a supreme Victorian grandeur and colonial triumph. The nostalgia which in 1606 the play conjured up for its first audiences, in recalling a Virgin Queen who had dispatched her favorites to colonize and conquer on her behalf, was capable of re-enactment in the already nostalgic Edwardian England of 1906. Similar recollections of Empire may have lain behind the connections drawn by a reviewer of Trevor Nunn's 1972 Stratford production with the magnificent Tutankhamen exhibition in London, which vast crowds queued to see almost as if it had been a theatrical production (*Gloucester Citizen*, 16 August 1972).

It seems more than coincidence that Shakespeare's play began to be revived in the nineteenth century once a woman ruler was on the throne, and has been produced more frequently in the twentieth century than ever before, when another woman – a second Elizabeth – is on the throne. The play was obviously the ideal choice for the lean post-war austerity years. 1951 marked the Festival of Britain and the celebratory partnership of Leigh and Olivier in the double Shaw/Shakespeare bill. 1953 – Coronation year – saw the triumph of Redgrave and Ashcroft at Stratford. Audiences could forget the war and their own privations in the supreme fantasies of Shakespeare's play, which celebrated a queen as they themselves were happy to do. After all, it was Elizabeth II herself who insisted, against the advice of the Government, on the Coronation's being televised in 1953, an act which brought the monarchy to the people as supreme spectacle, as Cleopatra herself is, and as Elizabeth I had herself been.

The meanings which accrue to Cleopatra under these circumstances seem less challenging to male power structures than they did when Cleopatra was played by a dispossessed male. Jonathan Dollimore has proposed that the original challenges of the play might be recaptured in performance by having the women played by men, and "all male roles would be played by women. . . . The woman playing Antony and the boy playing Cleopatra would subvert the very idea of sexual difference and sexual identity upon which the romantic, the moralistic, the sexist, the racist, and the decadent interpretations all at some stage rely" (Dollimore 93). In 1606 the boy actor played to an audience capable of remembering a woman ruler who not only *staged* herself as powerful, but possessed *real* power. The mingling, in the single role, of contrary images of authority and subjection has not been recaptured in the modern theatre.

This is in itself surprising, since by 1972, when Janet Suzman played Cleopatra, the Women's Liberation movement had developed a consciousness in some audiences of the social conditioning of women. How was Cleopatra to be viewed in relation to the power structures of the Roman world? As oppressed or oppressor? Glenda Jackson's Empress became subsequently linked in the public mind with her own passage from actress to politician, *via* the television role of Elizabeth I. In the 1980s and 1990s, a new ruler was in evidence in Thatcher's Britain, a figure viewed as ambiguously as ever Cleopatra might have been. However, in writing about various post-Thatcher productions, H. Neville Davies talks only of Antony and Enobarbus. Without a woman ruler available to men and women outside the theatre, the production of contradictory meaning within the play becomes impoverished. Who cares about the woman ruler? She has landed us in the soup and is out of the competition. Curiously, that situation reinvents Dryden's romantic and depoliticized version of the play, simultaneously revived, alongside these productions of Shakespeare's play, at the Almeida theatre in Islington in 1991.[12]

Shakespeare's play was from its first performance in competition with Daniel, and later on with Dryden.[13] But the competition with Dryden has, oddly enough, continued to be enacted surreptitiously even when Shakespeare's text seems to have won the theatrical day. George Rylands wrote of the Olivier/Leigh performance that "Laurence Olivier and his clever producer, Michael Benthall, sharing Dryden's nostalgia for heroism in a disillusioned age, played the tragedy as *All for Love or the World Well Lost.* The public prefer it so; and most of Shakespeare's critics have agreed with the public" (Rylands 141). The same tendency was noticeable in both Peter Hall's 1987 production of the play for the National Theatre with Dench and Hopkins, and in John Caird's 1992 RSC *Antony and Cleopatra.* Writing in the *TLS* in 1987, Barbara Everett – one of the very few women to write publicly about a production of this play – declared that "Peter Hall has given us a major rendering of something curiously like Dryden's Restoration *All for Love*" (*TLS*, 24 April 1987, quoted in Williamson 79). Caird's production embodied a Thatcherite statement, from a material base, in a post-Thatcher recession, where escaping into Romantic love heralds a return to theatrical and political conservatism, as surely as Dryden's *All for Love* had done in the Restoration.[14] Antony was played by Richard Johnson who, twenty years earlier, had played against Suzman; his past glories as Antony were, as many unkind reviewers pointed out, the past theatrical glories of an ageing actor as well as those of Shakespeare's military commander enslaved by love. John Peter in *The Sunday Times* declared that "when he says 'The beds in the east are soft' he might be recommending the Alexandria Hilton." Clare Higgins as Cleopatra was a "magnificent maneater." The reviewer concluded: "At the end the lovers are miraculously resurrected, and embrace in silhouette against a stormy turquoise sky. I could not believe my eyes" (8 November 1992, Shakespeare Centre Library). Dryden's version of the play, like so many later productions of *Antony and Cleopatra,* tried to unite the audience behind a bourgeois Cleopatra and a public-school educated Antony, with Octavia providing a lynchpin of respectability. Of the Cleopatra who scorned a squeaking boy performer – herself and not herself – there remained in Caird's production of Shakespeare's play, as in Dryden's adaptation, no trace.

Brecht declared that theatre should elicit a rational response from the audience, instead of mass emotion. *Antony and Cleopatra* more than any other Shakespeare play creates a peculiar detachment in audiences. Cool individuals leave the theatre after Octavius's final speech often apologizing to themselves and others for feelings of disappointment and disorientation. Shakespeare in this play is perhaps more experimental in his treatment of audience reaction than in any other, leaving his characters in unresolved competition – who *did* win at the end? Cleopatra, who cheated Octavius of his triumph? Antony, who received such marvellous acclaim after his death? Octavius, who contained them both in his epitaph? Or Enobarbus, whose death was more moving than anyone else's? The last act belongs to Cleopatra, and must have been the boy actor's theatrical triumph, as is the last scene of *The Taming of the Shrew.* But in a theatre where Cleopatra is played by a woman, that original boy actor's performance is complicated beyond measure by notions of the masculine and the feminine in circulation amongst a disparate and fragmented audience. If Shakespeare's boy Cleopatra had been able to gaze into the mists of time and see sensuality portrayed by a woman's body in come-on mode, and a play about power, competition, and gambling applauded when one of the competitors never even starts the race (Holland 183), he might have been more afraid of a woman playing his part than of a squeaking boy Cleopatra. The boy player and the playing woman have both vanished as if they had never been.

Cleopatra's regal playing with male desire makes the play a peculiarly Elizabethan one in its most precise sense, despite its Jacobean date. It also makes it difficult to recreate the play in the late twentieth century, not least because of its political incorrectness. Transposed into our modern world, Elizabeth I might be in court for the sexual harassment of men. In the modern theatre, however, it is difficult to read Cleopatra, as both critics and directors often seem to, as sacrificed to male control, contained within either the Roman model of restored order or a vision of transcendent Romantic love. Either way, as a drama of dominance or of ultimate subjugation, *Antony and Cleopatra* seems to exorcize its own disruptive capacities and returns us with sighs of relief to a real world where men are in control and people like Antony lose their jobs. Edification for ever.

But Cleopatra, as performer and critic of performance, is always in control of her own play: in control of Antony, of discourse, of her own image-making, and of the audience. She lost the sea battle; but the theatre is hers, as she revels in an arena which, in the last act, is supremely her own. In our age this play ought to be produced as a statement about women's control, not about women's weakness, because it exposes the performative nature of gender categories, offering us a world we can recognize.

The audience in *Antony and Cleopatra* participate in the play's awareness of its own theatricality, becoming fragmented and disparate in their reactions. Men and women watching the play are implicated in its dissolution of gender boundaries, each individual challenged by the representations of sexuality on stage, and never allowed by the dramatist to submerge that sense of separation into a comfortable group consciousness. Shakespeare himself engaged in a dialogue not only with inherited narratives, but with the political world, in which performance also, for James as for Elizabeth, encompassed the triumvirate of military, sexual, and theatrical action. The consciousness of images in the process of being made and controlled, at the center of which stood in Shakespeare's theatre the ambiguous figure of the boy actor, returns the play to its ludic and performative center, where underlings upstage their betters. The great men in the play may be world-sharers in Shakespeare's globe, but the gods in the gallery can and do forsake them, as Hercules in the end forsook Antony.

NOTES

1 *Antony and Cleopatra*, ed. Bevington, 5.2.215–20. All quotations are from this edition.

2 16 August 1972, Shakespeare Centre Library, 71.2 (c.83). All reviews of this production are quoted from this collection.

3 Baker 323. The story is quoted from Baker in Lamb 54, an otherwise authoritative account.

4 Butler 140. The whole of Butler's section on "Bodily Inscriptions, Performative Subversions," 128–41, is particularly illuminating for *Antony and Cleopatra*.

5 Jardine's arguments, 9–36, are answered by McLuskie 120–30.

6 All three reviews appeared on 16 August 1972.

7 *Daily Express*, 29 April 1953, Shakespeare Centre Library, 71.2 (c.40). All reviews of this production are from this source.

8 Cartwright, 269, notes the upstaging of Caesar in the final scene. My essay was already written when I read Cartwright's brilliant commentary on the play in terms of audience engagement with the players.

9 Dollimore, 489, has proposed that Cleopatra is best presented as a camp creation, pointing to Vanessa Redgrave's "alternative" modern dress production with Tony Richardson in 1973: "Camp is one further means whereby the artifice of the theatre is turned back upon what it represents."

10 Fitz 298: "Critical attitudes toward Cleopatra seem to reveal deep personal fears of aggressive or manipulative women."

11 Yachin, 6, in a different context, argues: "To a degree, Shakespeare has surrendered the production of meaning to his audiences."

12 Davies 111–30. The 1991 productions discussed by Davies were at the Birmingham Repertory Theatre (director John Adams); the all-black Talawa Theatre Company production at the Everyman Theatre, Liverpool, and subsequently at the Bloomsbury Theatre; and Tony Hogarty's production at the Shaw Theatre, Camden, and subsequently at the Lyric, Hammersmith.

13 Rees, *Samuel Daniel* 91–3, provides details from Daniel's 1607 text of his *Cleopatra* (dedicated to Mary Sidney as a response to her *Antonie* – translated from Garnier) about the hauling up of Antony to Cleopatra's monument ("in rowles of taffety") and the body getting stuck and swinging above the gaze of the spectators, which suggest his own presence at a production of Shakespeare's play.

Dryden's play was produced on the Restoration stage and subsequently throughout the eighteenth century to the complete exclusion of Shakespeare's, with the exception of Garrick's revival, which flopped. John Kemble put on a production in 1813 which mixed the two texts, but again was unsuccessful in pleasing audiences (see Stone 20–38).

14 Charnes 3; Armstrong 1–14. Armstrong singles out Michael Bogdanov's English Stage Company for its radical productions of Shakespeare.

REFERENCES

Armstrong, Isobel. "Thatcher's Shakespeare?" *Textual Practice* 3 (1989): 1–14.

Baker, Herschel. *John Philip Kemble: The Actor in His Theatre.* Cambridge, Mass.: Harvard University Press, 1942.

Bevington, David, ed. *Antony and Cleopatra.* Cambridge: Cambridge University Press, 1990.

Billington, Michael. *Peggy Ashcroft.* London: Murray, 1988.

Boaden, James. *Memoirs of Mrs Siddons.* London: Henry Colburn, 1827.

Bullough, Geoffrey. "*Antony and Cleopatra.*" *Narrative and Dramatic Sources of Shakespeare.* London: Routledge & Kegan Paul, 1977.

Butler, Judith. *Gender Trouble.* London and New York: Routledge, 1990.

Campbell, Thomas. *Life of Mrs Siddons.* London: Effingham Wilson, Royal Exchange, 1834.

Cartwright, Kent. *Shakespearean Tragedy and Its Double: The Rhythms of Audience Response.* University Park: Pennsylvania State University Press, 1991.

Charnes, Linda. "What's Love Got To Do With It? Reading the Liberal Humanist Romance in Shakespeare's *Antony and Cleopatra.*" *Textual Practice* 6 (1992): 1–16.

Cixous, Hélène. "The Laugh of Medusa." *New French Feminisms.* Ed. Elaine Marks and Isabelle de Courtivron. Hemel Hempstead: Harvester Wheatsheaf, 1981. 245–64.

Cook, Judith. *Women in Shakespeare.* London: Harrap, 1980.

Davies, H. Neville. "In the Public Eye: *Antony and Cleopatra* Now." *Shakespeare from Text to Stage.* Ed. Patricia Kennan and Mariangela Tempera. Bologna: CLUEB, 1992. 111–30.

Dollimore, Jonathan. "Shakespeare, Cultural Materialism, Feminism and Marxist Humanism." *New Literary History* 21 (1990): 471–93.

Dusinberre, Juliet. "*The Taming of the Shrew*: Women, Acting and Power." *Studies in the Literary Imagination* 26 (1993): 67–84.

Findlater, Richard. *Michael Redgrave, Actor.* London: William Heinemann, 1956.

—— *The Player King.* London: Weidenfeld & Nicolson, 1957.

Fitz, L. T. "Egyptian Queens and Male Reviewers: Sexist Attitudes in *Antony and Cleopatra* Criticism." *Shakespeare Quarterly 28* (1977): 297–316.

Granville Barker, Harley. *Prefaces to Shakespeare.* London: B. T. Batsford, 1930.

Harington, Sir John. *A Tract on the Succession to the Crown AD. 1602.* Ed. Clements R. Markham. London: J. B. Nichols & Sons, for the Roxburghe Club, 1880.

Holland, Norman N., Sidney Homan, and Bernard J. Paris. *Shakespeare's Personality.* Berkeley, Los Angeles, and London: University of California Press, 1989.

Holland, Peter. "Shakespeare Performances in England, 1992." *Shakespeare Survey 46* (1994): 159–89.

Jameson, Mrs. [Anna]. *Shakespeare's Heroines.* London: George Newnes, 1897 [1832].

Jankowski, Theodora A. "'As I Am Egypt's Queen': Cleopatra, Elizabeth I, and the Female Body Politic." *Assays: Critical Approaches to Medieval and Renaissance Texts* 5 (1989): 91–111.

Jardine, Lisa. *Still Harping on Daughters: Women and Drama in the Age of Shakespeare.* Brighton: Harvester, 1983.

Kerr, Walter. "Cleopatra: The Games She Plays." *New York Times*, Section 2, 17 September 1967. *Shakespearean Criticism 17.* Ed. Sandra L. Williamson. London and Detroit: Gale, 1992.

King, Laura Severt. "Blessed When They Were Riggish: Shakespeare's Cleopatra and Christianity's Penitent Prostitutes." *Journal of Medieval and Renaissance Studies* 22 (1992): 429–49.

Lamb, Margaret. *Antony and Cleopatra on the English Stage.* London and Toronto: Associated University Presses, 1980.

Levine, Laura. "Men in Women's Clothing: Anti-theatricality and Effeminization from 1579 to 1642." *Criticism* 28 (1986): 121–43.

Lowen, Tirzah. *Peter Hall Directs Antony and Cleopatra.* London: Methuen Drama, 1990.

McLuskie, Kathleen. "The Act, the Role, and the Actor: Boy Actresses on the Elizabethan Stage." *New Theatre Quarterly* 3 (1987): 120–30.

Marks, Elaine and Isabelle De Courtivron, eds. *New French Feminisms.* Hemel Hempstead: Harvester Wheatsheaf, 1981.

Maus, Katherine Eisaman. "'Playhouse Flesh and Blood': Sexual Ideology and the Restoration Actress." *English Literary History* 46 (1979): 595–617.

Montrose, Louis. "'Shaping Fantasies': Figurations of Gender and Power in Elizabethan Culture." *Representations* 1 (1983): 61–94.

Olivier, Lawrence. "*Antony and Cleopatra.*" *On Acting.* London: Simon & Schuster, 1986. *Shakespearean Criticism 17.* Ed. Sandra L. Williamson. London and Detroit: Gale, 1992.

Orgel, Stephen. "Nobody's Perfect: Or Why Did the English Stage Take Boys for Women?" *South Atlantic Quarterly* 88 (1989): 7–29.

Rackin, Phyllis. "Shakespeare's Boy Cleopatra, the Decorum of Nature and the Golden World of Poetry." *PMLA* 87 (1972): 201–11.

Rastall, Richard. "Female Roles in All-Male Casts." *Medieval English Theatre* 7 (1985): 21–51.

Rees, Joan. "An Elizabethan Eyewitness of *Antony and Cleopatra*?" *Shakespeare Survey 6* (1953): 91–3.

—— *Samuel Daniel.* Liverpool: Liverpool University Press, 1964.

Rylands, George. "Festival Shakespeare in the West End." *Shakespeare Survey 6* (1953): 140–6.

Schmitt, Natalie Crohn. "Theorizing about Performance: Why Now?" *New Theatre Quarterly* 6 (1990): 231–4.

Scott, Michael. *Antony and Cleopatra: Text and Performance.* London: The Macmillan Press, 1983.

Shakespeare Centre Library. Review volumes 71.2 (c.83), 71.2 (c.40).

Shakespeare, William. *Antony and Cleopatra.* Ed. David Bevington. Cambridge: Cambridge University Press, 1990.

Shaw, Bernard. *Three Plays for Puritans.* Harmondsworth: Penguin, 1946 [1901].

Singh, Jyotsna. "Renaissance Antitheatricality, Antifeminism, and Shakespeare's *Antony and Cleopatra.*" *Renaissance Drama* ns, 20 (1989): 99–121.

Sprengnether, Madelon. "The Boy Actor and Femininity in *Antony and Cleopatra.*" *Shakespeare's Personality.* Ed. Norman N. Holland, Sidney Homan, and Bernard J. Paris. Berkeley, Los Angeles, and London: University of California Press, 1989. 191–205.

Stone, George Winchester. "Garrick's Presentation of *Antony and Cleopatra.*" *Review of English Studies* 13 (1937): 20–38.

Terry, Ellen. *Four Lectures on Shakespeare.* Ed. Christopher St. John. London: 1931.

Tynan, Kenneth. *Curtains.* London: Longmans, Green & Co. Ltd., 1961.

Williamson, Sandra L. *Shakespearean Criticism 17.* London and Detroit: Gale, 1992.

Wingate, Charles E. L. "Cleopatras of the Stage." *The Cosmopolitan* 11 (May 1891): 3–13.

Yachnin, Paul. "'Courtiers of Beauteous Freedom': *Antony and Cleopatra* in Its Time." *Renaissance and Reformation* 15 (1991): 1–20.

5

LOOKING FOR MR. SHAKESPEARE AFTER "THE REVOLUTION"

Robert Lepage's intercultural *Dream* machine[1]

Barbara Hodgdon

At bottom, dreams are nothing other than a particular *form* of thinking.
(Freud, *The Interpretation of Dreams* 5: 506 n. 2)

Waking from his "most rare vision," Bottom is at a loss to "say what dream it was" or even to "expound" it until he seizes on the idea of having Peter Quince write a ballad which will make his dream readable or, more accurately, sing-able. Characteristically, however, Bottom desires authorial control over Quince's interpretation: he provides a title – "Bottom's Dream" – and a gloss – "because it hath no bottom" – simultaneously naming and (uncharacteristically) disavowing himself as the ballad's subject. As an early modern interpreter of dreams, Bottom tropes a relation between dreamers, dreams, and their discursive representation that figures the concerns of twentieth-century reception studies, which seek to map the relations between a text and its readers in order to understand how distinct affective and interpretive experiences, produced historically in specific social formations, shape the cultural destinies of a text.

My project does not attempt to expound Bottom's dream but to explore what inferences are facilitated by similar instances of naming and disavowal in the discourses surrounding Robert Lepage's production of Shakespeare's *A Midsummer Night's Dream*, which ran in repertory at London's Royal National Theatre from 9 July 1992 through 6 January 1993. Drawing on contemporary critical and cultural studies, such work moves beyond text-centered analyses and takes a contextual and materialist approach which situates historical spectators and their reading strategies as the primary objects of investigation.[2] Consequently, I offer neither a self-referential thick description nor a performance-driven account of the theatrical aesthetics or semiotics of either "Shakespeare's" or "Lepage's" *Dream*, except in so far as to note what textual and/or theatrical signs might prompt a particular reading.[3] To do so can, to be sure, offer a certain notion of culture and of intercultural performance, but almost invariably such accounts tend to locate codes and the production of meaning in relation to the collaborative efforts of the writer–director–actor–designer and so privilege the creative processes at work within an exclusively enclosed world of theatrical culture. Rather than assuming that the performance text itself contains or produces immanent meanings or focusing on the marks of its making and its makers, I want to consider its status as an event constituted by the concrete conditions of its spectators.[4] For it is in the "discursively saturated materiality" (Giroux and Simon 98) of the historical circumstances in which a performance is seen that it makes its demands for narrative intelligibility. What I shall be pursuing, then, is how readers' first-night encounters with Lepage's production marked a particular *event*: the emergence of Shakespeare's *Dream* as a national cultural property, an instance in which theatre, to appropriate Herbert Blau's phrase, "becomes like ideology itself, . . . something other than what it appeared to be" (*Appearances* 37). Traces of that event appear in various print materials – including some twenty-three reviews, primarily from the British press; interviews with Lepage and with his actors; and the souvenir program for the production, containing both images and quoted excerpts. To analyze these traces, textually as well as culturally, is to write a history that not only characterizes the social significance of that event in relation to a particular interpretive community but also reveals how what might be called a cultural logic of the postcolonial circulates equally in Lepage's performance text and its attendant discourses.

I will return to the question of how that logic operates shortly, but first I want to call attention to my own position as an historically mediated reader who is clearly imbricated within the analytical results. Because I saw Lepage's *Dream* on press night, I occasionally interweave my own observations with those of the reviewers I cite. However, it is important to bracket the distinctions between their politics of location and my own, for I am neither a native informant nor a participant observer privy to insider narratives or backstage gossip, but a traveler and collector of sorts who speaks from an appropriately problematic intercultural space – appropriate not simply because situating myself on a border or margin marks a fashionable place to be, but also because, as an American academic in London, I watched a *Dream* staged by a Québécois (until recently, the artistic director of the French theatre of the Canadian National Arts Centre) which featured a multicultural cast made up of British, Québécoise, Anglo-Indian, Anglo-West Indian, and Anglo-African performers. Unlike those of the critics, however, my account has neither been constrained by a late-night deadline nor offered up for immediate, widespread public consumption; rather, it is a product of recollection, addressed to a fairly specialized, presumably academic readership. In so privileging my own voice, I also wish to make two points. First, that because the discursive formation surrounding any historical event (and theatrical performances are no exception) is contradictory and heterogeneous, no reading of that event is unified; and second, that my analyses avoid categorizing reviewers' responses, Lepage's comments, or my own observations into preferred, negotiated, or resistant readings. What follows, then, represents field-work – a "story of the night told over" which does not, as Hippolyta would have it, "[grow] to something of great constancy" but rather aims to illuminate the cultural meanings of Lepage's *Dream* to particular spectators in a specific sociohistorical moment and so to contribute to discussions about the spectorial effects of performed Shakespeare.

The use-value of such a study lies in its ability to clarify how sociologies of taste and value and contextual protocols for reading determine frameworks for making meaning from materially inscribed theatrical data. Here, Tony Bennett's concept, reading formation, by which he means a set of intersecting discourses that productively activate a text, is especially useful, for not only are theatrical representations always produced within cultural limits and theoretical borders, but clearly spectators "read" performed Shakespeare (perhaps more so than other dramatic texts) through knowledges drawn from literary as well as theatrical cultures, knowledges which are necessarily implicated in particular economies of truth, value, and power, serving to mark one performance as a more acceptable interpretation than another.[5] Also important to a study which dissolves a performance text into its reading relations is what Janet Staiger calls "historically constructed 'imaginary selves,' the subject positions taken up by individual spectators" (*Interpreting* 81); tracking these provides insight into how individuals as well as social groups use cultural forms in the process of defining themselves. As will become apparent, certain shared contexts of reading and theatrical formations[6] and constructed identities of the self in relation to historical conditions which undergird the interpretive strategies for, and affective responses to, Lepage's *Dream* make it possible to read these discourses not only as a struggle over the meaning of theatrical signs but as symptomatic of current cultural anxieties about gender, race, and nationality.

* * *

Across the range of materials on Lepage's *Dream*, one particular reading strategy consistently emerges: the construction of binary oppositions indicative of categories linked in a hierarchic relation that is fundamental to mechanisms of ordering and sense-making in Western – especially European – cultures. Peter Stallybrass and Allon White argue that cultures "'think themselves' in the most immediate and affective ways" through such oppositions, which are often duplicated across various discursive realms and symbolic systems, especially psychic forms, the human body, geographical spaces, and the social order. Repeatedly, one symbolic system evokes another to justify its ordering; within such figurations, the categories of high and low bear an especially powerful symbolic charge which structures all other elaborations: "the top *includes* the low symbolically, as a primary eroticized constituent of its own fantasy life." The result, they claim, is "a mobile, conflictual fusion of power, fear and desire in the construction of subjectivity: a psychological dependence upon precisely those Others which are being rigorously opposed and excluded at the social level. It is for this reason that what is *socially* peripheral is so frequently *symbolically* central" (1–6). Using precisely similar hierarchical relations, the review discourse maps Lepage's *Dream* as a transgressive domain where intersecting points of antagonism between high and low, between "Shakespeare" and his "Other," signal powerful dissonances within British culture. In that discourse, figurations of place, body, national as well as ethnic identities, and gendered subjectivity interconnect and are used to shore up commonly held cultural codes, values, and norms and to reassert literary, theatrical, social, and political boundaries; moreover, such figurations are further marked out by the use of metaphor and analogy.

Perhaps the most overriding opposition articulated by reviewers can be expressed as a fort-da game played with two structuring absences: what Nicholas de Jongh called "Shakespeare's old *Dream*, as we have come to know it" (de Jongh), complete with Athenian palace and Mendelssohn's wood, and Peter Brook's 1970 Royal Shakespeare Company white-box production, widely acclaimed as *the* theatrical event of the decade and subsequently mythologized (by John Styan) as the culminating moment of a "Shakespeare revolution," ensuring its canonical status.[7] This binary not only marks out a history of *Dream*'s theatrical formations but tropes a nexus of its supposed cultural functions in constructing a perfected national community. On the one hand, it evokes a geography that no longer exists and an imaginative space riddled with desire. As Angela Carter writes:

> The English wood offers us a glimpse of a green, unfallen world a little closer to Paradise than we are. . . . This is the true Shakespearian wood – but it is not the wood of Shakespeare's time, which did not know itself to be Shakespearian, and therefore felt no need to keep up appearances. No. The wood we have just described is that of nineteenth-century nostalgia, which disinfected the wood, cleansing it of the grave, hideous and elemental beings with which the superstition of an earlier age had filled it. Or, rather, denaturing, castrating these beings until they came to look just as they do in those photographs of fairy folk that so enraptured Conan Doyle. It is Mendelssohn's wood. . . . However, as it turns out, the Victorians did not leave the woods in quite the state they might have wished to find them. (89)

None the less, both this magical, enraptured, and quintessentially *English* wood and the Athenian patriarchy offer locales where a late-twentieth-century spectator (even one who has read Jan Kott) may still come away refreshed, having been offered the promise of correctly channeled desire, of accessing anxiety over destabilizing identities or positionalities – those of sex, gender, ethnicity, and class – only to have it brought to rest. On the other hand, situating Brook as the cultural presence who lurks in the margins of Lepage's *Dream* opens onto a discourse that hailed him into the space of genius to legitimate him as Shakespeare's "true" heir, the maestro who had reinvented non-illusionistic theatre (see Styan 206–12). Moreover, reviewers constructed him in terms of his own work: the only quotation in the souvenir program for Brook's production, frequently cited in whole or in part by reviewers, came from his own manifesto, *The Empty Space*: "Once the theatre could begin as magic: magic at the sacred festival, or magic as the footlights came up. Today it is the other way round. . . . We must open our empty hands and show that really there is nothing up our sleeves. Only then can we begin" (108–9). At least two review headlines – "Peter Brook's Creative Dream" (Trewin) and "Peter Brook's most original Shakespeare play" (Bannock) – conflated author with director-auteur, a move that, in positing dual (or synonymous) personalities as the origins for the performance text, has ideological import for humanist social formations (see Staiger, *Interpreting* 95). *The Times*, seeking to discern the relationship between his "bizarre . . . delight" and "the original," even evoked Plato's doctrine of Forms to argue the congruence of "Mr. Brook" and "William Shakespeare": "for all the trapezes, juggling, helical wire trees, and general non-Elizabethanism, the Stratford production is not just good theatre but a *true production* of the *Dream*" (my emphases).[8] That such "truth" had emerged at the site of Shakespeare's birth touched off a myth of origins in which *Dream* could be reclaimed as a kind of foundational center for British culture.

Just as, in Louis Montrose's reading of *Dream* as an early modern cultural production, the Amazonian space of gendered otherness operates as a mythological formation against which dominant heterosexuality is tested and eventually reinstalled (31–64), Brook's production serves a similar mythic function for Lepage, and he both extends and interrupts the process of filiation that positions him as Brook's heir. For in the 1990s, it is no longer "the author" alone whose presence determines meanings; rather, as Blau maintains, the symbolic economy of previous theatrical productions activates a constant self-reflexivity whereby performance gets constructed against itself (*Appearances* 80–1).[9] Although Irving Wardle claimed to have been the first to "lumber Lepage with a comparison to Peter Brook which has been clanking along behind him ever since" and on reviewing his *Dream* was "glad to have the chance to strike off this ball and chain," Lyn Gardner's comments on Lepage's previous work clearly framed it through Brook's 1970 *Dream*: "highly visual but not afraid of the literary, . . . combining the lushness of opera with the spectacle of circus, the excitement of carnival, and the fluidity of film." When Lepage had first staged *Dream* in 1988 at Québec's Théâtre du Nouveau Monde, his design – three vertical staircases that represented the hierarchical levels of textual reality (spirits, noble Athenians, worker-comedians) and were mounted on a turning platform in the shape of England[10] – prompted Micheline Cambron to recall Brook's equally forthright critique of *Dream*'s traditional theatrical display of gauze-winged fairies, muslin mists, and painted trees. Yet, in writing of how one theatrical sign (or production) can evoke another so that both, simultaneously "present," reverberate in memory, Cambron could not efface her desire for the glacial purity of Brook's *Dream*, which for her, as for many, had become a theatrical fetish.

Indeed, my own initial reaction to Lepage's mise en scène – Michael Levine's black upstage screens surrounding a stage covered with grey mud, a watery pool at its center, over which hangs a light bulb suspended on a long flex – was that it engaged Brook's production through a process of negative quotation. As a chronotope of theatrical culture – that is, an organizing, historicizing image – Levine's environment signaled Lepage's impudent raid on Brook, a deconstructive move that turned his dazzling white-walled "empty space," where Shakespeare's spoken text became a squash ball bouncing off its pristine surfaces, topsy-turvy down. And when Angela Laurier's Puck, costumed in a red leather body suit which bared one breast, scuttled slowly into the center of the pool, reached up and took out the single point of light, it was also apparent that Lepage's much darker *Dream*, like his precursor's, was committed to forcing a confrontation between spectator and the materiality of actors' bodies that, unlike Brook's, would eventually displace character in favor of the self-validating presence of the performer (cf. Blau, *Appearances* 165).

Positioning Brook as the model for *Dream*'s cultural capital spawned further binaries: "earth-shattering" vs. "mud-spattering"; "fantastically air-borne" vs. "stubbornly earthbound" (Bayley); "authentic magic, comic joy, and rigorous attention to the verse" vs. "pervers[ity], humourless[ness] and vile [speech]" – "a lugubriously eccentric vision that reduces even the best performers . . . to mud-caked puppets" (Billington). Those critics who could not discover "Shakespeare's jokes . . . submerged beneath the splashing games" (Wardle) either wrote joke titles – "Dreaming in the goo"; "Mudsummer's Night's Dream"; "Puck in Muck" (Nightingale, *Times*; Spencer; Edwardes) – or, by performing their own comic moments, mapped out fissures between high and low culture, as in Ian Shuttleworth's "Peter Brook wrestles Ken Russell in a dark, bonkers circus version of *Chariots of Fire*."

Voicing the minority opinion, Benedict Nightingale thought it "the most original *Dream* since Peter Brook's version two decades ago, and the most strange and disturbing since – but there I have no memory to match it" (*Times*). Yet Nightingale's memory seems to have its own empty space, for twenty years before, titling his review "Dream 2001 AD," he labeled Brook's production "Shakespeare as he might be conceived by a science fiction addict or, indeed, performed by enthusiastic Vegans," adding, "Big

British Peter . . . has laboured and brought forth, among other things, Mickey Mouse" – a reference to Brook's Bottom, whose black bulb nose, black leather ears, and huge black clogs had translated the traditional, and dearly-beloved, ass's head. Singling out "gabbling, writhing lovers," "fairies in baggy pyjamas, like Japanese wrestlers," and a Puck in "billowing yellow silks and a blue skullcap" like some "fantastical Chinese rabbi," Nightingale complained that both plot and characterization suffered and stacked up associations with Disneyland, Billy Smart's Circus, International Wrestling on ITV, August Bank Holiday, the Isle of Wight, and "the grind and clank of the industrial Midlands" to cheapen it further. Since identical objections – especially with regard to character, the perceptual locus of hidden cultural assumptions[11] – trace through much of the review discourse for Lepage's *Dream*, reading Nightingale's past and present reviews as Louis Montrose does Simon Forman's dream (32–5) might ascertain not only what this particular changeling boy desired from performance but why he found "brilliantly imaginative" performative signs analogous to those he had once marked off as alien – or, more significantly, oriental – and marginalized as mass culture entertainment.

If regarding his reviews as dream-texts might explain how Nightingale forgets (or represses) his own previous statements, comparing the two certainly displays the complex interdependence of the categories he evokes and explodes the permanence of such structuring oppositions. Recall Stallybrass and White. "What is socially peripheral is . . . symbolically central. . . . The primary site of contradiction, the site of conflicting desires and mutually incompatible representation, is undoubtedly the 'low'" (4). In rejecting what he sees as popular and sentimental, Nightingale reveals, one might argue, his latent desire for the "low," at least in so far as it represents a non-Shakespearean "other." But what also seems to be apparent has to do with how the fantasies of one particular reader are linked to reading formations. For Nightingale's wish to disavow Brook's *Dream* is tied to its lack: "His manic decoration has deprived it of suffering, fear, horror and, apart from one moment, when Bottom's phallus is crudely mimed by the fairies, even of lust" ("Dream 2001"). These emphases on fear and suffering, together with the notion that in no play is "eroticism expressed so brutally," emerge from Kott's reading of *Dream*, which he cites.[12] That Lepage's *Dream*, using Shakespeare's text as a machine for performing the body erotic, fulfilled Nightingale's dark Kottian tastes, particularly in its representation of the lovers' nightmare struggles on the production's two stages – the mud and the bed, the primordial ooze and the site of sex and dreams – and in Titania's seduction of Bottom, observed by an Oberon who responds by fondling Puck, suggests that it confirmed a *literary* reading formation which (although he does not mention Kott's name) remained more firmly installed in Nightingale's memory than either his own response to or review of Brook's production.

* * *

Rather than pursuing the relationship between Nightingale's dream-reading formations and his psyche, I want to explore two especially crucial oppositions which trace through both Lepage's interviews and the review discourse: seeing vs. hearing; body vs. voice – interrelated terms that catch up values associated with national theatrical cultures and, more particularly, with "native" vs. "foreign" Shakespeares. Dennis Kennedy summarizes what has become a widely accepted distinction between English and foreign-language Shakespeare: "unable to place the same emphasis on Shakespeare's verbal resourcefulness, foreign performances have explored scenographic and physical modes more openly than their Anglophone counterparts, often redefining the meaning of the plays in the process" (*Foreign* 6). Although Lepage brought to the National his acknowledged skill as an image maker whose work is grounded in the physical materiality of the performative body,[13] his *Dream* is neither a production mounted in a foreign country nor, strictly speaking, an "import," even though many reviewers came close to figuring it as a local production from India. And in this case, Shakespeare's "native" *textual* identity was disturbed not by the problematics of translation, but by several sorts of tensions – between individual performers' acting styles and between idiosyncratic speech patterns (marking those performers as non-native "others") and the King's English.

As a Québécois performance artist who emerges from a bilingual culture and whose own theatre texts interweave French and English (and in *Dragons Trilogy*, Chinese), Lepage had foregrounded the traffic between linguistic and cultural identities in his previous work with Shakespeare's texts, most particularly in *Romeo and Juliette* (1989), where distinctions between English-speaking Montagues and French-speaking Capulets were specifically linked to differing sexual identities and both illuminated and critiqued the fragmentation underlying the Canadian myth of bilingual unity.[14] Remarking on his own linguistically situated identity, Lepage quotes one of *Dream*'s actors: "In French, you don't speak of an audience, you say 'spectateurs,' . . . in the English culture, the word is important." This statement, he says, defines the problems non-native speakers of English face with Shakespeare: "we're really struck by *seeing* how to *do* it instead of trying to *hear* it" ("Robert Lepage" 33; my emphases). Largely through his encounter with Shakespeare's "authentic" text (as opposed to either Victor Hugo's romanticized nineteenth-century translations or Michel Garneau's more recent "tradaptations"), Lepage claims to be reconsidering the "magical power" of words and music to evoke images ("Robert Lepage" 35).[15] Here, he seems to be subscribing to Brook's belief in Shakespeare's *textual* power. Yet in describing himself as "very caught by the image," he argues less for a doubled signifying system where, as in Brook's 1990 *Tempest*, all that was said or thought was also represented by a visual or tactile materiality of signs, than for the *physical* performative power that drives the present-day theatrical marketplace, predicated more than ever before on an economy of "physical capital," with representations of the body as the site of exchange value.[16] "There's a lot of work to be done," he maintains, "to convince people that you can transmit theatre physically, that the text, even if you don't hear it, is respected in what a spectator sees and feels" (Lepage, quoted in Wolf).

Once again, the reviewers who acclaimed Brook's *Dream* provide a touchstone for the difficulties the critical community had with discerning "Shakespeare" in the "chronic strangeness" of Lepage's "huge underground swamp" (de Jongh, Rutherford). Even those most cautious about the circus gimmickry could sense Shakespeare's authentic textual presence in Brook. Wrote Gavin Millar, "Brook's images are drawn from the text and constantly refer to it"; J. C. Trewin, summarizing the majority opinion, waxed eloquent:

> [H]owever Brook illustrates Shakespeare, it is Shakespeare that matters. Brook has simply polished the mirror. . . . [He] gets us to listen because he treats the Dream as something none of us has heard or seen before. . . . Always he gets the verses to reach us as if it were new, spoken by characters who are never the stereotypes of an hundred revivals. . . . We are made to imagine: sight and hearing are sharpened.

By contrast, reviewers of Lepage's *Dream* complained of the actors' carelessness with words, of an inability to hear, and of physical activity distracting attention from the dialogue; even Nightingale acknowledged that "some good lines are lost in the physical ado." "How much," mourned Steve Grant, "would someone who hadn't seen or read the play learn about its structure, meaning and beauty? Not much." Michael Coveney spoke for the majority when, evoking Peter Hall's insistence on observing meter, he wrote, "actors speak the words, not the lines." Predicated on Foucault's dictum that seeing punctures time-worn codes of saying (32–69), Lepage's striking anatomy lesson – deploying mime, dance, music, and lighting as means of frustrating the linear, the narrative, and the rational – had turned the wor(l)d upside down.[17]

Reviewers' responses to one particular moment aptly illustrate what was at stake in inverting – or, to some, perverting – the relationship between hearing and seeing. Just as in Lepage's *Dragons Trilogy*, where a character delivered a meditation on the importance of the bicycle in China from a moving bicycle, Theseus spoke his lecture on cool reason supplanting the inventions of lunatics, lovers, and poets against an upstage image of the story of the night being replayed as a child's infantile romantic game of musical chairs, which mockingly reinstalled the floating subject positions that Theseus would pin down and dismiss to the margins of experience. Here, the remarks of two reviewers point to a tension between dominant and emergent reading formations. Objecting to "moronic upstaging that wilfully sabotage[s] the speeches," Martin Hoyle lamented Lepage's deliberate demystification of time-honored themes; Clare Bayley, however, wished "that some of the speeches could be over more quickly and the next vision of wonder revealed." Not surprisingly, critics fantasized a top-down directorial move to erase the word and undermine the authority of Shakespeare's immortal lines. No one associated the image with a likely pop-culture analogue, Madonna's "Keep It Together" (from her *Blond Ambition Tour*), or thought of the chairs not as signs of themselves but as a quotation of other spectacles, other events – a low–high rip-off by a director who situates his foundational experiences of theatre and theatricality not in Canadian theatrical culture, which he describes as "not reflecting anybody's identity," but, more globally, in Genesis and Jethro Tull concerts and in Peter Gabriel's highly theatrical rock shows.[18] A long program note on the gamelan, a Javanese instrument constructed especially for the production and parodied in the mechanics' playlet, suggests the importance Lepage places on music to ground his work and to enhance (or displace) the sound of Shakespeare.

Curiously enough, in this particular nexus of sight and sound, Allan Mitchell's patrician Theseus was the only actor reviewers did not trash for o'ertopping or muffling Shakespeare's language. Played as blind, he becomes the figure both for the traditionally codified performance techniques of English-speaking theatre that Lepage was accused of debasing and for the reviewer who not only represses all that he sees in favor of hearing but whose ear, attuned to received standard pronunciation, invalidates what might be called the sound of the other. As Pierre Bourdieu writes, verbal manners function as valuable cultural currency through which members of the ruling class seek to maintain their social positions: not only are such manners one of the key markers of class, but they are also the ideal weapon in strategies of distinction that seek to mark distance and maintain national as well as cultural boundaries (66). Erecting as well as policing such boundaries was, after all, a foundational principle of the theatre where Lepage staged *Dream.* At a 28 January 1946 press conference given by the combined Old Vic and Shakespeare Memorial National Theatre committees, Viscount Esher had remarked that "the National Theatre would reclaim the English language from American vulgarizations" (quoted in Elsom and Tomalin 85). And in the 1949 British House of Commons Debate on the National Theatre, Oliver Lyttelton (a Tory M.P. and chair of the Shakespeare Memorial National Theatre Trust) asserted that the "National Theatre would preserve from pollution the language in which the dramatic works are played [and] would help to keep undefiled the purity of the English language" (quoted in Kruger 128). If such comments reflect an anxious reclamation of what the Second World War had placed in jeopardy, clearly neither Lyttelton nor Esher could have anticipated that the future might bring a French, much less a French-Canadian, assault on the Shakespearean "mother tongue."

The ideologies driving the opposition between hearing and seeing – an intellectual conservatism that favors the finite (voice) over the infinite (sign) (Buzacott 16) – became most apparent, however, as they were articulated across the bodies of two central performers, Puck and Bottom. Without exception, critics lauded Angela Laurier's "unforgettably unearthly performance" (Wardle): an "amazing, jointless, acrobatic and androgynous Puck . . . [who] takes on the likeness of any creature from any element" (Tinker) – "a woman who is nothing less than a two-legged Kama Sutra" (Grant). They seemed eager to relive either her initial appearance, angling crab-like across the stage, with legs where her arms ought to be; her gravity-defying spin, ten feet off the floor, to put a girdle round the earth; or the moment when she attaches herself to Bottom's back "like an incubus, waggling feet doing an eloquent job as ass's ears" (Hoyle). But most were also clearly troubled by a presence that grafted together supposedly incompatible categories: high/low culture; male/female; animal/human; "French-Canadian"/Shakespeare. One strategy involved qualifying their amazement by aligning her physical virtuosity with that of a circus performer or contortionist to fashion her either as a mass-culture misfit who disordered all expectations of the human body or a freak-show artist performing Indian rope tricks. Another not only was more forthrightly misogynistic but sought, by demonizing her marred language, to subordinate and efface her dazzling performance by marking her body as resistant to Shakespeare's lexical authority. Said one, "She isn't Puck, what with her funny accent and one breast hanging out, but she's a cute act" (Hurren); carped another: "she negotiates English verse with all the nimbleness of Inspector Clouseau: "wat 'empern 'omesperns 'ave we swaggereeng 'ere?" (Taylor).

Somewhat similar anxieties condensed around Timothy Spall's Bottom, driven, it would seem, by more threatening territorial imperatives. As the only mortal who crosses boundaries, Bottom opens up a subject position for (predominantly, though not exclusively male) theatre critics not only to live out their dreams of acting on a real stage rather than writing about it, but also to experience a first-rate sexual fantasy – in this case, with Sally Dexter's "gorgeously snake-like" Titania (Grant), who hangs, bat-like, suspended upside-down in space until, waking to Bottom's song, she ravishes him. Clearly disturbed by the public primordial scene which Nightingale had relished, one critic compared it to a rape (which indeed it is) while another, remarking on the voyeuristic spotlight that seeks out Bottom's groaning ecstasy, divorced himself further from the sight by claiming to be alienated (Coveney, Hoyle). Even more significantly, by coding Spall's body with an impressive list of American stereotypes – "a Brando-smitten narcissist" (Wardle), "a reincarnation of . . . your seventies macho man with medallion, platform shoes and naff American drawl" (Dunn), "flaunting his Liberace wig, bare chest and Californian swagger" (Nightingale,

Times) – reviewers kept Bottom's dark Kottian bestiality at a distance. In a series of transparently xenophobic blocking moves, most disavowed the sight of themselves bouncing orgasmically with Titania on the creaking bedsprings of Lepage's ubiquitous prop by figuring him as a stateside other. But Michael Billington, who saw and heard a "hopelessly unfunny Bottom impersonating, of all people, Laurence Olivier," suggested an even more profound transgression: to parody Olivier on the stage that bears his name in the theatre he had been partly responsible for founding was to strike deep at the heart of British national theatrical culture.

When it came to the visual spectacle and imagistic prowess that undergirds Lepage's directorial reputation, critics marked out cultural and geographical distinctions in a discourse tangled with nationally naturalized assumptions, as though replaying voices from a nineteenth-century past. Those appalled at the mud-wrestling spectacle overlooked the program's initial citation – lines taken from that quintessential Edwardian, Rupert Brooke – "One may not doubt that, somehow, good / Shall come of water and of mud./ And, sure, the reverent eye must see / A purpose in liquidity" ("Sightlines"). Instead, their eyes seized on the connections to Hades and Dante's dark wood (Nightingale, *Times*; Rutherford), and turned photographs and excerpts documenting European as well as Asian and African rites of passage into "adolescent tussles" (Paton) or "inter-sex wrestling" (Nathan); only a few picked out the program's appeal to a "Jungian ancestral psyche springing from its root beneath the earth" ("Sightlines") – and then only to suggest that "Freudian undercurrents" (Grant) were somehow more appropriate to *Dream* than Jung's elemental ooziness (Dunn). Despite Titania's weather-report (*MND* 2.1.81–117[19]) – the "authenticity" of which Lepage discovered late in the rehearsal period and evoked to shore up his choice of *mise en scène* which, he maintained, came out of a preliminary workshop ("Robert Lepage" 36) – what critics saw was a *Dream* which floated away from Shakespeare as well as theatrical history on Lepage's sea of mud.

"It is true," writes Freud, "that we distort dreams in attempting to reproduce them. . . . But this distortion is itself no more than a part of the revision to which the dream-thoughts are regularly subjected as a result of the dream-censorship" (5: 514). In attempting to revise what many construed as a disfigured or missed encounter with Shakespeare, reviewers repressed any potentially post-imperial guilt to write Lepage's *Dream* into a discourse which reinvented English history. Titania's Indian boy bore much of the textual brunt for critics, one of whom compared the opening scene, where an Indian Philostrate poled a bed containing the four sleeping lovers – Theseus and Hippolyta posed at its corners – across the muddy pool, to "some strange ceremony in the upper Ganges" (Billington). Moreover, animalistic metaphors aided the distancing move that pushed images and performers into the space of the primitive, away from "civilized" First World cultures. Those who had apparently never stood on Waterloo Bridge looking down toward the National Theatre at low tide figured the pool as an "African salt-lick where animals come to drink" (de Jongh) and the "reptilian sprites" who slithered through it (Wardle), "eagerly sniffing stray mortals as if about to sink their teeth in," as "mud-covered, blue-faced Congolese boys" (Hoyle). Although Angela Laurier's Québécoise Puck was, strictly speaking, the only non-British citizen in the cast, many of *Dream*'s major performers (with the exception of Allan Mitchell's Theseus) had their passports revoked and were constructed as colonials: an American Bottom, an Asian Hippolyta (Lolita Chakrabarti), an African Oberon (Jeffrey Kossoon). Given these moves, it seems curious that no reviewer noted that pairing Sally Dexter's Titania, a white Englishwoman, with Kissoon's African Oberon threatened to replicate the fear of miscegenation that traces through *Othello*, or that the Athenian court, presided over by an English Theseus and an Asian Hippolyta, reversed the gender and racial differences so obvious among the fairies. Lepage's own rationale for his cross-cultural casting, he claimed, had nothing to do with race or with tokenism, "get[ting] across the idea that black and white should work together." Rather, he found it interesting "to have a black Oberon who brings all of his blackness because he's the night . . . and also when you see this man walk across the stage he carries all of Africa or West India with him . . . ; [with Oberon and Titania], you see this part of the world meeting another . . . and suddenly the colour of your skin or your accent are poetic icons."[20] Lepage's transcultural poetics, however, faded into unreadability; instead, his "poetic icons" foregrounded the symbolic centrality of colonized others within Britain, so that traces of interracial and intercultural tensions surfaced, displaced, in reviewers' comments on who could or could not speak blank verse or on unsuitable and bizarre performance styles.

But if what seemed either harsh or unfamiliar, including the "oriental scratch and jangle" (Coveney) of the Javanese gamelan, might be associated with the colonial other, those images reminiscent of "Peter Brook's Third World aesthetic visions" (Coveney) – such as Levine's black upstage dream screen rising to reveal "a pink African dawn" (de Jongh), the "aboriginal chanting that turned Theseus' encomium to his hunting dogs into a tribal set piece," and the four golden showers which cleansed the muddy lovers (Hoyle) – were tinged with enough post-imperial nostalgia to be worth collecting. It would be no exaggeration to say that when critics – Richard Eyre, the National Theatre's artistic director, among them ("Robert Lepage" 35) – objected that Lepage's *Dream* collapsed forest and court into the muddy space of the other, what was clearly at stake was a contamination of the social space described by John of Gaunt as "This other Eden, demi-paradise, / This fortress built by Nature for herself, . . . / This precious stone set in the silver sea" (*R2* 2.1.42–3; 46). Certainly in terms of the theatrical space itself, on press night the reviewers' grumbling body language could be read as a sign of the extent to which they saw themselves on the margins, while Lepage, masquerading as Caliban, took over the stage to refigure a *Dream* peopled with representatives of Empire.[21] And if Theseus, the blind (British) rationalist, seems the perfect onstage figure for such reviewer-colonizers, the cover for the production's souvenir program provides an even more tellingly contradictory image. Juxtaposing male body fragments that seem tied to different historical periods, it detaches the act of dream-vision from the sleeping self and redirects it onto the spectator. Not only, then, does the dreamer's body become the object of the spectator's gaze, but right at its center, Angela Laurier's Puck gazes through a large hole in his back – the Empire turning the othering look back on itself (see illustration p. 82).

Lepage himself might or might not entertain such a reading. Beyond mentioning how "polluted the whole system built around Shakespeare is . . . polluted with all these zillions of little cultural references that are wrong," he certainly did not, in his interviews with either Christie Carson or Richard Eyre, figure himself as an imperial iconoclast (Lepage, "Collaboration" 31–6; "Robert Lepage" 23–41). In neither, however, are his ideas on theatre, interculturalism, and interpretation seriously challenged. Not only can he avoid or deflect questions because he is at the center, but he is permitted to express himself in a rather graceful and liberal exchange which tends to position him as a postmodern high-culture artist, closer to the kind of figure to whom Linda Hutcheon's writing gives value than to, say, the more complex, intensely problematic position Kwame Appiah describes for a postcolonial, postmodern subject.[22]

If, as Appiah argues, the "post" in both those terms is a space-clearing gesture that opens up a position from which to construct one's self (145–50) – and to fashion one's dream of a canonical text – then Lepage and his production can stake a claim to being both postcolonial and postmodern. Certainly his *Dream*, which yokes divergent cultural materials and identities into pastiche, collage, and bricolage, is oppositional to the grand literary and theatrical narratives that would draw national and cultural boundaries around "Shakespeare" and manage "his" meanings. As such, his practice can be aligned with Fredric Jameson's notion of the postmodern as a cultural dominant ("Cultural Logic"). But in so far as Lepage's own claims for his free-floating play of imagistic borrowings threaten to dismantle politics as a transformative social practice, his production falls within what Teresa Ebert calls ludic postmodernism, a sphere which she identifies as "postpolitical" and describes as a textual practice that seeks open access to the free play of signification in order to disassemble the dominant cultural policy which tries to restrict and stabilize meaning (887). In the case of Lepage's *Dream*, however, the ludic swerves away from the postpolitical to appear as the theatrical equivalent of T. S. Eliot's *Wasteland* – a modernist otherness-machine for essentializing

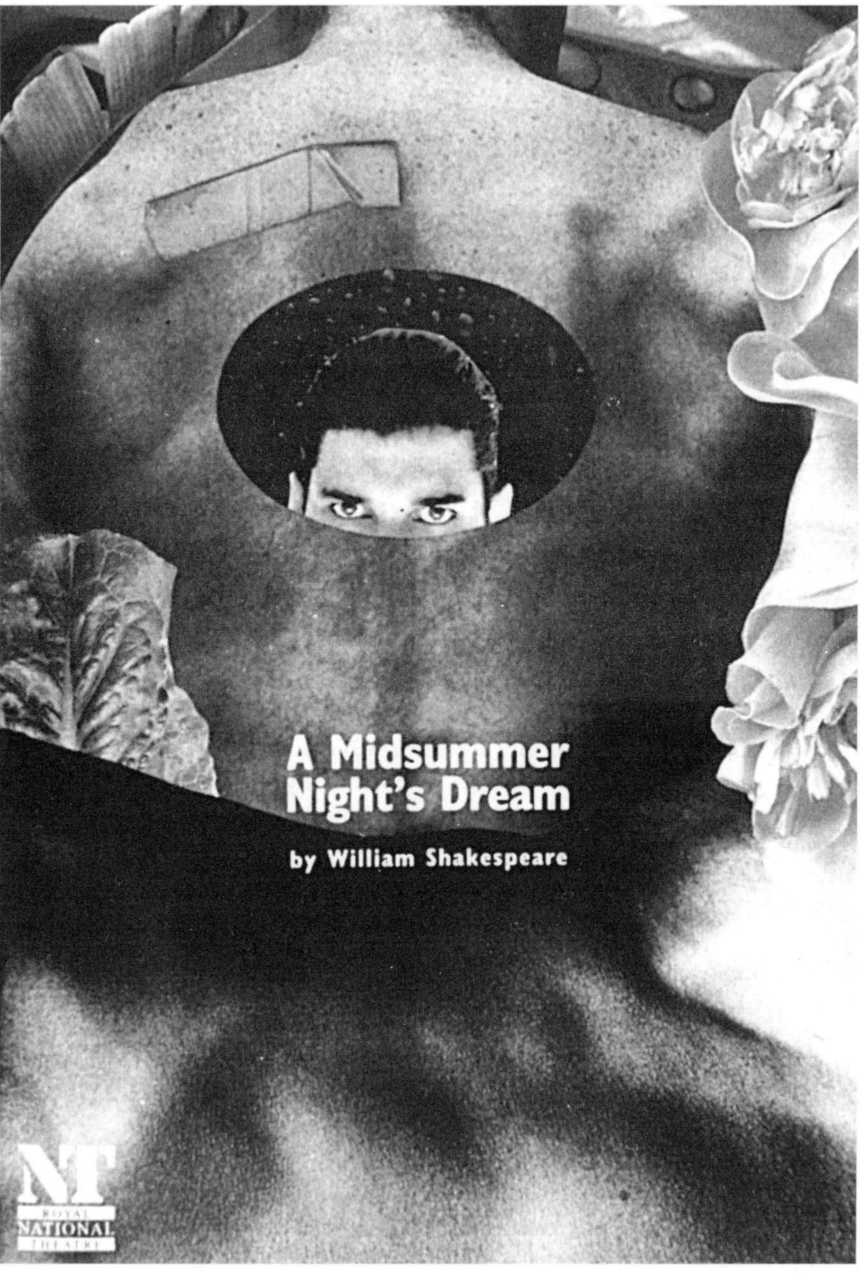

Program cover for Robert Lepage's production of *A Midsummer Night's Dream* at the Royal National Theatre

cultures.[23] Such a move, of course, also recalls Brook's idealized notions of mediation, exchange, and intercultural transfer, a "culture of links between man and society, between one race and another, between micro- and macrocosm, between humanity and machinery, between the visible and invisible, between categories, languages, genres" (*Shifting Point* 239). For just as Brook claimed to have found, for *The Mahabharata*, a "new" universal theatre language based on Indian ritual, myth, and anthropology, Lepage sought in Indonesian culture a philosophy and spirituality which matched his interpretation of the play as based on a hierarchy of good and bad spirits that meet in the human being, who is animated by the conflict within.[24] Was he aware that the Indonesian national motto is Unity in Diversity? Or that in Indonesia, resistance to unity is especially strong, distinguished as it is by over three hundred distinct ethnic groups spread among thirteen thousand islands stretching from the tip of Southeast Asia to the west coast of Australia? Did he recall the moment of Indonesian genocide in East Timor, for which the United States provided military and diplomatic support?[25] To provide such a context is to trouble Lepage's "orientalism" (if it can be called that), to expose the contradictions in his desire to adopt a culture's mythology but without its attendant historical materiality, turning it into an abstraction which can be evoked in the name of transcultural unification or universal harmony.

If Brook's utopian vision of a theatrical practice that can erase barriers between cultures to express a shared truth has evolved considerably[26] since his *Dream*, that production also marks a particularly contradictory nexus of intercultural exchanges. Among its repertory of signifying surfaces were a number of "Eastern" borrowings: orientalist performance techniques, costumes based on those worn by Chinese acrobats, Indian raga, and Asian incantations. Yet those reviewers who did remark such signs tended to fold them into "circus," an appropriately comfortable space of childlike delight where the thrill of performance itself could be celebrated. What made such a move acceptable? For one thing, since the circus had already received a high-culture gloss from Beckett's clowns (borrowed, in turn, from silent film), reviewers (Nightingale excepted) found it easy to appropriate "low" culture in a hegemonic or ideological way to prove their own cultural supremacy. A similar functional transformation of signs applied to Brook's actors. Always (already) expected to speak beautifully, they might now be credited with exhibiting acrobatic physical dexterity: the cultivated, reserved British body could, after all, move between high and popular culture. But figuring Brook's *Dream* as a circus also suppressed another strand of discourse. In aligning the production's Oriental simplicity with a verbal as well as visual stylistic purity that contributed to restoring "Shakespeare," several reviewers recalled Brook's uncomfortably confrontational *US*, his Artaudian protest against the Vietnam War. But they did so primarily to contrast *Dream*'s triumphant alliance between actors and audience, not to remember, for instance, the 1970 bombings in Cambodia. Here, Styan's title, *The Shakespeare Revolution*, functions as the perfect trope for such acts of remembering and forgetting, in which China's Cultural Revolution – which stopped all artistic reproduction for a decade – reappears as a Westernized ghost, attached to the name of Brook as well as that of Shakespeare.

In pointing to these dream-like transformations of knowledge-making, I do not mean to diminish the undoubted significance for *theatrical history* of Brook's *Dream*: to do so would be to betray a fixed pole-star of pleasure in my own Shakespearean dream-memory. Instead, I wish to problematize what is at stake in writing a history of theatrical aesthetics with "Shakespeare" at the center and to gesture toward another. I would argue not only that Lepage takes *Dream* in a direction Brook had mapped out, but that its performance strategies emerge from a present-day moment when the Orient appears not, as Edward Said writes, "as a theatrical stage affixed to Europe" (63) but *on* European stages, where its pure performative disciplines and supposed "simplicity" have repeatedly, as productions by Brook and Ariane Mnouchkine bear witness, served to revitalize impoverished Western theatrical traditions of realism and naturalism. But if the Orient has become a haven, it has also produced a Zen-like form of theatrical practice that, risking a kind of ahistorical nirvana, can lead to theorizing productions as archives or museum displays without legends, empires of plundered signs[27] masquerading as installation art. As Patrice Pavis argues, "our era and our western guilty conscience encourage both an alliance with foreign cultures and a functional transformation of all signs into a post-modern 'supracultural' product that is icily but fatally beautiful" (*Theatre* 211). As icy and beautiful as Brook's *Dream*, perhaps. But hardly Lepage's, which seems more an instance of what Pavis calls the "culture of sensuality," nourishing itself by importing Indonesian cultural styles like tea, as when Lepage incorporates the Catchak, a Balinese monkey chant, to greet Theseus and Hippolyta in the hunting scene. Yet when asked by Richard Eyre whether there is a danger in being a cultural tourist, Lepage replied,

> It depends how you borrow from other cultures and what your interest is in borrowing from that culture. . . . I'm in search of what I am. . . . I'm not trying to take good ideas from other people or other people's culture, I'm trying to see how that relates profoundly or universally to what I want to say or want to do.
>
> ("Robert Lepage" 38)

Mythologizing his own subjectivity, Lepage goes to Shakespeare to test himself and in the process produces a *Dream*-text which legitimates his own intercultural artistry.[28] On the one hand, in so far as Lepage's "borrowings" not only serve as raw material for his own experiments in intercultural connections but contribute to fashioning himself as an individual socio-theatrical subject, he seems entirely complicit with the colonial practices he would deny. On the other, it seems possible that, faced with doing Shakespeare at a royally sanctioned London venue, Lepage's reliance on Indonesian psychic and symbolic forms was a move toward finding a space outside of either the British or the French Empire – an Archimedean point from which to explore and critique the insularity of British "Shakespeare-culture."

Cultures, of course, are like dreams: collections of signs, a traffic in images that can be potentially estranging, both for those practitioners who work in the space between cultures and for spectators of intercultural performances. Certainly, codes and conventions that are easily read by those within a particular culture may be opaque to outsiders who, in decoding them, turn them toward their own, more familiar "shaping fantasies" (see Zarrilli 25). Where Lepage imagined constructing a metaphysical universe – one operating not horizontally, as in film, but vertically ("Robert Lepage" 37) – in a theatrically pure, utopian "empty space," what the reviewers wrote over his performers' bodies and his stunning oneiric images was a sociohistorical discourse. Voicing his suspicion of theorists like Victor Turner who believe that in performance some transcultural communitas may be achieved, Blau writes, "Performance is a testament to what separates"; if indeed anything in it can cross cultures, it is the universal sense of a primordial breach suggested by the performer who, "in a primordial substitution or displacement, is born on the site of the Other."[29] Despite his avowedly universalist intentions, Lepage inadvertently erected a dream-screen to which his own sense of the unconscious as a Jungian catch-all for a world-soul or a transcultural humanity seemed oblivious. There is, in other words, a Jamesonian political unconscious that threads through his *Dream* which, in seeking to mystify and naturalize culture, Lepage completely ignores (Jameson, *Political*). The reviewers' vocabulary of oppositions gives that thread a pattern of interpretation, one mobilized by an historical moment of cultural anxiety in which a rising number of colonized "immigrants" and the promise of a united Euroculture threaten to erase the idea of Britain. Operating according to James Clifford's "salvage" paradigm (73–8), their discourse voices a desire almost antithetical to the merging of worlds Lepage's *Dream* proposes: the desire not only to rescue something "authentic" out of an encounter with performed Shakespeare, but to keep intact the boundaries of national – and theatrical – cultures. This desire, it could be argued, remains "true" enough to Shakespeare's *Dream*, with its closural reassertions of class and gender hierarchies, that it can be drawn into view as the "right" sort of dream to have – a move that, for most of its reviewers, situates Lepage's production in the nightmare space of the monstrous.

There is always, of course, the desire for some authentic field of dreams that will remain constant throughout the years. As a symbolic map of "Englishness," the discourse encircling Lepage's *Dream* marks that space and that time – part of a past reminiscent of all that once was good and could be again.[30] But given Shakespeare's recent adventures within contemporary cultural production, that nostalgic *Dream* has become a folk-cultural activity – an organic, mystical ritual recapturable for present-day Britons, if at all, only in the near-annual productions in Regent's Park. Nearly twenty-five years after the so-called Revolution, what "Shakespeare," and especially performed Shakespeare, is now caught up in is an attempt to incorporate the global array that forms the imaginative landscape of contemporary cultural life and includes crossings, graftings, and modes of articulation between high- and low-culture media as well as among nations. That dream-field has already produced, and will continue to produce, theatrical performances which, to evoke the Derridean turn of *Wayne's World,* might be called "Shakespeare . . . NOT!" or, more appropriate to this case, the other's dream.[31] In seeking to negotiate further that distinctly multicultured as well as intercultural terrain, future studies need to take place not at the locus of examining director-auteurs and the ideotexts of their mise en scènes or the theatrical apparatus itself, but at the point of historical reception, where "theatre" collides with spectators who may transform it into "a strange, eventful history." For it is there, at the site of knowledge-making and its attendant power, that questions similar to those Gayatri Spivak poses, though in a slightly different context, seem precisely the ones to ask (150). Curiously and coincidentally, they are questions that Bottom, Shakespeare's intercultural dreamer, his own subjectivity called into question by a ravishing Other, might well find familiar: Who is this other dreamer? How is he – or she – named? Does he – or she – name me?

NOTES

1 Earlier versions of this essay were read at the 1993 Shakespeare Association of America conference in Atlanta and at the 1993 ACTR/ARTC and ACCUTE conference in Ottawa; a shorter version entitled "Splish Splash and the Other: Lepage's Intercultural *Dream* Machine" appeared in *Essays in Theatre/Études théâtrales* 12:1 (November 1993). My thanks to the editors, Harry Lane and Ann Wilson, for providing materials on Lepage's work and for granting permission to reprint.

2 See Staiger, *Interpreting* 1–81 and "Taboos" 143–4. Staiger's work on film texts offers a more precise materialist model than most work on theatre reception or studies of audience.

3 For an account that differs from mine, see Crowl.

4 The notion of the performance text as an event is adapted and extrapolated from de Certeau's discussion of "events" as a structuring foundation for historiographical writing (xiv–xv, 81).

5 See Bennett 206–7. Often, such knowledges are text-based – that is, a performance is judged "correct" or valid insofar as Shakespeare's *language* appears on the stage.

6 I construct the term "theatrical formation" from Bennett 206–7. See also Carlson, "Theatre."

7 Even reviewers who had not seen Brook's production evoked it, though it was also the case that these critics were more likely to endorse Lepage's *Dream* than were those for whom Brook's production remained a foundational memory. For Brook's *Dream*, see Styan 206–37. See also Croyden 229–86, Loney, and Selbourne.

8 All reviews of Brook's *Dream* are from press books in the Shakespeare Centre Library, Stratford-upon-Avon.

9 However, in the case of performed Shakespeare, the author – or, perhaps more appropriately, the authorial *text* – remains a central touchstone of judgment.

10 Intriguingly, given Canada's postcolonial status, no critic mentioned the English map.

11 See States 374. Pavis notes that one characteristic of what he terms postmodern performance is that text and plot are no longer at the center (*Theatre* 61). Significantly, Lepage's emphasis on actors' bodies tends to deconstruct "character" and to privilege the body as the locus of *overt* cultural assumptions.

12 Lepage's souvenir program includes this excerpt from Kott's essay, "Titania." See "Sightlines," n.p.

13 Lepage's previous and current work is grounded in the materiality of actors' bodies, especially in *Vinci* (1985–6), *Polygraphe* (1987), *Echo* (1989), *Needles and Opium* (1991–4), *Coriolanus* (1992–3), *Macbeth* (1992–3), and *The Tempest* (1992–3). For a fine assessment of the last three, see Salter, "Between Wor(l)ds."

14 The trope of fragmenting and reuniting cultures runs through Lepage's work, in particular *The Dragons Trilogy* (1988–91), *Tectonic Plates* (1990–1), and *Needles and Opium*.

15 For insightful comments on Garneau's tradaptations and his "collaborative" work with Shakespeare's texts, see Salter, "Wor(l)ds" and "Borderlines."

16 On Brook's *Tempest*, see Pavis, "Wilson" 277. I borrow "physical capital" from Seltzer 45.

17 For the notion of the World Turned Upside Down, see Stallybrass and White, *passim*.

18 Lepage, "Robert Lepage" 24. The chairs "motif" also appears in Lepage's *Tectonic Plates*. For the mention of Gabriel, see Lepage, "Lepage Interview" 15. My thanks to Carson for sharing her transcript of this interview, sections of which appear in Lepage, "Collaboration," and for granting permission to cite her transcript.

19 Citations to Shakespeare are from Wells and Taylor.

20 Lepage, "Lepage Interview" 4. In this section of Carson's transcript, Lepage also speaks of deliberately casting Scots mechanicals "because they're red-haired and white-faced and it might be a clownier ambiance if we had good Scots who are kind of . . . naturally alive and funny. But some people said, 'Oh, you want to show the different class, the Scots are the workmen and the Brits are the court?' Well, if that comes out, then that is a comment that I am not responsible for."

21 For an account of how Caliban functions as a metaphor for postcolonial self-fashioning, see Vaughan and Vaughan 144–71.

22 I find Hutcheon's formulations problematic largely because, unlike other theorists of the postmodern, she excludes popular culture. See Appiah 145–57.

23 Suleri speaks of being treated as an "Otherness-machine" (105), a phrase Appiah adopts (157) and which I also appropriate. Exactly where "modernism" ends and "the postmodern" begins is, of course, an ongoing theoretical debate.

24 See Lepage, "Collaboration" 34–5. For pertinent assessments of Brook's *Mahabharata*, see Dasgupta, Case, and Bharucha. For Brook's responses to accusations of cultural raiding, see Brook, "Theatre."

25 See Wallis 274–5. On East Timor, see Chomsky.

26 Evolved, it would seem, toward near-aphorisms. See Brook, *Open Door.*

27 I borrow "empires of signs" from Barthes.

28 A process continued in his 1993–4 "Shakespeare Cycle" – *Macbeth, Coriolanus,* and *The Tempest. Macbeth* especially was grounded in an orientalism borrowed from Akira Kurosawa's 1957 film *Throne of Blood,* moments of which Lepage specifically quoted: at the opening, Macbeth and Banquo mimed riding through misty woods; in the closing sequences, a fall of arrows threatened to pin Macbeth to his castle walls.

29 Blau quoted in Carlson, *Theories* 514. For Turner and others, see Schechner and Appel.

30 I paraphrase Terence Mann's (James Earl Jones) "People Will Come" speech toward the end of *Field of Dreams.*

31 For essays attending to a wide range of productions and issues, see Kennedy, *Foreign.* See also Kennedy, *Looking*; Pavis, *Theatre*; and Elsom. For Mnouchkine's Shakespeares, see Kiernander 106–22.

REFERENCES

Appiah, Kwame Anthony. "The Postcolonial and the Postmodern." *In My Father's House: Africa in the Philosophy of Culture.* New York: Oxford University Press, 1992. 137–57.

Bannock, Sheila. *Stratford-upon-Avon Herald* 4 September 1970.

Barthes, Roland. *Empire of Signs* (1970). Trans. Richard Howard. New York: Hill & Wang, 1982.

Bayley, Clare. *What's On* 15 July 1992. Rpt. in *Theatre Record* 12 (1992): 823.

Bennett, Tony. "Texts, Readers, Reading Formations." *The Bulletin of the Midwest Modern Language Association* 16:1 (1983). Rpt. *Modern Literary Theory.* Ed. Philip Rice and Patricia Waugh. London: Edward Arnold, 1989. 206–20.

Bharucha, Rustom. "Peter Brook's *Mahabharata*: A View From India." *Theater* (Spring 1988): 6–20.

Billington, Michael. *Guardian* 11 July 1992. Rpt. in *Theatre Record* 12 (1992): 822.

Blau, Herbert. *To All Appearances: Ideology and Performance.* London and New York: Routledge, 1992.

—— "Universals of Performance; or, Amortizing Play." *SubStance* 37–8 (1983).

Bourdieu, Pierre. *Distinction: A Social Critique of the Judgement of Taste.* Trans. Richard Nice. Cambridge, Mass.: Harvard University Press, 1984.

Brook, Peter. *The Empty Space* (1968). Harmondsworth: Pelican Books, 1972.

—— *The Open Door: Thoughts on Acting and Theatre.* New York: Pantheon, 1993.

—— *The Shifting Point.* New York: Harper & Row, 1987.

—— Interview. "Theatre, Popular and Special; and the Perils of Cultural Piracy." By David Britton. *Westerly* 32:4 (December 1987): 67–73.

Buzacott, Martin. *The Death of the Actor: Shakespeare on Page and Stage.* London and New York: Routledge, 1991.

Cambron, Micheline. "Autour du 'Songe d'une nuit d'été': les escaliers de la mémoire." *Cahiers de théâtre Jeu* 48 (*Échos shakespeariens*) (1988): 45–8.

Carlson, Marvin. "Theatre Audiences and the Reading of Performance." *Interpreting the Theatrical Past: Essays in the Historiography of Performance.* Ed. Thomas Postlewait and Bruce A. McConachie. Iowa City: University of Iowa Press, 1989. 82–98.

—— *Theories of the Theatre: A Historical and Critical Survey, from the Greeks to the Present.* Ithaca, NY: Cornell University Press, 1984.

Carter, Angela. "Overture and Incidental Music for *A Midsummer Night's Dream.*" *Saints and Strangers.* New York: Viking Penguin, 1986.

Case, Sue-Ellen. "The Eurocolonial Reception of Sanskrit Poetics." *The Performance of Power: Theatrical Discourse and Politics.* Ed. Sue-Ellen Case and Janelle Reinelt. Iowa City: University of Iowa Press, 1991. 111–25.

Chomsky, Noam. "The United States and East Timor." *Towards a New Cold War: Essays on the Current Crisis and How We Got There.* New York: Pantheon, 1982. 337–70.

Clifford, James. "The Others: Beyond the 'Salvage' Paradigm." *Third Text* 6 (Spring 1989): 73–8.

Coveney, Michael. *Observer* 12 July 1992. Rpt. in *Theatre Record* 12 (1992): 823.

Crowl, Samuel. "Shakespeare's Body: Robert Lepage's Earthy *Dream.*" Paper circulated at Paul Yachnin's 1994 Shakespeare Association of America seminar, "Playing with Theory."

Croyden, Margaret. *Lunatics, Lovers and Poets: The Contemporary Experimental Theatre.* New York: McGraw-Hill, 1974.

Dasgupta, Gautam. "*The Mahabharata*: Peter Brook's 'Orientalism'." *Performing Arts Journal* 10 (1987): 9–16.

de Certeau, Michel. *The Writing of History.* New York: Columbia University Press, 1988.

de Jongh, Nicholas. *Evening Standard* 10 July 1992. Rpt. in *Theatre Record* 12 (1992): 823–4.

Dunn, Tony. *Tribune* 17 July 1992. Rpt. in *Theatre Record* 12 (1992): 821.

Ebert, Teresa. "The 'Difference' of Postmodern Feminism." *College English* 53.8 (December 1991): 886–903.

Edwardes, Jane. "Puck in Muck." *Time Out* 24 June – 1 July 1992.

Elsom, John, ed. *Is Shakespeare Still Our Contemporary?* London and New York: Routledge, 1989.

Elsom, John and Nicholas Tomalin. *The History of the National Theatre.* London: Cape, 1978.

Field of Dreams. Dir. Phil Alden Robinson. With Kevin Costner, Amy Madigan, and James Earl Jones. Universal, 1989.

Foucault, Michel. "The Spectacle of the Scaffold." *Discipline and Punish: The Birth of the Prison.* Trans. Alan Sheridan. New York: Random House, 1979. 32–69.

Freud, Sigmund. *The Interpretation of Dreams* (1900). Vols. 4 and 5 of *The Standard Edition of The Complete Psychological Works of Sigmund Freud.* Ed. James Strachey, 24 vols. London: Hogarth, 1953–74.

Gardner, Lyn. *City Limits* 3 February 1989.

Giroux, Henry A. and Roger I. Simon. "Pedagogy and the Critical Practice of Photography." *Disturbing Pleasures: Learning Popular Culture.* Henry Giroux. London and New York: Routledge, 1994. 93–105.

Grant, Steve. *Time Out* 15 July 1992. Rpt. in *Theatre Record* 12 (1992): 821–2.

Hoyle, Martin. *Plays and Players* August 1992: 35.

Hurren, Kenneth. *Mail on Sunday* 12 July 1992. Rpt. in *Theatre Record* 12 (1992): 822.

Hutcheon, Linda. *The Politics of Postmodernism.* London and New York: Routledge: 1989.

Jameson, Fredric. "The Cultural Logic of Late Capitalism." *Postmodernism, or The Cultural Logic of Late Capitalism.* Durham, NC: Duke University Press, 1991.

—— *The Political Unconscious: Narrative as a Socially Symbolic Act.* Ithaca, NY: Cornell University Press, 1981.

Kennedy, Dennis. *Looking at Shakespeare.* Cambridge: Cambridge University Press, 1993.

Kennedy, Dennis, ed. "Introduction: Shakespeare without his language." *Foreign Shakespeare: Contemporary Performance.* Cambridge: Cambridge University Press, 1993.
Kiernander, Adrian. *Ariane Mnouchkine and the Théâtre du Soleil.* Cambridge: Cambridge University Press, 1993.
Kott, Jan. "Titania and the Ass's Head." *Shakespeare Our Contemporary.* Trans. Boleslaw Taborski (1964). New York: W. W. Norton, 1974. 213–36.
Kruger, Loren. *The National Stage: Theatre and Cultural Legitimation in England, France, and America.* Chicago: University of Chicago Press, 1992.
Lepage, Robert. Interview. "Collaboration, Translation, Interpretation." By Christie Carson. *New Theatre Quarterly* 9:33 (February 1993): 31–6.
—— "Lepage Interview, 30 May 1992." By Christie Carson. Author's transcript.
—— Interview. "Robert Lepage in discussion with Richard Eyre." 19 November 1992, Lyttelton Theatre, Royal National Theatre, London. *Platform Papers #3: Directors.* London: Royal National Theatre, 1992. 33–41.
Loney, Glenn, ed. *Peter Brook's Production of William Shakespeare's "A Midsummer Night's Dream" for the Royal Shakespeare Company.* New York: The Dramatic Publishing Company, 1974.
Millar, Gavin. *Listener* 3 September 1970.
Montrose, Louis Adrian. "'Shaping Fantasies': Figurations of Gender and Power in Elizabethan Culture." *Representing the English Renaissance.* Ed. Stephen Greenblatt. Berkeley: University of California Press, 1988. 31–64.
Nathan, David. *Jewish Chronicle* 17 July 1992. Rpt. in *Theatre Record* 12 (1992): 821.
Nightingale, Benedict. "Dream 2001 AD." *New Statesman* 4 September 1970.
—— *The Times* 11 July 1992. Rpt. in *Theatre Record* 12 (1992): 821.
Paton, Maureen. *Daily Express* 10 July 1992. Rpt. in *Theatre Record* 12 (1992): 822.
Pavis, Patrice. *Theatre at the Crossroads of Culture.* Trans. Loren Kruger. London and New York: Routledge, 1992.
—— "Wilson, Brook, Zadek: An Intercultural Encounter?" *Foreign Shakespeare: Contemporary Performance.* Ed. Dennis Kennedy. Cambridge: Cambridge University Press, 1993. 270–90.
Rutherford, Malcolm. *Financial Times* 11 July 1992. Rpt. in *Theatre Record* 12 (1992): 820.
Said, Edward. *Orientalism.* New York: Random House, 1978.
Salter, Denis. "Between Wor(l)ds: Lepage's Shakespeare Cycle." *Theater* 24:3 (1993): 61–70.
—— "Borderlines: An Interview with Robert Lepage and Le Théâtre Repère." *Theater* 24:3 (1993): 71–9.
Schechner, Richard and Willa Appel, ed. *By Means of Performance: Intercultural Studies of Theatre and Ritual.* Cambridge: Cambridge University Press, 1990.
Selbourne, David. *The Making of A Midsummer Night's Dream: An Eye-Witness Account of Peter Brook's Production From First Rehearsal to First Night.* London: Methuen, 1982.
Seltzer, Mark. *Bodies and Machines.* London and New York: Routledge, 1992.
Shakespeare, William. *William Shakespeare: The Complete Works.* Ed. Stanley Wells and Gary Taylor. Oxford: Clarendon Press, 1986.
—— *Macbeth* (1978). Trans. Michel Garneau. Montréal, Québec: VLB Éditeur, 1981.
—— *Coriolan.* Trans. Michel Garneau. Montréal, Québec: VLB Éditeur, 1989.
—— *La Tempête.* Trans. Michel Garneau. Montréal, Québec: VLB Éditeur, 1989.
Shuttleworth, Ian. *City Limits* 16 July 1992. Rpt. in *Theatre Record* 12 (1992): 822.
"Sightlines." *A Midsummers Night's Dream* souvenir program. London, Royal National Theatre, 1992. N.p.

Spencer, Charles. *Daily Telegraph* 13 July 1992. Rpt. in *Theatre Record* 12 (1992): 824.

Spivak, Gayatri Chakravorty. "French Feminism in an International Frame." *In Other Worlds: Essays in Cultural Politics.* New York and London: Methuen, 1987. 134–53.

Staiger, Janet. *Interpreting Films: Studies in the Historical Reception of American Cinema.* Princeton: Princeton University Press, 1992.

—— "Taboos and Totems: Cultural Meanings of *The Silence of the Lambs.*" *Film Theory Goes to the Movies.* Ed. Jim Collins, Hilary Radner, and Ava Preacher Collins. London and New York: Routledge, 1993. 142–54.

Stallybrass, Peter and Allon White. *The Politics and Poetics of Transgression.* London: Methuen, 1986.

States, Bert O. "The Phenomenological Attitude." *Critical Theory and Performance.* Ed. Janelle G. Reinelt and Joseph R. Roach. Ann Arbor: University of Michigan Press 1992. 369–79.

Styan, J. L. *The Shakespeare Revolution: Criticism and Performance in the Twentieth Century.* Cambridge: Cambridge University Press, 1977.

Suleri, Sara. *Meatless Days.* Chicago: University of Chicago Press, 1989.

Taylor, Paul. *Independent* 11 July 1992. Rpt. in *Theatre Record* 12 (1992): 823.

The Times. 29 August 1970.

Tinker, Jack. *Daily Mail* 10 July 1992. Rpt. in *Theatre Record* 12 (1992): 824.

Trewin, J. C. *Illustrated London News* 12 September 1970.

Vaughan, Alden T. and Virginia Mason Vaughan. *Shakespeare's Caliban: A Cultural History.* Cambridge: Cambridge University Press, 1991.

Wallis, Brian. "Selling Nations: International Exhibitions and Cultural Diplomacy." *Museum Culture: Histories, Discourses, Spectacles.* Ed. Daniel J. Sherman and Irit Rogoff. Minneapolis: University of Minnesota Press, 1994. 265–81.

Wardle, Irving. *Independent on Sunday* 12 July 1992. Rpt. in *Theatre Record* 12 (1992): 820–1.

Wolf, Matt. "Robert Lepage: Multicultural and Multifaceted." *New York Times* 6 December 1992. II. 5. 1.

Zarrilli, Phillip B. "For Whom Is the King a King? Issues of Intercultural Production, Perception, and Reception in a *Kathakali King Lear.*" *Critical Theory and Performance.* Ed. Janelle G. Reinelt and Joseph R. Roach. Ann Arbor: University of Michigan Press, 1992. 16–40.

6

SHAKESPEARE, VOICE, AND IDEOLOGY

Interrogating the natural voice

Richard Paul Knowles

1993 was the twentieth anniversary of the publication of Cicely Berry's *Voice and the Actor,* the first in a series of voice texts that have profoundly influenced the acting of Shakespeare in English. These include Berry's second book, *The Actor and His Text*; Kristen Linklater's *Freeing the Natural Voice* and *Freeing Shakespeare's Voice*; and Patsy Rodenburg's *The Right to Speak* and *The Need for Words,* the latter of which, published in 1993, rounds out an informal trilogy, twenty years in the making, of paired volumes on voice and text respectively. I would argue that any actor with a serious interest in performing Shakespeare in English in the last two decades has at one time or another come under the direct or indirect influence of one or more of these books. I would also argue that *Voice and the Actor,* together with the approaches to voice and text that it introduces, has been as pivotal in the history of Shakespearean performance in the twentieth century as the production that provided its impetus – Brook's *Dream.*[1]

Of the six books that I will examine here, three – *Voice and the Actor, The Actor and His Text,* and *Freeing the Natural Voice* – have become canonical texts for acting teachers, voice coaches, and players of Shakespeare, while the other three – *Freeing Shakespeare's Voice, The Right to Speak,* and *The Need for Words* – having only recently appeared, have already become required reading. These books and the methods they represent are in part a reaction to what was perceived to be the classism, racism, and élitism of earlier voice and speech training, as concentration on "proper" accents and manners gave way in the 1960s and 1970s to an attempted (if occasionally naive) democratization of the theatre. This manifested itself in a new "openness" in the work of directors such as Peter Hall, Peter Brook, and Trevor Nunn, even as the "golden cello" musicality of John Gielgud's delivery gave way as a model to the new focus on clarity and meaning in the vocal styles of actors such as Ian Richardson, Ian Holm, and Michael Williams.[2] The so-called "radical" RSC that emerged as a part of this shift is related, as Christopher J. McCullough has shown, to the link between the RSC under Hall and Nunn (both "Cambridge educated and fervent

Leavisites") and the Cambridge "school" of the 1940s and 1950s as represented by E. M. W. Tillyard and, pre-eminently, F. R. Leavis.[3] Not surprisingly, as Alan Sinfield argues ("Royal Shakespeare"), the RSC has proven in practice to be something less than radical, and to function most often in a culturally affirmative fashion (in Marcuse's sense), for reasons that I hope this essay will illustrate.[4]

The voice texts I am examining emerged from the same late-1960s cultural context as Hall, Brook, Nunn, and the RSC. They also derive from British traditions of actor training that claim implicitly to provide a neutral and universal set of tools that will be useful to all actors in all situations. As Jacqueline Martin says, "[British] training has been designed to produce all-round actors, who can cope with the classics, musical, fringe and West End theatre as well as radio and television" (161). In spite of these claims, however, I propose to read these books as cultural productions which themselves do particular kinds of ideological work, "allowing" actors to make their "free" choices not, as Rodenburg puts it, for "any speech activity" once the voice is "primed to respond effortlessly" and "ready to range anywhere" (*Need* 88), but in fact only within a particularly circumscribed range.

It may seem unfair to interrogate printed texts written by voice coaches and teachers rather than the methods they employ in their studios and rehearsal halls, but I would argue that these books have had major influence independent of their authors' and others' authorized application of their techniques, and that *as* texts, these books encode and reinforce ideological structures and assumptions that are both deeply embedded in theatrical discourse and too easily overlooked or mystified when their methods are applied in practice. Indeed, I want to focus less on the exercises that are the books' central contributions than on the rhetorical contexts within which those exercises figure, and out of which they are developed. I want to focus, that is, precisely on those portions of the books that actors looking for help will tend to skip over. My approach is materialist: I will treat voice training as one of the material conditions for the production of meaning in the contemporary performance of Shakespeare that is routinely overlooked in performance criticism. I am less interested in how well the methods "work" than in *what* (ideological) work they *do*.

But first, some history. As I suggested above, and as is the case for so much of the mythologized contemporary tradition of Shakespearean production in English, it all began with Peter Brook. In the beginning was the *Dream*, and the *Dream* was the word; it is not incidental that the first *words* in the first of this tradition of voice texts are delivered by Brook, as the author of the Foreword to *Voice and the Actor*. Berry pays tribute to Brook as a kind of "onlie begettor," citing the experience of working on his *Dream* as having given her confidence in her work, and drawing on that experience to lend Brook's authority to her method (Parker 32–3).[5] The significance of her relationship with Brook, whose working methods and influence are too well known to rehearse in detail, has to do with his role as a kind of signifier, the culmination of what J. L. Styan has called "the Shakespeare revolution," a movement that purportedly began with Poel and reached its fullest realization in Brook's *Dream* and in the coming into currency of his 1968 catch-phrase title, *The Empty Space*.[6] While Styan focuses on Brook's "white box" set and its merging of modernist staging practices with "Elizabethan-style" open stages in a so-called "neutral arena" that "allows" Shakespeare to speak for himself, as it were, unfettered by intrusive scenic decoration or illusion – and while Brook himself uses "the empty space" metaphorically to construct a supposedly neutral, open, and exploratory rehearsal process – Berry, Linklater, and Rodenburg aspire to the construction of the actor's voice and body as empty space, the neutral conduits through which "Shakespeare" can speak directly, uncontaminated by accidentals of historicity. But empty spaces of whatever kind, I suggest, are to the theatre what common sense is to critical practice (Belsey 1–36): vacuums to be filled by the unquestioned because naturalized assumptions of (dominant) ideology.

Jacqueline Martin, in a book-length account of *Voice in the Modern Theatre* that uses Shakespeare as its touchstone and boasts an approving Foreword by Cicely Berry, traces (41–7) from Stanislavski to Brook "the trend . . . towards 'liberating' and 'freeing,' and a more psychological approach to analysis," together with "a new found desire for truth" (as opposed to a different construction of what "truth" *means*). In doing so, she constructs a genealogy that precisely parallels Styan's treatment of stage space from Poel to Brook. She finds in Stanislavski an attempt "to free the body of unnecessary tension and to develop the voice, so that it would express externally the delicate inner expressiveness of the creative process" (50), and she constructs a teleology of voice that follows this narrative through to Brook in terms that will be familiar to readers of Berry, Linklater, and Rodenburg. Wolfsohn, for example, is said to have "*discovered* [my emphasis] that the voice is not the function solely of any anatomical structure, but rather the expression of the whole personality"; that "the voice and the person are one and when one of them is expanded so will the other be"; and that "the actor releases emotional blocks in order to realize creative potential more fully" (64). Grotowski, whose influence on Brook was direct, is said to have made the "discovery" that training the voice involved "learning to release psycho-physiological blocks rather than trying to force the 'natural' voice to learn unnatural techniques" (72). A discussion of Brook is the culmination of the chapter. Martin cites Brook's maxim that "the voice has to be open and ready. The emotions have to be open and free," and she notes that "he prefers the actor whose voice and creative abilities are open to nature and the instincts of the moment" (77).

The actor who achieves this openness will achieve, it is suggested, "a more universal statement," and will find "the primitive nature of man beneath the veneer of civilization and language" (79). She quotes Brook's directive that "you must act as a medium for the words. If you consciously colour them you're wasting your time" (80); and she cites an actor's explanation that "Brook wanted the text to play them, rather than they the text. By employing these means, he felt they would be forced to experience the metaphysical moment when the author first created the words" (80).[7] In the beginning.

In his appeal to this metaphysical moment of authorial (and authoritative) creation Brook is echoing the twentieth century's most influential Shakespeare critic, A. C. Bradley, whose stricture that readers of Shakespeare should aim at "making the same process occur in themselves as occurred in the poet's head"[8] also underscored the work of Leavis and through him, much of the work of the RSC. As Terence Hawkes has demonstrated, moreover, Bradley's influence as a "character critic" has reinforced the individualist/universalist reading of Shakespeare that has proven ultimately to be both conservative and élitist (*Shakespeherian Rag* 27–50).

Brook's Foreword frames *Voice and the Actor* within a context that is completely congruent with the views Martin reports. Significantly, he praises Berry's conviction that while "all is present in nature our natural instincts have been crippled from birth . . . by the conditioning, in fact, of a warped society." He also commends the ways in which she will work with an actor to "set the voice free" and "liberate his [*sic*] hidden possibilities" in order to allow the actor to be "true to 'the instinct of the moment'." Finally, Brook cites Berry's conviction that "life in the voice springs from emotion," and praises her concentration less on "uninspiring technical exercises" than on "deep experience" and "a growth in human relationships."

Partly through the influence of Berry, Linklater, and Rodenburg, these views inform the (re)production of Shakespeare throughout Britain and North America, most directly and demonstrably in the work of the RSC, as evidenced by the profile and influence of Barton's *Playing Shakespeare*, Rutter's *Clamorous Voices*, the *Players of Shakespeare* volumes, and books such as Antony Sher's *Year of the King* (Sher wrote the Foreword to Rodenburg's second book). I want to position Brook in this context not as the genius whose thoughts on voice shaped a generation of performances, but as a site at which various cultural and ideological forces coalesced. In fact, I would argue that the influence of Berry on the RSC has been significantly more direct than that of Brook, or arguably of any other single figure, though as a voice coach (gendered female) she has been less celebrated.[9]

The main features of the post-Brook school of voice texts have to do with the ways in which these books participate in what Alan Sinfield calls "the twin manoeuvres of bourgeois ideology [to] construct two dichotomies":

> universal versus historical and individual versus social. In each case the first term is privileged and so meaning is sucked into the universal/individual polarity, draining it away from the historical and the social – which is where meaning is made by people together in determinate conditions, and where it might be contested.
>
> ("Give an Account" 141)

The way in which these texts execute these manoeuvres is largely through their construction of *freedom* (by far the most frequently used word in the books, sometimes occurring ten or more times on a single page), *nature* and the natural (as opposed to civilization, repression, education, or restraint), *identity* or *character* ("human" and dramatic), and "*Shakespeare*" (or "the text"). These terms are related differently in each book to the concept of "expression" – of self, of Shakespeare, of "our common humanity" – or what Brook calls "an expression of inner life" (Foreword).

"Freedom" is among the most slippery of these concepts, and as I have suggested it lies at the heart of each of these texts. In *Voice and the Actor*, Berry offers a definition and explanation: "I prefer to use the word 'free' to the word 'relaxed,'" she says, "as the latter gives the impression of being floppy and heavy, and therefore perhaps dull, whereas 'free' implies being relaxed but ready for action, alert but not tense" (22). In spite of not always being this careful to foreground the limitations of her choice of word and phrase, and in spite of frequent lapses into associations with such things as personal liberation and interpersonal honesty (or even democracy), Berry uses freedom in her first book primarily to convey this sense of relaxed readiness. She presents her exercises, that is, as methods by which to "allow" – a word most often used, ironically, in the imperative mood – "the text," or "Shakespeare," to speak through the body "naturally," unencumbered by the actor's conscious or conditioned shaping – what Brook has already introduced as "the conditioning . . . of a warped society" (Foreword 3). The actor/reader is repeatedly urged to "allow the words to do their own work" (108), to "take their own value" and "lead you" (124), to "allow the rhythm to take you" (124), confident that, if "you" do, "the meaning will be clear" (108).

Freedom, then, is constructed in *Voice and the Actor* as a kind of surrender: instinctive and involuntary (11, 24, 116, 132) rather than conscious (15, 22, 31, 101); flexible, relaxed, and malleable (12, 53, 80) rather than tense, anxious, or resulting from muscular effort (12, 13, 31, 37); and deriving from a "clean slate" rather than preconceived ideas (13). The assumption that *the text* will speak once the actor is "totally open to receive it" leads Berry to reject as "a waste of time . . . work on any text that is second-rate" (17) and to focus her exercises on canonical (usually British) authors – Dryden, Milton, Hopkins, Thomas, and of course, pre-eminently, Shakespeare. The determination of what is "first rate," apart from prescribed authority and tradition, is to some degree veiled in *Voice and the Actor*, but there are intimations that will be more fully developed by Berry herself, and particularly by Linklater and Rodenburg, in subsequent books. Clearly, however, even here, what "freedom" will do for actors is to restore a "natural," "childlike" access to "self," a psychological "depth" that puts them in touch with something that is at once their true (individual) selves, our common (universal) humanity, and Shakespeare. This construction of freedom directly feeds both the individual/universal vs. the social/historical axis, and the construction of Shakespearean essentialism that the RSC inherited from Leavis's Cambridge. In doing so, it prescribes a certain range within which an actor's choices can be made, a range circumscribed by conceptions of character (human and dramatic), of dramatic texts, and of Shakespeare, that are ideologically coded (and foreign to anything that Shakespeare would have recognized).

* * *

Berry extends her range in her second book, maintaining her primary focus, as the title suggests, on *The Actor and His Text*, but clarifying her understanding of the relationships among text, actor, and character. As Jacqueline Martin notes (172), the emphasis here shifts from "making the voice free" to "making the language organic, so that the words act as the spur to the sound" (Berry, *The Actor* 11). Again, of course, this requires a "first-rate text," together with a particular conception of human identity and dramatic character, all found, "naturally," in Shakespeare. Berry begins, in *The Actor and His Text*, with the premises that an actor works by "finding the reason for the words he [*sic*] has to speak [and] relating them both to his own experience and to the motive of the character, in order to make them authentic" (18). She finds that "in Shakespeare the motive of the character and the way the character expresses himself coincide in a positive way" (10), concluding that "the words must be a release of the inner life, and not either an explanation of it or a commentary on it" (18–19). She determines that the actor must remain "free to our basic primitive response to [the language] – primitive in the sense of being less consciously organized, and less culturally based" (19).

The belief in an essential, inner truth that lies somewhere prior to or beneath conscious control and cultural conditioning is deeply embedded in *The Actor and His Text*, beginning with Berry's belief that language itself is "primitive in essence" (19): "Words," she says, "evolved out of noises which were first made to communicate basic needs" and which "can arouse quite basic and primitive responses in us" (19–20). This is particularly true, she feels, of poetry, which "contains a fierceness and a reality perhaps at a different temperature than that of naturalistic writing" (32), and she quotes approvingly Edith Sitwell's remark that "poetry is a suppressed scream" (33). Each of the elements of verse speaking she subsequently examines derives from a Rousseauesque belief in the honest savagery or childlike "innocence of communication" (48) that precedes the corruption of civilization, that sets up a binary opposition between emotion and intellect, privileging the former, and that approaches a kind of universality. Rhythm, for example, is related to "our atavistic verbal memory" (37), music provides "a meaning beyond the grammatical sense . . . which is not far removed from our pleasure in nursery rhymes" (47), and "pleasure in rhyme is a very basic instinct, which has nothing to do with class or education, simply with a delight in the turning of a word, as in children's rhymes" (77).[10]

It is more difficult now to accept the naivety of this position than it was in the 1960s and early 1970s, particularly since Derrida has demonstrated in *Of Grammatology* the "privileged place . . . Rousseau occup[ies] in the history of logocentrism," and the ideological role played by the "phonologism" and "the motif of presence" behind the privileging of the spoken over the written word in which post-Berry voice training takes part (Derrida 97).[11] There is, moreover, in *The Actor and His Text* and its progeny, an element of nostalgia for a truth that is simple, direct, and expressive, and that is related to nostalgia for a supposed Elizabethan innocence:

> We live at a time when people are less articulate about their feelings. As we become more educated in the sense that we have more information, we become less in tune with our instincts, and so our response to words becomes only literal: we stop feeling the emotional life of the language. In Elizabethan times, for instance, because the majority of people were not literate they relied much more on verbal communication: stories, information, whole histories of families were passed on by word of mouth. Complicated pneumonics were often used to do this, and these latter probably contributed to an ear for word games and rhymes; it was to do with a whole fabric of life. Today, our dependence on the media – where so much of the talk is there to fill out time in a knowing way – on machines, on the speeding up of life that technology produces, on urbanization, the breakdown of family units, the breakdown of community involvement: all these factors contribute to less real verbal communication between people. (48)

Real communication between people, then, is constructed by Berry as verbal, emotional, and unsophisticated, and truth derives from "the less conscious responses [which] come from a deeper current within us" (23) than "our logical, conscious thought" (25). The exercises in *The Actor and His Text* are therefore designed to "make us ready for the intuitive response" (24) and allow the breath to take the words "down to a physical level, deeper than the intellect" (27), and are packaged in such a way that physical depth – deep breathing – is silently conflated with emotional depth, psychological depth, and the "deep meaning" of language, especially Shakespeare's.

Berry argues that "the further down into the centre [another word with many uncontrolled associations here] we take the breath, the more in touch the breath is with our feelings, and therefore the more the voice will respond to the texture of the language" (274). Ultimately, she constructs a series of binaries – depth vs. surface, nature vs. civilization or artifice, emotion vs. reason, even vowels vs. consonants or open vs. closed vowel sounds (101) – in which the first terms are linked and privileged through an association with truth and honesty, while the second are related to the corruptions of an essentially dishonest intellectual and cultural conditioning. And of course these binaries are constitutive of the individualist/universalist vs. social/historical polarities that function effectively to inhibit politicized readings and political dissent.

* * *

As its title would suggest, Kristen Linklater's *Freeing the Natural Voice* shares with Berry's books a faith in the possibility of achieving a "natural" physical and emotional "freedom" to provide access to transcendent truths. It also takes much further Berry's Rousseauesque faith in a purity of expression that Linklater associates with "horses," "babies," and "small children" (43), because it "resembles instinctual reflex on an animal level" (53). More explicitly than Berry, Linklater believes that unlike the culturally conditioned intellect, the body cannot lie[12] – "we can trust the involuntary processes," she says in *Freeing Shakespeare's Voice* (20) – and she consequently seeks, like Berry, to root speech in a primal realm of "pure" vocal expression:

> Language began instinctually, physically, primitively. The extended roar of pain, pleasure, or rage, was articulated into more detailed communication by muscles in the body responding to the demand of an evolving intellect. The intellect, needing to convey increasingly precise information, deployed muscles in the mouth to distinguish positive from negative reactions and gradually to describe objects and facts and handle the minutiae of language. It is inconceivable that when the mouth first started to make words it did so in a manner divorced from its normal exercise of chewing, biting, kissing, sucking, licking, snarling, lip-smacking and lapping. All these were practical activities with sensual rewards and palpable side effects. . . . Words have a direct line through the nerve endings of the mouth to sensory and emotive storehouses in the body. . . . That direct line has been short-circuited, and the beginning work to release the built-in art of eloquence must be to re-establish the visceral connection of words to the body. (173–4)

Much of this sorts comfortably with the approach of Berry; but as Linklater's title suggests, and her work with American method actors will have reinforced, Linklater's first book focuses less on freeing the *text* to speak directly than on gaining access through American psychotherapeutic principles (which tend to construct the individual unconscious as pre-social[13]) to a neuro-muscular state of receptiveness that will allow "organic" sensory impulses to spring from the actor's psychological and physical "center" to *inform* the text. Despite Linklater's intention "to make available the deepest and widest extent of our humanity for Shakespeare's poetry to work on" (209), the emphasis of *Freeing the Natural Voice*, unlike that of Berry or Rodenburg, is on the "individual" through whom the text is "revealed," and on the process through which "interpretation of the text [is] released from within" (185).

This emphasis surfaces in exercises that are introduced by the suggestion that "feelings respond more quickly to an image than a word" (141), and that involve imagistic associations which are privileged over the text that inspires them. "Allow the breath to be affected by the pictures, not by the words that inspire them," she prompts. "Do not let the words dominate, let them pick up the feeling of the images and be influenced by them" (141). This is not an isolated instance; the privileging of feeling over image and image over text culminates in the book's final chapter, in which Linklater first addresses the issue of text directly, and uses the image of the dramatic script as mere fertilizer for the actor's creativity (193). By logical extension, "pure" voice training seems in Linklater to become a therapeutic end in itself, "unencumbered," as she says, "by external material such as words" (193).

Linklater's movement away from the accidentals of cultural conditioning that constrain the voice, towards freeing "the individual emotional and imaginative capacity" in the service of "the human truth it expresses" (45), is ultimately an individualistic and generalizing one. In attempting to *transcend* cultural conditioning en route to "the atmosphere of universal experience" (186) she allows for the *effacement* of cultural and other kinds of difference and is in danger of throwing out the particular baby with the generalizing wash of her rhetoric. All vowels and no consonants make Will a dull boy.[14]

* * *

Linklater published her second book, *Freeing Shakespeare's Voice*, in 1992, sixteen years after the appearance of *Freeing the Natural Voice*. The parallel titles are not incidental; the second book makes explicit what Linklater's first had implied: that if you look sufficiently deeply into yourself, freeing your natural voice and body and discovering your most profound psychophysical center, you will find Shakespeare. Only then will you be able to "plumb the depths of the human condition and tell the truth" (31). Shakespeare's words, she argues, "re-present the aroused internal human condition" (43). Again, Shakespeare, human nature, truth, and the human condition are by implication unchangeable, and acting shaped by Linklater's methods will necessarily function hegemonically to affirm the individualist/universalist polarity and the societal status quo.

Freeing Shakespeare's Voice is the most deeply ideologically coded of the books under discussion, and it is very much of its time in its embodiment of a 1990s "new-age" mysticism.[15] At the same time, however, it draws ahistorically on Shakespeare and on an idealized "Elizabethan World Picture" (she frequently cites Tillyard) to deal with anxieties about "Marxism, feminism, colonialism and other -isms," all of which serve Linklater merely as "continuing proof of Shakespeare's relevance to any current or future examination of the [by implication unchangeable] world" (64).

Linklater's version of Elizabethan England asserts Tillyard's élitist "chain of being" as the governing principle of life (cf. 57–72),[16] and she accordingly constructs many of her exercises around the concept of "degree" and the metaphor of the ladder. In doing so, she inscribes a wildly ahistorical and hierarchical ideology, conflating Ulysses's decontextualized version of degree in *Troilus and Cressida* with Keith Johnstone's "theatre sports" status games, and both of these with the English class system. She subsequently "marr[ies] the age of psychology," by which she means the present, "with the [Elizabethan] age when Man, Nature and the Cosmos coexisted in immutable degree" (64). Believing in the natural virtues of unified subjectivity, in the "harmony to which human nature aspires" (129) and in "the unity that leads to a truthful performance" (46),[17] Linklater constructs methods of reading that, she admits, "may seem to be teetering on the precipice of interpretation."

> But I would like to claim that this is not interpretation, it is reading the clues. In coming as close as possible to Shakespeare's mind and voice we can feel our feet on intelligent ground and can use this ground as a jumping-off point for interpretative choice. (71)[18]

In application, however, Linklater's assumptions – about the Elizabethan context, "reality," the text, acting, character, human identity, and universal human nature – narrowly constrain the range of interpretive choice for the actor, and what begins as "what is most apparent" quickly comes to seem arbitrary. When she turns to analysis of the scene between Richard and Anne in *Richard III*, for example, she determines that

> the passion that surely mounts in [Anne] is terror ("clever" interpretations of character could arrive at different conclusions, but here we start from what is most apparent from the given circumstances and the text). Richard's . . . ambition is the driving [passion], and in this scene he must convince Anne that he passionately loves her. . . . [T]he falling in love, must seem real [to Anne]. It can only seem real if it is experienced as real by the protagonist; therefore Richard must tell the truth when he says that his love for Anne drove him to murder. (87)

This is not interpretation, presumably, because it's true.

Freeing Shakespeare's Voice concludes with a section on "The Contexture," in which the assumptions that underlie the rest of the book surface most explicitly. In a chapter on "Today's Actor in Shakespeare's World" Linklater discusses the "alchemical" craft by which the actor's psyche "rearranges itself" in order to become that of the character, for "it is the artistic goal of any real actor to become the person [not, significantly, the character] s/he is playing" (187). In doing so, the actors "flesh their characters to archetype," and move "from particular to universal meaning" (188). Citing Tillyard again, and further cementing the alliance between contemporary voice theory and the Cambridge of the 1940s and 1950s, she notes that the world of the Elizabethans was "organized to withstand the constant threat of chaos by the strict order of the Great Chain of Being [which] formed an existential circle within which the psyches of Shakespeare's men and women had a particular logic." Linklater laments that "that embracing circle has been replaced in our world by a patchwork of communal philosophies stitched unevenly together by the political, economic, technological and psychological ideologies that inform the 'civilized' cultures of the industrialized nations," but she nevertheless asserts that through "our likeness to the Elizabethans," and with the help of Freud – by which, again, she seems to mean normalizing American schools of psychotherapy – "we can walk and talk with Shakespeare on familiar ground." In fact, she asserts, after "the theatre fluctuated between babble and bubble" for centuries of Restoration "froth" and nineteenth-century "manners," it is now "the first time *since* Shakespeare's time that the plays can be fully realized." For "not until the twentieth century were the plays respected as what they are rather than what someone wished they were," and "not until the present time has society been in tune with the Elizabethans on a fundamental human plane" (189–90). It is here that voice training most explicitly connects with the fundamental precepts of the "Elizabethan revival" in staging and with Styan's "Shakespeare revolution": the belief that "free" and "open" principles of staging (analogous to rehearsal processes at the RSC and elsewhere) "allow" contemporary audiences direct access to Shakespeare's transcendental intentions that has been unavailable since the seventeenth century.

In her chapter on "Shakespeare's Voice in Today's World," Linklater attempts to struggle with the ideological implications of her method, and the chapter plays out considerable anxiety about its own politics. Early on she presents a vision of Shakespeare and theatre as therapy, both on an individual level and through what she calls "catharsis within a community" (196). Therapy constructed in this way, of course, conspires with the individualist/universalist biases in these texts to suggest that social problems are the function of psychological problems, or what Linklater has earlier called "neuroses" (5). There is no point working for social change when what an individual really needs to do is to get therapy, adjust, and "return" to an ahistorical "normal."

In the interests of "therapy/healing" (197), Linklater believes that the study of voice can help to redress "our present-day issues of economic inequality, race, prejudice, corruption" (201) by taking us deep within ourselves, and deep within our culture. For "to understand another culture deeply, one must understand one's own." According to Linklater's logic, within "our" individual psyches – somewhere beneath cultural conditioning – we find the deepest truths about ourselves, about human nature, and about those things that all cultures presumably share – those things that, like Shakespeare, transcend the accidentals of historicity. "Actors of cultural origins other than the Greco-Roman/Western one will not be disappointed in meeting Shakespeare's language," she asserts, because "the absorption of the sounds and rhythms of another language into one's living systems puts one on the path to an empathetic understanding of all cultures." "Theoretically," she feels, averting issues surrounding the construction of canons, and avoiding the question of *whose* classics she is referring to, "right-minded people know that the classics should reveal to the audience a universal message plumbed from the depths reverberating deep below national or racial distinctions" (201). Linklater's formula for the redress of inequalities begins to sound very like a recipe for cultural imperialism, or what I think of as the "we-are-the-world" school of interculturalism.

Linklater's assertions are discomforting enough in their use of a Western cultural icon as the font of universal truth, but they are made more so by the fact that her final chapter,[19] entitled "Whose Voice? *The Man*," argues the Oxfordian case for Edward DeVere's authorship of the plays. Linklater introduces the chapter by saying "I cannot, in all conscience, end this book which trumpets so loudly and so often the word 'Truth,' without bowing my head and my knee in the direction of Edward Devere" (209). She goes on to state that the sort of insight "Shakespeare" has into the lives of both the lower classes and the aristocracy "would seem more likely . . . [to have] come from the top down rather than from the bottom up" (213). However peripheral the chapter itself and its conclusion may be to the book's focus on vocal technique, this argument is the logical culmination of its ideological underpinnings, which clearly reinforce North American Anglophilia as embodied in "ye olde" Shakespeare Festivals across the continent, in imitation and emulation of British voice and other training, and most notably in the disproportionate postcolonial "cultural cringe" (Ashcroft 12[20]) before the RSC in most North American performance criticism of Shakespeare.

* * *

Patsy Rodenburg's *The Right to Speak* and *The Need for Words* share many of their central principles with other volumes I've been examining, particularly those by Cicely Berry, with whom Rodenburg taught for nine years at the RSC. Their similar construction of language, Shakespeare, character, and human identity need not be rehearsed again. *The Right to Speak* differs from the others, as its title would suggest, in its having responded to the cultural and political climate of the 1990s by constructing differently than Linklater those pressures which constrain freedom of expression. The whole book, in fact, rests on the conflation of different senses of the word "freedom," the effect of which is to construct "freeing the natural voice" as a route to social and political liberation and empowerment. There is incipient recognition here that gender and class distinctions are culturally constructed, and that repression often functions hegemonically by internalizing behaviors as "natural" that are in fact learned. Rodenburg constructs a version of the "natural voice" that is "habit free, guilt free" (32), and free of learned social and psychological blocks and repressions.

This distinction between Rodenburg and her predecessors is more apparent than real, however, at least in terms of its impact on the construction of dramatic character. To begin, the "rights" for which she pleads are explicitly gendered female (27, 67, and *passim*), and associated with the "natural" vs. the analytical, the rural vs. the urban (66–70), and the so-called "right to be children all over again" (105 and *passim*). In addition to the reinscription of these familiar tropes, which equate the female with the natural, rural, and childlike, and despite the rhetoric of liberation and empowerment, *The Right to Speak* ultimately places responsibility for repression squarely within the realm of the psychological: Rodenburg frequently prods her reader-actors to "*give yourself* the right to breathe" and to "*choose* to have freedom of expression" (104, 147, my emphases), and she insists that they not "deny themselves" their vocal rights and privileges (145). These instructions may provide self-confidence and aid in various kinds of vocal work, but they also function in the way of most naturalistic drama, together with the techniques used to produce it, to deflect social unrest to the level of individual psychological adjustment.

For the most part, the focus of *The Right to Speak* remains on the link between deep psycho-physical awareness and culturally transcendent truths. Like Berry and Linklater, Rodenburg conflates physical and psychological depth, and opposes both to the intrusive and impure influences of the conscious mind:

> As the breath goes lower and lower past its superficial and then its normal capacity in the throat and upper chest, then down through the chest and diaphragm where a more intense capacity lies, and then deeper, yet deeper into the abdomen and pelvis, it settles down into and disturbs a habitation untouched by the intellect and rationality. When it does hit bottom it sometimes dislodges a vital clue to our being – the secret life held down under the deepest of breaths. (88–9)

"The free and lower breath," she claims, "gives us access to our feelings" (147), and "when pain, loss, betrayal, love, joy or delight becomes so great to the point of bursting, we always break through to a heightened plateau of communication" (25). At this heightened point, in Rodenburg's view, we are ready to encounter "the great classical plays of all cultures that confront the universal issues of humankind" (26).

With *The Need for Words* Rodenburg completes the pattern, established by her predecessors, of publishing a first book, as her subtitles indicate, on "working with the voice" and a second on "voice and the text," though unlike Berry and Linklater she does so in the course of a single year. *The Need for Words* is characterized by the familiar conflation of physical and psychological depth with freedom, truth, and the natural (configured as primitive, childlike, unsophisticated, and female), but it is different from the other works in its reiterated focus on the "need" for individual expression.

Arguing that "simply needing a word will bypass all the circuits of tension and allow us easy access to the voice" (52), Rodenburg constructs this need as (among other things): "a need to communicate" (14, 58); a "need for access to words that should naturally excite and liberate us" (15); a "need to be specific and emotive," which is "not an academic need" (10),[21] but the "need to breathe" (92); and "the need for spoken truth" (142). She explores the ways in which "useless tension cuts off need" (91) and "our whole culture has been designed to inhibit us from speaking by laying barriers in the path of our need for words" (18). Turning to text and delivery, she talks of how one "learns to need the words because the listener needs to hear them" (141), because "an audience will quickly detect that the speaker doesn't need the text in a deeply personal way, that he or she has made no intimate investment in what is being said" (155). When she talks of "needing the words to take you through the journey of the text" (31) and consequently of "mak[ing] the listener need each word in the chain of a thought" (32), Rodenburg is constructing linear metaphors of journeys and chains much in the way we have seen Berry and Linklater do, and much as she later in the book constructs a "universal" need for Aristotelian linear narrative.[22] And, as in Linklater, there is a spiritual dimension to this, since "in the beginning was the Word" (7), and "when the word is made flesh it really does dwell among us" (49).

It is clear that "need" in this text has as many uncontrolled associations as does "freedom" in the others, even shifting on occasion into the realm of the needs of the characters (219), conflating actor with character in a telling slippage. But throughout *The Need for Words* individual psychological needs and their expression are paramount, as Rodenburg tries to find a "method of tapping into an individual's capacity or emotional life, from which the need to speak Shakespeare's words must ultimately spring" (34). She is most comfortable asserting "an individual's inner truth and need" (14), and slips from the individual "human being" to the universal "we" with alarming alacrity in passages referring to "*our* most vital needs as *a* human being" (3, my emphasis). And "we" "*need* Shakespeare" (Rodenburg's emphasis) because "it is generally agreed that Shakespeare's plays and sonnets explore with enormous compassion and variety all the great dilemmas facing human beings in conflict" (167).[23] "Shakespeare's brilliance," she continues, "is that he seems to be able to speak to us all over those hundreds of years and across every cultural bias and barrier. He is a genius because he understands our likenesses as well as our individuality" (171), which for Rodenburg amount, it seems, to the same thing. And as in most liberal humanist endeavors, the construction of likenesses that are rooted in the definition and control of the "universal" by the socially dominant is more culturally significant than are the threatening projects of respecting or producing cultural and other differences.

Not surprisingly, gaining "the right to speak" and finding "the need for words" finally translate into the conflation of self-knowledge, universal truth, and Shakespeare, all "found" in and "expressed" through the transcendent body and voice, and *when* expressed, providing an individual cathartic release that Rodenburg constructs as "liberating" (*passim*). "Essentially," she argues, in a legitimating appeal to what Foucault (131) calls "the author function," "the speaker has to become the vessel for the text" (88), "connecting across time to the writer writing the words onto paper" (97).[24] The strands of the argument come together in a great ahistorical paean to the individual's connection with truth, harmony, and the universal value of great writing as the ultimate achievement of the need for words:

> When a speaker connects to a text in a genuine way you continually sense an invisible, harmonious thread stretching between writer and speaker. Time instantly collapses and the world lives again in a timeless zone. . . . The speaker becomes the writer's vessel just as the writer is a vessel of other unseen creative forces. The greatest writers, the ones who endure over centuries, are like messengers of a huge universal consciousness and the speaker must serve the needs of such texts with particular care. . . . When this connection is made, then, we have achieved the need for words. All points of the triangle achieve measured satisfaction and harmony. (96–7)

For all Rodenburg's recognition in *The Right to Speak* that the forces which restrict vocal, physical, and psychological freedom can be social and external, in spite of her claims in *The Need for Words* that Shakespeare "wrote for king and commoner alike" (33), and in spite of her disclaimers of "vocal imperialism" (*Right*, 5), it is clear that in her view it is the actor's mind, body, and habits – not society – that must change for liberation to be achieved. The actor influenced by these books will learn to construct characters whose psychological depths and difficulties will remain the focus of interest, and whose psychological adjustment, as a "return" to some universalist state of normalcy, will continue to provide cathartic reversals, recognitions, and closures for audiences who will continue to leave the theatre with calm of mind, all passion spent.[25]

* * *

Voice training is only one of many ideologically coded theatrical practices that shape meaning in contemporary Shakespeare production, and it is clear that voice work is contained by, and only capable of functioning within, institutional and professional contexts that limit any potential it might have for invention, intervention, or dissidence. This is particularly true when a Head of Voice of the stature of Rodenburg is appointed by the National Theatre on only a part-time basis. It is also clear, however, that the ideological underpinnings of the books examined here, deriving as they do from the transcultural, psycho-physical work of Peter Brook and others, would themselves, in the short rehearsal periods afforded contemporary British and North American productions, tend either to resist or comfortably contain any genuinely oppositional attempts to stage the plays, attempts which cannot succeed if they function at the level of theme, content, or directorial concept but ignore the ideological structures embedded in every branch of theatrical discourse. It is not surprising that in productions of Shakespeare throughout the 1970s and early 1980s, "Brechtian," for example, tended to describe a *style*, limited to fashionable elements of design stripped of their political purposes and neutralized by actors who on at least some level were attempting to "become" the characters they were playing. Even now, directors who attempt something different on the level of process will almost invariably be working at cross-purposes with the training and presuppositions of their casts. Any attempt to circumvent traditional rehearsal practices is likely to be confronted by the self-protective instincts of actors who believe their training to be ideologically neutral, and who when challenged will guard their professional reputations against directors who "don't know how to work with actors," or "don't understand what actors *do*."

It is similarly unsurprising that the work of politically oppositional directors such as Michael Bogdanov is so often contained and gentrified in practice, that it sits comfortably at conservative, state-supported institutions such as the RSC, the National Theatre, or Ontario's Stratford Festival, or that it surfaces in amicable co-operative ventures between Bogdanov's English Shakespeare Company and the Mirvish family, who own London's Old Vic and Toronto's Royal Alexandra theatres, but are best known in Canada for "Honest Ed's," Toronto's most garish discount department store. Produced through actors with the kinds of voice and other training I have outlined here, and through institutional structures that are fully congruent with that training and with the currently dominant multinational brand of "corporate humanism,"[26] even Bogdanov's socialist attempts at cultural intervention can result only in variations on what Alan Sinfield has taught us to call "Shakespeare-plus-relevance" ("Introduction"

159) – titillatingly "rad" in content, but comfortably contained and rendered functionally familiar by its modes of production.[27]

NOTES

1 In an article by K. Parker, Berry is said to have cited Brook's way of working with actors as a major influence that "gave her the confidence in using particular exercises, about handling language and so on" (31).

2 For evidence that the battle to abandon "proper" accents has not yet been won, see Hodgdon.

3 See McCullough 39, who quotes Peter Hall's claim that "I am a radical, and I could not work in the theatre if I were not," from Addenbroke (66). The quotation about "fervent Leavisites" derives, via McCullough, from Janet Watts, "The Nunn Story," *Observer Colour Supplement* (2 May 1982): 39.

4 See Marcuse 88–133. My analysis of voice texts participates in the cultural materialist project represented by Dollimore and Sinfield, Holderness, and Sinfield's *Faultlines* 1–28 and 254–302. It also concerns itself with the class and commercial interests of "the Shakespeare industry" as analyzed by Hawkes in *That Shakespeherian Rag* 1–26 and *Meaning by Shakespeare* 141–53; and by Gary Taylor, *Reinventing Shakespeare* 298–411. The RSC and its voice work have been major players in Styan's "Shakespeare Revolution," which, together with the "protestant" Leavisite/New Critical doctrine of unmediated literary analysis, promoted an ahistorical myth of "free" access to Shakespeare on Elizabethan and modern open stages that effaces or mystifies cultural contexts and inhibits social change.

5 The back-cover blurb to *Voice and the Actor* makes much of Berry's experience on Brook's *Dream* and of Brook's claim in the Foreword that Berry's book is "so necessary and valuable."

6 Styan observes that "it seems no coincidence that the new direction and focus of scholarly thinking about Shakespeare, together with the new freedom from constrictions of realism and the proscenium arch, should culminate in Peter Brook's landmark production of *A Midsummer Night's Dream*" (6).

7 Martin is quoting Brook from Innes 185; from Brook's 1968 film of *The Tempest*; and from Selbourne 23.

8 Quoted by Cooke 184.

9 Berry's influence is acknowledged by Juliet Stevenson (Rutter *et al.* 43); by Rodenburg (*Right* xiii); by Jacqueline Martin in her discussion of Barton and the RSC (33–6) as well as in her analysis of Berry (171–5); and less directly in the arguments in Barton of actors such as Ian McKellen (who wrote a Foreword to *The Right to Speak*). But her influence is apparent in all of the actors' discussions of playing Shakespeare cited above.

10 Berry's denial that what she is discussing has to do with class or education plays out an anxiety that all these texts share. Berry, Linklater, and Rodenburg go to considerable lengths to deny their participation in the classism, racism, and élitism associated with earlier schools of voice and speech training. Rodenburg raises the question of "vocal imperialism," but in *The Right to Speak*, lists "race, culture and social mobility" as "outside the scope of this book" (7). These denials mask an anxiety about Shakespeare and other canonical authors' providing "the best" texts for voice work, and about "proper" accents and "correct" delivery – an anxiety deflected to the realm of truth to a "self" which is somehow also universal. A related anxiety surfaces in a note to *The Actor and His Text*: "At the time of writing I chose to use *he* rather than *he/she*, believing it

to be less cumbersome. I now regret this, and I apologize to those whose feelings may be offended" (11). The 1993 edition (with a Foreword by Trevor Nunn) is entitled *The Actor and* The *Text*, but retains the masculine pronoun in the text, together with this apology. These anxieties culminate in Linklater's new-age mysticism and her defence of the Oxfordians, on the one hand, and Rodenburg's liberal-feminist views of empowerment on the other. Rodenburg alone addresses gender as an issue in voice training, or acknowledges that the culturally conditioned behaviors from which her exercises are designed to free "us" are gendered, and does so only in *The Right to Speak.*

11 See also 97–268. While some linguists might question the applicability of Derrida's critique to an expressive medium that is "always already" oral, and for which the physicality of voice production is primary, sociolinguists such as Bakhtin/Volosinov (Volosinov, *Marxism*), including Edward Sapir, Benjamin Whorf, and Max Adler, have engaged in politicized analyses which see voice production and oral expression as inevitably social (at least in practice). For an account of the debates in contemporary linguistics see Newmeyer, especially 106–26 and 133–40.

12 The myth that access to the body provides access to culturally transcendent truth is pervasive in voice training. Director Guy Sprung, in "Mountain Changes: The SFU/Equity Showcase Voice Intensive," however, describes a debate which problematizes the most basic assumptions of voice training:

> A controversy broke out in one session about the natural position of the tongue when it is at rest. Does it lie with the tip touching the back of the lower teeth, or does it lie with the tip resting gently against the upper palate, touching the back of the upper teeth? I ascribed the discussion to the fact that the disputants grew up speaking two different languages . . . and hence may have two different positions of "natural" rest for their tongues. (18)

Ellen O'Brien has argued in a letter to me that this example problematizes issues of *articulation*, which is learned, rather than breath, phonation, or resonance, which she claims are instinctive. I would argue that the body is also culturally conditioned at this more fundamental level.

13 For a critique of Freud and his followers on these grounds see Volosinov, *Freudianism.*

14 It is worth noting the incongruity between the rhetoric of "freeing" something "natural," "allowing" the true self to speak (and again, "free," "let," and "allow" are most often used in the imperative mood), and the frequent adjuration to "*recondition* your whole way of communicating" (94, my italics), resulting in "*re-programming*" (94, 103, and *passim*), "reconditioning your use of yourself" (111).

15 An examination of the ideological coding of Linklater's derivation of the origins of language from the sacred, magical, and mystical is beyond the scope of this paper, but see Hornbrook's analysis of Rousseauesque faith in the natural goodness and creativity of children, 150; and Greenblatt's questioning of who controls the sacred, 21–65.

16 Hawkes notes, *That Shakespeherian Rag* 109, that Tillyard's book has as much to do with the context of its first publication in wartime Britain as with its Elizabethan subject matter. It is significant that in addition to *The Elizabethan World Picture* Linklater draws heavily on Caroline Spurgeon's *Shakespeare's Imagery and What it Tells Us* and Frances Yates's *Theatre of the World*, texts which, like Tillyard's, assume a humanist essentialism and a hierarchical world view that are fully in line with the ideological underpinnings of her own work.

17 Linklater's concentration on unity and identity distinguishes her work from Berry's, at least in practice. According to Juliet Stevenson, Berry teaches actors that "you need not, *should* not, be bound by notions of psychological consistency," but should follow the language, which "tells you who the character is moment by moment, word by word" (Rutter *et al.* 43).

18 There is something else interesting being played out in this denial that voice training and coaching are interpretive. Voice coaches since Berry have increasingly encroached on teaching the reading of text, while denying that they are playing a directorial function. To do so would result in their being banished from rehearsal halls by directors jealous of their privileges. All of this is part of an organizational structure that is not only hierarchical, but gendered. The role of the voice coach (almost always a part-time position) is constructed as a service function, *allowing* interpretation to take place, and it is gendered female. As such it may *not* encroach upon the creative realms of playmaking and directing which, particularly at the RSC and the National, are gendered male.

19 A short chapter precedes this, in which Linklater, following Canadian text coach Neil Freeman, argues for the use of the Folio, claiming that "all serious Shakespeareans refer to the First Folio and some swear by it as by the bible" (204). She demonstrates the danger of following Freeman when she notes that "the First Folio is venerated by actors because legend has it that secrets of the actual performance readings of Shakespeare's actors are encoded in the punctuation, the spellings and the capitalizations of the Folio script" (205).

20 Quoted from Arthur Phillips, "The Cultural Cringe," in *The Australian Tradition: Studies in a Colonial Culture* (Melbourne: Cheshire, 1958).

21 There is a disturbingly anti-academic and anti-intellectual flavor to Rodenburg's work, as there is to most voice texts produced in Great Britain, where the attempt to correct the classism and élitism of earlier work has included what is perceived as a too cerebral approach to classical acting.

22 "A story must maintain the listener's interest," she argues. "Its trajectory is measured by a beginning, a middle and an end. . . . *We all like* stories told to us in narrative form. *All of us naturally* listen to words constructed in the order of 'what happens next'" (99, my emphasis). She goes on to instruct her readers on how to "find" linear narrative structures in the texts they confront – even, I would argue, when they are not there.

23 This passage reinscribes conflict as the basis for dramatic, and by extension human, action. In both of her books, and explicitly in *The Need for Words*, Rodenburg assumes that "most great pieces of writing are about struggle," and advises that "we often have to list the pros and cons, the positive and negative forces that are in conflict inside a piece of writing" (156), reinscribing binary division and conflict as "inside" any text, rather than as constructed by these methods of analysis.

24 Harry Berger, Jr., "Bodies and Texts," *Representations* 17 (Winter 1987) 153, talks of how invoking the Author functions as a "principle of closure, of semiotic inhibition . . . to privilege certain readings and control 'unruly meanings'."

25 I do not wish to suggest that the actor must take responsibility for the promotion of social change, or that the power structures of the theatre industry would allow this. Actors who want to work will work within current structures or be fired – and the same may be said for voice coaches. I *do* want to suggest that the material conditions of voice and other training need to be interrogated if change is to be possible through theatre, and that vocal texts might usefully demystify their structures and develop radical methodologies to help make change possible rather than to reinforce the status quo. Most importantly I want to insist that performance criticism of Shakespeare pay attention to the

conditions and practices that shape the production of meaning in the material theatre.

26 I borrow this phrase from the Canadian Federation for the Humanities, who present a "Corporate Humanist Award" annually for significant published contributions to the arts.

27 I would like to thank Harry Lane, Ann Wilson, and the late Michael Quinn, who read earlier drafts of this essay; members of Skip Shand's 1993 Shakespeare Association of America seminar on "Actorly Reading," particularly Skip, Cary Mazer, Barbara Hodgdon, Lorraine Helms, and Susan Specter; and most of all Ellen O'Brien, who was extremely generous in her response in spite of her anxiety about some of what I say. Finally, I want gratefully to acknowledge the editorial help of James Bulman.

REFERENCES

Addenbroke, David. *The Royal Shakespeare Company*. London: Kimber, 1974.

Ashcroft, Bill, Gareth Griffiths, and Helen Tiffin. *The Empire Writes Back: Theory and Practice in Post-Colonial Literatures*. London: Routledge, 1989.

Barton, John. *Playing Shakespeare*. London: Methuen, 1984.

Belsey, Catherine. *Critical Practice*. London: Methuen, 1980.

Berry, Cicely. *The Actor and His Text*. London: Virgin, 1987. Repr. 1992 as *The Actor and The Text*.

—— *Voice and the Actor*. London: Harrap, 1973. Repr. 1987.

Brockbank, Philip, ed. *Players of Shakespeare: Essays in Shakespearean Performance by Members of the Royal Shakespeare Company*. Cambridge: Cambridge University Press, 1985.

Brook, Peter. *The Empty Space*. Harmondsworth: Pelican, 1972.

Cooke, Katherine. *A.C. Bradley and His Influence on Twentieth Century Shakespearean Criticism*. Oxford: Clarendon, 1972.

Derrida, Jacques. *Of Grammatology*. Trans. Gayatri Chakravorty Spivak. Baltimore: Johns Hopkins University Press, 1976.

Dollimore, Jonathan and Alan Sinfield, eds. *Political Shakespeare: New Essays in Cultural Materialism*. Ithaca, NY: Cornell University Press, 1985.

Foucault, Michel. "What Is an Author?" *Language, Counter-Memory, Practice: Selected Essays and Interviews*. Ed. Donald F. Bouchard. Trans. Donald F. Bouchard and Sherry Simon. Ithaca, NY: Cornell University Press, 1977. 113–38.

Greenblatt, Stephen. *Shakespearean Negotiations*. Berkeley: University of California Press, 1988.

Hawkes, Terence. *Meaning by Shakespeare*. London: Routledge, 1992.

—— *That Shakespeherian Rag*. London: Methuen, 1986.

Hodgdon, Barbara. "Splish Splash and The Other: Lepage's Intercultural *Dream* Machine." *Essays in Theatre/Études théâtrales* 12:1 (November 1993): 29–40.

Holderness, Graham, ed. *The Shakespeare Myth*. Manchester: Manchester University Press, 1988.

Hornbrook, David. "'Go play, boy, play': Shakespeare and Educational Drama." *The Shakespeare Myth*. Ed. Graham Holderness. New York and London: Manchester University Press, 1988. 145–59.

Innes, Christopher. *Holy Theatre: Ritual and the Avant Garde*. Cambridge: Cambridge University Press, 1981.

Jackson, Russell and Robert Smallwood, eds. *Players of Shakespeare 2: Further Essays in Shakespearean Performance by Players with the Royal Shakespeare Company*. Cambridge: Cambridge University Press, 1988.

Johnstone, Keith. *Impro: Improvisation and the Theatre.* London: Faber & Faber, 1979.
Linklater, Kristin. *Freeing the Natural Voice.* New York: Drama Book Publishers, 1976.
—— *Freeing Shakespeare's Voice: The Actor's Guide to Talking the Text.* New York: Theatre Communications Group, 1992.
Marcuse, Herbert. *Negations: Essays in Critical Theory.* Trans. J. Shapiro. Boston: Beacon, 1968.
Martin, Jacqueline. *Voice in the Modern Theatre.* London: Routledge, 1991.
McCullough, Christopher J. "The Cambridge Connection: Towards a Materialist Theatre Practice." *The Shakespeare Myth.* Ed. Graham Holderness. Manchester: Manchester University Press, 1988. 112–21.
Newmeyer, Frederick J. *The Politics of Linguistics.* Chicago: University of Chicago Press, 1986.
Parker, K. "Goodbye, Voice Beautiful." *Plays and Players* 382 (July 1985): 32–3.
Rodenburg, Patsy. *The Need for Words: Voice and the Text.* London: Methuen, 1993.
——*The Right to Speak: Working with the Voice.* London: Methuen, 1992.
Rutter, Carol *et al. Clamorous Voices: Shakespeare's Women Today.* Ed. Faith Evans. London: The Women's Press, 1988.
Selbourne, David. *The Making of 'A Midsummer Night's Dream': An Eyewitness Account of Peter Brook's Production from First Rehearsal to First Night.* London: Methuen, 1982.
Sher, Antony. *The Year of the King: An Actor's Diary and Sketchbook.* London: Chatto & Windus, 1985.
Sinfield, Alan. *Faultlines: Cultural Materialism and the Politics of Dissident Reading.* Berkeley and Los Angeles: University of California Press, 1992.
—— "Give an Account of Shakespeare and Education, showing why you think they are effective and what you have appreciated about them. Support your comments with precise references." *Political Shakespeare.* Ed. Jonathan Dollimore and Alan Sinfield. Ithaca, NY: Cornell University Press, 1985. 134–57.
—— "Introduction: Reproductions, interventions." Dollimore and Sinfield 130–3.
—— "Royal Shakespeare: Theatre and the Making of Ideology." Dollimore and Sinfield 158–81.
Sprung, Guy. "Mountain Changes: The 1991 SFU/Equity Showcase Voice Intensive." *Canadian Theatre Review* 71 (Summer 1992): 15–19.
Spurgeon, Caroline. *Shakespeare's Imagery and What it Tells Us.* Cambridge: Cambridge University Press, 1935.
Styan, J. L. *The Shakespeare Revolution: Criticism and Performance in the Twentieth Century.* Cambridge: Cambridge University Press, 1977.
Taylor, Gary. *Reinventing Shakespeare: A Cultural History, from the Restoration to the Present.* Oxford: Oxford University Press, 1989.
Tillyard, E. M. W. *The Elizabethan World Picture.* Harmondsworth: Penguin, 1972.
Volosinov, V. N. *Freudianism: A Marxist Critique.* Trans. I. R. Titunik. Ed. I. R. Titunik in collaboration with Neal H. Bruss. New York: Academic, 1976.
—— *Marxism and the Philosophy of Language.* Trans. Ladislav Matejka and I. R. Titunik. Cambridge: Harvard University Press, 1986.
Yates, Frances. *Theatre of the World.* Chicago: University of Chicago Press, 1969.

7

ACTING SHAKESPEARE IN POSTCOLONIAL SPACE[1]

Denis Salter

I

Actors are ideological constructs, but how often is this point acknowledged? More often than not, at least in the North American context, actor training schools, *conservatoires*, BFA and MFA programs, and theatre-company apprenticeships tend to emphasize only three things: the exploration of one's unique interior life (imagination, psychology, and emotional makeup); the acquisition of physical skills; and the close(d) readings of so-called representative dramatic texts situated within a vague historical context. Politics, ethical values and debates, linguistic barriers, competing ideologies, differences in race, nation, class, and gender: these and related issues are often declared too irrelevant to warrant systematic inclusion within the curriculum, or they are gradually assimilated, and ultimately effaced, by conventional pedagogical practices.[2]

This state of affairs has serious implications for the kinds of Shakespearean acting that are seen and not seen on our stages, especially in postcolonial cultures like Canada, Australia, New Zealand, India, and South Africa. Shakespeare has been relentlessly naturalized in these countries as a universal, timeless, and canonical "genius" whose works, it is often assumed, should provide postcolonial actors with unmediated, unproblematized points of access. In this paper, I shall argue that this kind of "natural" relationship between text and actor has in fact been more assumed than real and has served to mask a whole set of ideological, aesthetic, and technical issues that now require full disclosure. Although I concentrate on Canada (with some reference to the paradox of Québec), I suspect that this preliminary and partial inquiry will also uncover a pattern of recurrent issues for Shakespearean acting in many emergent cultures at various stages of colonial and postcolonial "development."

In postcolonial nations like Canada, Shakespearean acting, and the training that has authorized it, has been nothing but ideological, even though vested interests have worked assiduously to mask this historical condition.[3] For postcolonial actors, Shakespearean texts are not value-free, atemporal, transcendent masterpieces that can yield up their meanings through direct and transparent actorly readings. As G. B. Shand has concisely put it, there is no such thing as a "neutral conduit": the actor, like the playwright, like the critic, like the audience, is "actually a predictive and essentialist conditioner of textual signification."[4] For postcolonial actors, Shakespearean texts often function as foreign objects that articulate imperialistic values of domination, exploring dramatic conventions, themes, and language from which they are alienated – to some degree – but to which they can nevertheless respond at some unconscious level. For postcolonial actors, Shakespearean texts are often, in fact, sources of estrangement. They are unfamiliar, seemingly unknowable, densely encoded and authored elsewhere; yet they are also partially understandable objects of wonder, existing here and now, sources of heightened perceptions that seem paradoxically to transcend temporal and cultural boundaries. Postcolonial actors therefore find it impossible to respond unequivocally to Shakespearean texts, and often find themselves needing to devise, if only unwittingly, the actor's interpretive equivalent of Paul Ricoeur's "demystifying hermeneutics" (Ricoeur 35).

But how is this process of demystification to take place when all the institutional and pedagogical practices suggest that postcolonial actors, given the right kind of training and discipline, should disavow their particular historical conditions to become no different from the kinds of actors working at, say, the RSC? This notion has been so pervasive that a number of Canadian actors have subscribed to it, sometimes against their better judgement. It wasn't until his final term at the London Academy of Music and Dramatic Art (LAMDA) in 1973 that R. H. Thomson realized that instead of making a career in England, he wanted to return home, to work as a Canadian actor in the emergent and indigenous Canadian theatre of the 1970s. "It seemed to my young thespian heart," he later recalled, "that to act was to be an expression of your own people, people you shared a country with and perhaps understood." But note the characteristic equivocation ("perhaps understood"): for postcolonial actors, there is inevitably a sense of dislocation between themselves and their own indigenous culture whose problematic identity they *must* seek to enact. Paradoxically, it was work on new Canadian scripts, with "grit, determination and individuality of style," that eventually allowed Thomson to return to Shakespeare, the playwright whom he had originally "rejected . . . in the Stratford, Ontario, context – as not being 'Canadian'" (Thomson 293 and 299).

The 1960s and 1970s were, for better or worse, the decades of Jan Kott-inspired productions of Shakespeare. Kott's argument that Shakespeare is indeed "our contemporary" may have inspired Peter Brook and other directors to give modern-day relevance to their interpretations; but it also served to alienate postcolonial actors even further from texts concerning which they already had a sense of divided allegiance. Kottian contemporaneity, in spite of its radical appeal at the time, is in effect an interpretive strategy that encourages deference to Shakespeare as it suppresses the suspicious and resistant textual readings that the postcolonial position activates. Slowly, gropingly, postcolonial actors have to understand that Shakespeare is not/was never/can never be *their* contemporary – at least, not in anything even remotely like the way he could be for Peter Brook and other artists of his generation for whom Shakespeare was not an Imperial(izing) text to be interrogated but a dead(ly) Tradition in need of revision. Indeed, it is the insight that Shakespeare belongs not to "us" but to "them" that postcolonial actors find oddly *liberating*. One of the central obligations for postcolonial actors is to learn to say "no" to the ostensible contemporary cuings in Shakespeare's texts. This means saying "no" to miscegenation (*Othello*), "no" to racism (*The Merchant of Venice*), and "no" to ethnocentrism (*The Tempest*), even while recognizing how certain contestatory performance traditions – Paul Robeson's Othello, Henry Irving's Shylock, David Suchet's Caliban, for example – have sought to overturn these kinds of monovalent textual readings.

The main difficulty for postcolonial actors encountering, and eventually deconstructing, Shakespearean texts is not really his characters, themes, aesthetic conventions, symbols, and dramaturgic formulae. The main difficulty is language, written and spoken. How indeed can the postcolonial margins write, speak, and act back to the imperial center when trying to articulate themselves through the very language that itself partially constitutes the problem of estrangement? Or as G. B. Shand has wittily posed the question: "[I]s breathing the commas a caving in to textual imperialism?"[5] These impediments to understanding are especially acute in predominantly white anglophone settler colonies – anglophone Canada, for example, but not francophone Québec – where one might expect the English language to be such a natural(ized) medium of expression that all the actorly obligations and options within the Shakespearean text should be readily discernible. The totalizing assumption seems to be that since we all speak English, we can all communicate with each other. Can't we – and, if not, why not?

When first negotiating with Shakespearean texts, postcolonial actors are often at a loss, though they may naively assume that this is somehow their fault. Shakespeare may write in English, but it is not an English that they necessarily know – or for that matter can be expected to know – with any degree of assurance. It is not contemporary – it is antique; it is not theirs – it is the distant yet nevertheless powerful language of the oppressor. It is not something they can act as they might wish; instead, it wants to act them. It seems to contain stage directions and actorly instructions written in a dense code that they must decipher if they hope to survive. As Ann Wilson has pointed out, appearances to the contrary, this language is *never* innocent: "What emerges with the celebration of Shakespeare and his Englishness is the political importance of maintaining the English language," and producing Shakespeare's plays (in a postcolonial context) "serves as [a] powerful tool of legitimating the privilege and cultural perspective of an élite" (Wilson 23). This is, moreover, an English that is not in any sense "natural," though it may seem so in those cultures where it has been thoroughly internalized through a process of ideological interpellation. Rather, it is an English that, like a foreign language, has to be studied to minimize its lexical, cultural, and temporal barriers, all of which will remain in one form or another, even after it has been (partially) mastered through a strategy of reverse textual colonization.

Shakespearean lexicons, the *OED*, annotated editions with full scholarly apparatus: these are useful scholarly aids, but using them may paradoxically enhance, rather than diminish, a sense of textual estrangement. Studying them seems a perverse way for an actor to try to authenticate his or her *own* "natural" voice. Denotations can be understood after endless practice and long hours with Arden editions; connotations, however, often remain elusive, and might never in fact get into the bloodstream; and although blank verse may be gradually demystified, working with purportedly "free" and "natural" approaches to verse-speaking – such as John Barton's *Playing Shakespeare* (and its teaching videos) – often makes postcolonial actors feel even more isolated within their own (disavowed) linguistic practices. What might be "natural" to the verse-speaking of the RSC actors, including an actor of postcolonial origins like Ben Kingsley, is not necessarily "natural" to everybody else. Once they have given themselves permission to speak in their own "natural" voices, postcolonial actors begin to dismantle the dated binary opposition of center and margins that has, until that point, made them into a ventriloquist's dummies, pretending to speak with their own voices when all along Shakespearean Textuality has been doing it for them.

Nobody, except perhaps madmen, children, criminals, and revolutionaries, wants to behave unnaturally – actors least of all. Their skill in animating a role and their popularity with audiences depend, of course, on how successful they are in realizing tacitly understood beliefs about what constitutes a "natural" performance. "Natural", however, does not exist in a temporal and spatial vacuum: it is always determined by specific historical, artistic, and ideological values. Exactly what those values are and how they are embodied through performance are issues that are routinely dodged, not only by theatre artists but also by theatre historians and performance theorists. These issues always seem too difficult or controversial. Perhaps too many people still have a vested interest in assuming that "natural," like Shakespeare himself, is a transhistorical, transcultural ideal that works best if left inviolate and unproblematized. Perhaps too many people still think "natural" means "naturalistic," an understandable, though inexcusable, conflation that leads to overdetermined historical commentaries on Constantin Stanislavski and Lee Strasberg. If, however, a critic decides that a certain actor is "natural" as, say, Richard III, what does this mean, and, if we don't know, shouldn't there be a way to find out?

At the very least, we should feel compelled to ask some exacting questions, even if we know that answers are not likely to be forthcoming. Natural by what standard? Natural in what ways? Natural to whom? Natural when and where? Why, how, and to what presumed ends has the natural been constituted, what kinds of characterological and actorly templates has it formed, and to what extent, if at all, do actors – postcolonial actors especially – feel compelled to be disciplined by, or to subvert, those templates?

In trying to answer these questions, it might be worth reminding ourselves about some of the axiomatic features of so-called "natural" acting in the history of Shakespearean performance. "Natural" acting has tended to function, I think, as a (mostly invisible) strategy of surveillance, designed to keep unnatural – meaning, unregulated and potentially dissident – discursive formations securely in their place. "Natural" acting has most often sought to remain faithful to an essentialized model of human character in which there is an exactly understood correspondence between that character's identity and its mode of stage representation according to a set of prescriptive values sanctioned not only by tradition but also the kinds of behavior that the larger social context is prepared to accept and to validate as natural. Natural values, when they are symbolically rearticulated by the actor's body, function as an extended reflex mechanism in which organic and spontaneous impulses are so carefully disciplined and so rigorously internalized that actor and character have become second nature to and for each other. Hence, acting Shakespeare "naturally" has regularly been an exercise in textual, interpretive, and performance *normalization*, in which the actor, disappearing as it were inside a role, becomes an intrinsic part of a great English theatrical Tradition that moves in a steady march from Burbage to Olivier, a Tradition to which Kenneth Branagh is now trying desperately to gain privileged access.

Acting Shakespeare *un*naturally is, however, a very dangerous thing to do: actors behaving this way will be routinely censured for not understanding Shakespeare, for not respecting traditions, for not being trained properly, and for not possessing that ineffable quality known as stage presence. In brief, they will be censured not just for being unnatural but for being aberrant, perhaps even subversive. Criticisms of this type can of course put an end to an entire career. Natural, however, should be understood as a relational – not as an absolute – critical term; it requires particularizing terms of reference so that it can be adjudicated differently in imperial, precolonial, colonial, postcolonial, and national contexts. When Robert Lepage was directing *A Midsummer Night's Dream* at the Royal National Theatre in London in 1992, he instructed the mechanicals to do bad imitations of Olivier as Richard III. This was very funny in the rehearsal hall and gave new life to what seemed a tired set of jokes; but according to Lepage, it backfired on the stage of the Olivier Theatre on opening night. "The laughter stopped, died away," Lepage has recalled, "as all the people in the theatre thought, 'What, they dare to do *this*, in the theatre named in honour of Olivier!'" Lepage's actors understood at that moment that their behavior was being read as a perversion of an ennobling, preeminently "natural" tradition; as Lepage concluded, "you can't change the style of acting and break with tradition unless these changes come out of a real need in the audience to experience things differently."[6]

The London audience was not prepared to allow Lepage and his cast of mostly postcolonial actors to perform *un*natural acts of textual and performative transgression on *their Dream*, on *their* Shakespeare, and on *their* Olivier; and the critics censured the production as a "*mud*summer night's dream" – an ethnocentric reference not only to the mud-bath in which much of the action was set, but to the acts of defilement with which Lepage, as a postcolonial outsider, seemed to them unduly preoccupied (Hodgdon 31–7). Would mimicking Olivier have seemed unnatural, however, if the production had first opened in Montréal, in Johannesburg, in New Delhi, or in Sydney? Or would such business have been praised as singularly natural – a legitimate and effective method by which postcolonial actors, in playing the "rude" mechanicals, might radically reinvent the art of Shakespearean acting by starting with the parodic inversion and displacement of the Olivier template?

Stage traditions notwithstanding, "natural" acting is never natural – it is always artificial – a distinctive style or mode of performance that has only been naturalized by traditions, by training practices, by critical standards, and by audience values. Although it is only by de-naturalizing Shakespearean acting that postcolonial actors can engage in the kind of ideological demystification that Lepage initiated in London, the very idea that Shakespeare *must* be subjected to this process has occurred to relatively few postcolonial actors; as a dissenting view, it was simply inconceivable amid the renewed spirit of Bardolatry created by the opening of the Stratford, Ontario Festival in 1953. To explain how the cultural ground had been carefully prepared for the building of the Stratford Festival requires an essay in its own right. But I do want to sketch in *some* of the lines of historical development here, to consider their consequences for the kind of Shakespearean acting that English-Canadian theatre has often felt compelled to sanction.

II

There has been, from as early as the nineteenth century onward, a collective disposition towards the kind of anglophilia that, in identifying certain styles of performance as natural, has also sought to authorize Shakespeare himself as a natural – that is, stable, lasting, and pervasive – symbol of imperial/colonial relations.[7] English-Canadian actors' attitudes towards Shakespeare, and towards definitive readings of his texts, have therefore tended to be nothing if not respectful, predicated on the assumption that it is they who must adapt themselves to Shakespeare, not Shakespeare who must adapt himself to them.

The perennial values informing English-Canadian Bardolatry are effectively summarized in a 1907 essay, "Shakespeare and the Latter-Day Drama" (14–18), by the Canadian poet, playwright, and critic Wilfred Campbell. More properly described as a diatribe, Campbell's essay fulminates against modern authors, including Tolstoy and Shaw, who have dared to make irresponsible and self-serving attacks on Shakespeare. Campbell's own view is unequivocal: Shakespeare is "the world's greatest dramatic writer," one who not only expresses "universally admitted sanity and human nature," but also those essential "national characteristics" – including "poise," "self-control," and the "power of self-improvement" – that "the north-western nations of Europe, especially the British, possess in no small degree." Neither Tolstoy nor Shaw can be taken seriously as a critic of Shakespeare: Tolstoy because he belongs, as a Russian, to a people who (like the Spanish) "have been marred in their origin and making," and Shaw because he cultivates, however cleverly, an attitude of "shallow cynicism." Shakespeare provides a salutary antidote to Tolstoy, Shaw, and their supporters, and to those modern playwrights, most notoriously Ibsen, who are determined to explore "unhealthy phases of personality and fancied hidden motives." Shakespeare, in marked contrast, forms a "*normal* standard" (emphasis mine), a set of poetic "ideals," as he seeks to promote "a sense of the greatness of human existence."

From Campbell's point of view, nineteenth-century actors such as Irving had only succeeded in "degrading" these ideals when they "endeavour[ed] to interpret creations such as *Hamlet* in a new manner, so as, in some cases, almost to produce a new creation." Actors must not, Campbell sermonizes, try to satisfy their own "abnormal ideals," they must not encourage audiences to acquire a taste for "the suggestive, the *unnatural*, and the immoral" (emphasis mine), and they must not invent characters independent of the requirements that Shakespeare has so clearly laid down. Rather, they ought to understand that Shakespeare's plays should be performed exactly as written, for in them "there is nothing abnormal, nothing disgusting or revolting, but all is largely human and *natural*" (emphasis mine). In realizing these stylistic principles, actors will not only ensure that the long tradition of Shakespearean acting remains "natural," but they will also make an exemplary contribution "to the development of the best ideals of the British race."

Campbell's argument, taken to its logical conclusion, suggests that if Shakespearean acting were to deviate *even slightly* from the aesthetic benchmark of the "natural," it would undermine not just Shakespeare's reputation but the very foundational values that the Elizabethan age has bequeathed both to the British nation *and* its dependent colonies. By publishing his essay in the *Canadian Magazine*, Campbell was in fact extending the implications of his argument to suggest that Canadian actors must learn how to act as "natural" as their English counterparts. Otherwise, like Ibsen, they will become degenerate and pessimistic; like Tolstoy's Russian people, they will risk becoming insane; like Shaw, they will become merely flippant; and like Irving in *The Bells*, they will wind up dishing out "pure horror" for its own sake. Shakespeare, Campbell concludes, has set a much higher artistic *and* moral standard than this, one that Canadian actors will have to aspire to if they are to succeed in maintaining the connection between themselves and the kinds of imperial values that Campbell takes pains to idealize in the poeticized trope of England=Elizabeth/Shakespeare=Canada.

Campbell thus helped to valorize an unbroken, centralizing, normalizing, and patently nostalgic tradition that continues to function in Canada as a site of resistance for those postcolonial actors who are prepared to explore the dialectical tensions between so-called natural and unnatural modes of performance. It is, I think, at the Stratford Festival where these dialectical tensions have been most tellingly concentrated – and where they have been most effectively effaced as well. When, in the early 1950s, that looming patriarch of British theatre, Tyrone Guthrie, insisted on building a neo-Elizabethan open platform stage in, of all places, Stratford, Ontario, many people felt persuaded that a singularly 'Canadian' style of performance would eventually emerge from what was billed as a daring New World experiment in classical actor training. As Guthrie himself liked to put it:

> It will only be, in my view, by evolving a distinctively Canadian comment on the classics that any satisfactory native dramatic style will be achieved. . . . Without some classical background actors, authors and audience will only flounder about, with no fixed stars to steer by, at the mercy of every violent current of popular opinion, blown this way and that by loud-mouthed Know-alls who propagate the doctrines which they believe to be fashionable and therefore profitable.
>
> (Guthrie 28–9)

I would argue, however, that notwithstanding Guthrie's high-minded, evangelizing, and authoritarian words, this experiment in classical actor training was in fact based on a set of reactionary ideals, similar to the ones outlined in Campbell's diatribe, and designed to ensure that an essentializing "Canadian-ness" – no matter how it might be defined in colonial, postcolonial, national, postnational, or (as now) global terms of reference – could *never* be expressed at Stratford, no matter how diligently Canadian actors might work to achieve it. As Michael Langham candidly explained in

1982, "[t]here was never anything Canadian about Stratford . . . that was a diplomatic thing Guthrie cooked up."[8]

Stratford raises the recurrent postcolonial question about place: where is – and therefore what is – the Stratford stage? As an acting space, it has an inherently conflicted identity, as it tries to achieve the perhaps impossible task of bringing two incommensurate worlds – the Old and the New – into a mutually productive relationship. It is *in part* an Elizabethan-derived, five-sided wooden platform, broken up into multiple acting levels to allow for fluid and swift changes of locale, and surrounded in a 220 degree arc by as many as 2258 spectators, not one of whom is more than sixty-five feet from the stage. Figuratively and literally, the Stratford stage has sought to transport Canadian theatre – and the culture it represents – backwards in time to the very spirit of the Elizabethan age. It has often provided Canadians with the comforting illusion that they have secured unique access to Shakespeare himself, and that along with William Poel, Harley Granville Barker, and other Elizabethan-inspired directors, they have been among the first to know – nine years before the Chichester Festival Theatre in England and ten years before the Guthrie Theatre in Minneapolis – the approximate staging conditions and actorly practices for which Shakespeare's plays were first written.

In addition to its recuperated Elizabethan features, however, the Stratford stage is *in part* a 1950s-style architectural design constructed from wood, steel, and concrete. Enhanced by austere decorative lines and a carefully controlled sense of spatial balance, the theatre's ostensible Shakespearean openness and flexibility are regularly compromised by its relentlessly modern architectural form. Since an actor is visible to only a portion of the audience at any given time, other sections of the audience are apt to feel alienated until the focus is shifted towards them. To create the *impression* of intimacy – and to prevent monotony – the thrust stage requires tightly arranged blocking patterns, neither too busy nor too static, in which each separate scene has to be vividly and concretely localized through the careful disposition of "realistic" sets, costumes, and properties.[9] In fact, paradoxically, it has often been through the pursuit of proscenium-style illusionistic effects – and through what Nathan Cohen derided as "a preoccupation with beautiful composition" – that the actors and audience have somewhat managed to circumvent the inherent limitations of the Stratford stage (Cohen 52).

Since actors are fully – indeed, mercilessly – exposed on this stage, they need to know exactly where they are; but finding answers to this question has by no means been easy. Is it an Elizabethan-style platform stage? or a modern "empty space" of seemingly infinite adaptability? Or is it an architectural hybrid, neither one style nor another, but, like the mid-Atlantic, something in-between? Where in fact is it located – in a tourist's version of Ye Olde England or in contemporary Canada? Where indeed is *here*, as Northrop Frye would have put it? Do the illusionistic, localized scenes that take place on this stage need a kind of hard-edged and austere postwar modernity to them, or an opulent Elizabethan sense of the ceremonial and the emblematic, or a bit of both? Once these answers are forthcoming it *might* be possible to answer the hardest questions of all: what kind of Shakespearean acting will seem "natural" here? what will seem "unnatural"? and how, if at all, can the postcolonial actor make the distinction? For the Canadian actor, is the Stratford stage in effect a decontextualized, ahistorical, pseudo-universal, *un*naturally hybrid space? As it lays claim, moreover, to past and present – England and Canada; Shakespeare then and Shakespeare now – does it tend to encourage conventional actorly readings and silently close down textual options as it seeks to disengage acting from the contemporary (Canadian) reality that should sustain it?

The Stratford stage, at least as Guthrie, Michael Langham, and invited guest directors were apt to use it in the 1950s and 1960s, apparently promoted an equivocal acting style in which a low-key, methodical, and psychologically-nuanced kind of modernity was grafted onto a gesturally and vocally heightened, externalizing quasi-Elizabethan kind of theatricality. In attempting to minimize the irreconcilable differences contained within this stylistic hybrid, actors like Christopher Plummer (Hamlet, 1957; Macbeth, 1962; and Antony, 1967), Lorne Greene (Brutus, 1955), and Bruno Gerussi (Ariel, 1962) were severely hampered by various forms of mimicry, ambivalence, and double-voicing. Herbert Whittaker's review of Plummer's 1957 Hamlet, directed by Langham, deftly summarizes these problems:

> Mr. Plummer's early scenes, in which he is setting forth the sick, bemused Hamlet, are too trickily laid out, too much filled with vocal invention, with extra meaning attempted and not pulled off. For example, his use of a dagger in the "To be or not to be" soliloquy was too ingenious: it took our attention from the character to the actor.[10]

Indeed, as Nathan Cohen once observed, the thrust stage's limitations meant that even Stratford's best actors – Tony Van Bridge, William Hutt, and Douglas Rain –

> cannot make speech sound like their *natural* [emphasis mine] mode of expression. They handle it as if . . . they were translating, with the speed and agility of UN experts, from a foreign language. . . . Although the accents are mid-Atlantic or as much like that as possible, the attack is very much pre-Suez West End and Stratford-on-Avon.[11]

Superfluous effects, rhetorical ostentation, excessive speed, *un*natural tones, foreign registers: these are the telltale signs of arrested development, decenteredness, and self-doubt that constitute the language of the postcolonial body when it is struggling to give voice to itself within the constraints of an indeterminate space.

"Act Elizabethan / Be Canadian": for the postcolonial actor, this perennial injunction at Stratford has (re)affirmed the existence of a divided identity in which the dialectical tension between natural and unnatural styles of performance has continued to remain frustratingly unresolved. In 1968, Nathan Cohen lamented that "after 15 years the nature of the [Stratford] company, its specific identity, eludes any definition."[12] Cohen seems to have hoped, without really believing it, that an identifiable *Canadian* style might eventually emerge. And yet his terms of reference were, and still are, historically invalid. It is, I think, an *unresolved* form of dialectical tension – where the differences between so-called natural and unnatural styles of acting will always remain problematic – that best defines the conflicted postcolonial performance-tradition that Stratford has bequeathed as its legacy for Shakespearean acting in English Canada.

III

The situation for postcolonial francophone actors in Québec is significantly different. For many of them – especially for Québécois(e) nationalist actors – Québec is *not* even vestigially a postcolonial society: it is an independent or sovereign nation, in principle if not (yet) in actual fact. Hence they are strategically positioned to assimilate Shakespeare, both as a practicing playwright and as a cultural metonymy, to their sovereignty through various acts of translation/adaptation – what poet and playwright Michel Garneau has concisely described as "tradaptation." In this new alliance of power and authority, Shakespeare does not figure as a crypto-imperialist demanding and receiving the kind of deferential attitudes that have prevailed at Stratford. Nor is he (re)presented as a symbol of English-Canadian cultural superiority that must be resisted at all costs. (Although English Canada is of course an important political influence in Québec, culturally it tends to function as an empty signifier: Campbell, for example, is not even an historical curiosity in Québec: he simply doesn't exist.) For Québec, Shakespeare is mostly a playwright of extraordinary dramatic interest through whom it can create explicitly allegorical – and sometimes carnivalesque – *re*readings of its own history. Displacing Shakespeare within allegorical frames of reference has a programmatic function: it seeks to nullify the universal/timeless values that are routinely ascribed to him by reconfiguring those values within a particularized, sometimes aggressively decolonized, context.[13]

In 1968 (the same year that Cohen lamented the lack of identity at Stratford), Robert Gurik recreated *Hamlet* as a precisely grounded, high-culture parody, entitled *Hamlet, prince du Québec.* In it, Hamlet represents Québec's protracted crises of identity, its sense of obligation to and betrayal by the past, its reluctance to act unilaterally to achieve self-determination, and its debilitating descent into chronic alienation and madness ("Nelliganism"). Horatio represents René Lévesque: a friend to Hamlet/Québec who, though well-meaning, is ultimately ineffectual; the Ghost of Hamlet's father represents Charles De Gaulle who instructs Hamlet to free Québec from the combined stranglehold of the English in Québec and the Catholic Church; and Polonius represents Lester Pearson/Canada: a loquacious, sententious, foolish, bumbling, and meddlesome old politician who is killed off, in a moment of sweet allegorical revenge, by none other than Hamlet himself. Hamlet's own death is not in vain: it signals the gradual emergence of a radically different political order in which Québec's independence seems more or less assured; as Hamlet puts it, "Qui . . . qui . . . nous sortira de la fange des compromis, de l'esclavage, qui brisera les chaînes qu'hypocritement nous avons nous-mêmes forgées. Il faut que ma mort serve aux autres" (95). As he dies, Hamlet rephrases De Gaulle's provocative declaration of Québec independence ("Vive le Québec libre!") so that it acquires a disturbingly elliptical combination of deceleration and hope ("Il faut . . . que vive . . . un . . . Qué . . . bec . . . libre" [95]). In gesturing here towards an ever-deferred (though still highly desired) utopian future, Gurik's *Hamlet* of course seeks to contest Shakespeare's ending; the climactic reciting/resiting of De Gaulle's words suggests, however, that the authority of Eurocentric textuality has by no means been completely dismantled.[14]

The Québec pattern of (re)appropriation-translation-adaptation means there is *not* a continuous tradition of essentialized or idealized actorly readings of Shakespeare's texts. Every production has been/must be an occasion for highly specific readings which, if anything, subvert even the possibility of an emergent tradition. Jean Cléo Godin has reminded me, for example, that the very phrase, "Shakespearean actor," makes no sense in the (francophone) Québec context. There is nothing comparable to the Stratford phenomenon in which actors such as John Colicos, Douglas Rain, Douglas Campbell, Martha Henry, Amelia Hall, Kate Reid, and William Hutt have been regularly associated with the "great" parts in the Shakespearean repertoire. In Québec, actors are simply actors, and although they might be popularly identified with certain Shakespearean roles – Jean-Louis Roux as King Lear, for instance – to them Shakespeare, no matter his high status as a classical author, always ranks second in importance to Molière. (On the other hand, Godin points out that the phrase "Tremblayian actor" – here he is thinking of someone like Rita Lafontaine – increasingly makes sense as a tradition of Michel Tremblay interpretations and performances is gradually built up: but then, Tremblay is in danger of becoming to Québec what Shakespeare is to English Canada – a canonical playwright whose authoritative position is a function of, and metonymy for, the culture for which he has been sanctioned to speak.) One might naively assume that the relative absence of a natural(izing) tradition of Shakespearean performance has granted Québécois postcolonial actors the kind of artistic autonomy that has been routinely denied to actors in English Canada. To a certain extent, Québécois actors do have a greater degree of freedom, partly because they can perform Shakespeare in their own language, rather than in a foreign language that inherently (re)produces estrangement.

But tradaptation is a fraught business: Shakespeare, like De Gaulle, is always present at some level of enunciation to govern the textuality of postcolonial performance. When Garneau first tradapted *Macbeth* into Québécois in 1978, he rejected, in an act of linguistic revolution, the so-called normative or standard French language of France in order to explore, celebrate, and authenticate the popular language of Québec with its unique mixture of archaisms, neologisms, and slang. Garneau's *Macbeth* indeed borrows liberally from Québécois, although it also incorporates his own attempts to invent a highly playful kind of poetic language that is as different in some ways from contemporary Québécois French as Shakespeare's *Macbeth* is from contemporary Canadian English. Yet Garneau's experiment produced a characteristically mixed response among postcolonial critics, actors, and directors. Ian C. Nelson and Curt Wittlin have argued, for example, that Garneau's "pervasive system of pseudo-phonetic orthography" (354) makes his *Macbeth* unnecessarily difficult for Québécois(e) actors to read during rehearsal even though, paradoxically, the play's idiom is one which they can handle "naturally" during performance. For Nelson and Wittlin, in trying to make his text accessible to actors, Garneau unwittingly erected barriers to understanding similar to those that Shakespeare's original texts have erected for English-Canadian actors. Hidden within this argument, however, is a prototypical example of colonial anxiety: in the spirit of Campbell writing in 1907, what these critics are really worried about is that Garneau's *Macbeth* is so irrevocably localized that it cannot measure up to – and is in fact a betrayal of – the Shakespearean ideal: "he does not fully succeed in creating a text which catches either the universality of the play or the loftiness of its idiom. It is unlikely to become a 'classic' version, except perhaps for a limited time in a narrow regional context" (358).[15]

When Lepage directed a revival of Garneau's *Macbeth* during Le Festival de théâtre des Amériques in Montréal in 1993, many of these issues resurfaced. Marie Brassard, who played Lady Macbeth, explained that although Garneau's "tradaptations are very beautiful," she none the less felt obligated "to serve Shakespeare . . . through Garneau" and wished at times that they had chosen the "nice, safe [François-]Victor Hugo translation instead" (quoted in Salter, "Borderlines" 72) – the one that Québec actors used to rely on before the linguistic revolutions of Garneau and other writers of his generation had taken place. As Lepage pointed out, the main difficulty with Garneau's *Macbeth* is that it is a hybrid text, simultaneously archaic and contemporary – "'*entre chien et loup*,' 'between the dog and the wolf,' that strange time between day and night – neither one thing nor the other." Actors, he noted, have to struggle to make the words sound "'natural'" so that the characters seem to be speaking in a language that belongs to them; otherwise "the whole production begins to fall apart" and "[t]he stylistic differences are then really glaring" (quoted in Salter, "Borderlines" 73). Lepage was of course not worried about so-called Shakespearean loftiness and universality; but he was worried that the language of tradaptation, like the language of the culture from which it originates, is so vulnerable to changing historical conditions that it might make actors feel completely unnatural, alienated from themselves and from the culture they are trying to serve.

I would argue that tradaptations, like postcolonial acting, should never be granted timeless status, for to do so would inadvertently reinforce the mystifying assumption that Shakespeare, and the values that he has been made to represent, can never be changed. Rather, tradaptations should be exercises in radical contingency, responsible only for the particular historical moment in which they attempt to decolonize and reinterrogate the Shakespearean text. They should vanish once their particular historical moment has passed and new tradaptations should take their place.

The recurrent question, whether Shakespeare's original text is retained or translated into another language, is this: what operations does Shakespearean Textuality perform on the actor's body? Brassard noted that the language of Garneau's *Macbeth* "puts weight on your body, as though you are a peasant working in the fields" (quoted in Salter, "Borderlines" 73). This is a vivid way of describing the sheer physicality of language, the way it (re)shapes the actor's own physicality and what it is capable, and incapable, of signifying. In postcolonial performance theory, as in materialist feminist theory, it is important to determine why, how, and to what ends Shakespearean textuality "speaks the body," making inviolate and autonomous subject-positions so difficult to achieve. Many postcolonial Shakespearean productions have run into both interpretive and performative difficulties because they have naively assumed that the actor's body is a *tabula rasa* that will actually take pleasure in being penetrated by textual authority. But the Shakespearean text and the body-text are frequently incommensurate, and indeed no amount of negotiation between them may be possible as they struggle independent of each other to reanimate a dying or dead corpus. The struggle will only come to an end when at least one of them is emptied of ideological significance; only then will mutually enhancing reinscription be possible. But, as this deliberately exaggerated way of expressing the problem suggests, the emptying of significance is in fact ontologically and epistemologically impossible. As Richard Paul Knowles's Shakespearean Association of America Seminar in 1992 so forcefully reminded us, Peter Brook aside, there is no such thing as an "empty space." The question then becomes: in the struggle between the body-text and the Shakespearean text, in this conflicted will to power, what new deferential order will emerge?

A favored postcolonial strategy of resistance has been to update and resituate the Shakespearean text. This has meant the usual dramaturgic remodeling (cutting, transposing, rewriting, perhaps modernizing diction and phrasing) together with the even more significant decision to place the text in a relentlessly specific time and place. In 1975, for example, Robin Phillips and David Toguri set their Stratford Festival production of *The Comedy of Errors* in the late-nineteenth-century U.S. Midwest; and in 1989, Lepage and Gordon McCall set their combined francophone/anglophone production of *Romeo and Juliette* [sic] on a stretch of the Trans-Canada Highway passing through a contemporary Saskatchewan farming community. The underlying assumption of these kinds of resitings is that the Shakespearean text will be forced to relinquish at least some of its prescriptive authority, that it will become more accessible, like a fetishized consumer product, to audiences conditioned by the values of late capitalism, and, finally, that it will become susceptible to actorly readings/performances happily rooted in localized forms of knowledge. Actors sometimes assume that these resitings will in fact give them permission to be "truthful" to their sense of who they are and "natural" within the language of their bodies through what seems to be an ideologically specific approach to the Shakespearean text now subject(ed) to *their* direct control. As the headlines in Liam Lacey's *Globe and Mail* review (7 July 1989) of the Lepage/McCall *Romeo and Juliette* punningly expressed it, "all the road's a stage for Shakespeare with a twist," "bilingual play drives home the reality of two solitudes."

The virulent reactions against these kinds of resitings indicate how extensively and dangerously they seem to put traditional ideological and cultural values at risk. Critics have routinely argued that resitings promote reductive interpretations, literalize Shakespearean poetry, particularize – and thereby destabilize – so-called universal frames of reference, challenge a rich legacy of canonical performances, and deform what the Shakespearean text so patently means.[16] All these arguments could be countered, I think, one by one; but doing so would be beside the point. In the postcolonial context, only one point is worth insisting on: instead of radically reconstituting Shakespearean textuality, resitings merely seek to extend its authority in seemingly "natural" ways. Resitings are, in fact, essentialist strategies that tend to remask an irreducible and ineradicable set of binary opposites – the Prospero/Caliban dichotomy or syndrome – in which the body of the postcolonial actor is overwritten by the imperialistic authority of the Shakespearean text.[17] Once the counter-discursive resistance of the postcolonial body is preempted, the inherent value of the Shakespearean text is effectively reinscribed, though it will often appear otherwise, especially when, as at the Stratford Festival, it has become reified as normative practice. The appropriative gaze of Shakespeare as cultural institution, at Stratford as elsewhere, can therefore never be entirely deflected. It continues to be reflected through mimesis as a form of subtle, but tyrannical, aesthetic discipline which stabilizes the monstrous Prospero/Caliban hierarchy to recolonize the times and places to which the Shakespearean text was *supposed* to have been adapted during its resiting.

If contemporary performance practices remain so immune to postcolonial rereadings of Shakespearean texts, what is to be done? In some situations, actors, encouraged by their directors, have retreated from ideological conundrums into the apparent ontological security of personal psychology. This strategy has been privileged in late industrial societies like the U.S. whose postcolonialism has been deliberately hidden beneath its status as a superpower. In the U.S., Method acting, for example, has functioned as the theatrical counterpart of the constitutional right to be a free, psychologically autonomous individual, pursuing and validating oneself within 'real' – and therefore normalizing – terms of reference. This is, however, an extreme case of ideological mystification and will only work if words like "free," "individual," "self," and "real" are so completely taken for granted that the body-text/social-context nexus remains constructed as value-free.

But is the self in fact so transparently knowable and so protected from ideological formations that it can continue to function, with any degree of legitimacy, as a free agent indifferent to national, cultural, racial, class, and gender differences? Method acting and its cognate practices have in fact attempted to function in precisely this way when imported from the U.S., but without mediation, into the training methods of influential actor-training programs like the National Theatre School of Canada (NTS). However, for postcolonial actors at NTS and similar institutions, trying to negotiate their initial relationship with Shakespeare, Method acting is often a source of imprisonment rather than freedom, contributing little to their tentative efforts to develop a personally enabling politics of location.[18] It tends to create an apparently objective, solipsistic rendering of character in which subtext, indirection, authenticity, and motivations (the parameters of the psychologically "real") are emphasized, together with the assumed fiction of psychological continuity, coherence, and interior truth. To a far greater extent than any other contemporary Western acting style, Method acting has a vested interest in being an art of sublimated pretence – in which actors disappear as autonomous identities, effaced within the transcendent, psychological reality of their characters. Method acting takes it for granted that ideology and the social order that it interpellates *do not exist*.[19] "I act, therefore I am": beyond this self-referential and self- generating, deliberately apolitical proposition, Method acting has refused to let the postcolonial actor go.

What postcolonial actors need to develop is a theory and practice of actorly agency – a way of achieving interpretive and performative autonomy – by means of, within, through, and finally, outside of, clearly separate(d) from the will to power represented by the Shakespearean text. Shakespeare, as textual authority, as cultural idea(l), as institutional practice, and as stage tradition, must not be allowed to go on speaking on behalf of postcolonial actors. They need to speak for themselves. But the question, as always, is *how*? It seems to me that at this particular historical moment there are only two choices. In direct response to the politics of location, the Shakespearean text will have to be radically and continuously disarticulated – a process in which the postcolonial actor's autonomy will always be at risk. Or, the Shakespearean text will have to go on being enacted *elsewhere* – but not (and not ever again?) in postcolonial space, where the actor's only remaining strategy of resistance to Shakespeare is absolute silence.

NOTES

1 This is a revised version of two interrelated papers. The first was written for the Shakespeare Association of America seminar, "Actorly Reading," directed by G. B. Shand, in Atlanta, Georgia, 1 April 1993; and the second for the International Federation for Theatre Research XIIth World Congress working-group, "Historiography of the Theatre: 20th Century," directed by Erika Fischer-Lichte, in Moscow, 10 June 1994. For helpful comments on various drafts, I am grateful to Per Brask, Jean Cléo Godin, Barbara Hodgdon, Richard Paul Knowles, Robert Lecker, Cary Mazer, Ed Pechter, Richard Plant, G. B. Shand, Joanne Tompkins, and Ann Wilson. I am also grateful to the Social Sciences and Humanities Research Council of Canada for financial support.

2 For a concise summary of these and related issues, see Richard Paul Knowles, ed., *Canadian Theatre Review* 71 (Summer 1992), a special issue on "Interrogating Theatrical Practice."

3 See Kurt Reis.

4 Written report on my draft version for the SAA seminar in Atlanta.

5 Ibid.

6 Interview with Lepage in Montréal, 26 May 1993.

7 See my article, "The Idea of a National Theatre" 79–80.

8 Quoted in Carole Corbeil, "It's Very Strange to be Back." I am grateful to Ric Knowles for bringing this interview to my attention.

9 My information about the form and function of the Stratford theatre is drawn from Nathan Cohen, "Theatre Today" 33–4; Dennis Kennedy 157–64; Richard Paul Knowles, "Shakespeare at Stratford"; and John Pettigrew and Jamie Portman, 1: 68–87.

10 *Whittaker's Theatre* 73. For additional comments on Plummer, as well as on Greene and Gerussi, see Pettigrew and Portman, 1: 108, 133, 161, and 195; and Herbert Whittaker, Introduction xx and xxviii.

11 "Stratford After Fifteen Years" 60.

12 Ibid. 58.

13 There is a growing body of critical literature on Shakespearean translation, tradaptation, and performance in Québec: see, for example, Annie Brisset; Jean Cléo Godin; Louise Vigeant; and a special issue of *les cahiers de théâtre Jeu* 48 (1988), "échos Shakespeariens."

14 Brisset has convincingly argued that Gurik's parody creates a complex double perspective:

> C'est à la fois le public québécois et l'adversaire englobé dans la personnification de l'anglophonie. D'où la nature agonique de ce discours, discours de l'action dont l'objet concerne l'aliénation politique, économique et culturelle de la société québécoise qui devrait se libérer du <colonisateur> anglophone. (186)

15 Brisset, however, expresses no such reservations, arguing instead that:

> [l]oin d'actualiser globalment le texte original, Michel Garneau préserve au contraire l'identité intrinsèque de *Macbeth,* mais il introduit ponctuellement des modifications qui transportent la tragédie de Shakespeare sur une autre scène, dans un passé recomposé où elle rebondit sous la forme d'une allégorie de la Conquête, tragédie réelle, vécue ici autre-fois, éclairant alors la situation vécue ici et maintenant. Ainsi le propos shakespearien s'intègre-t-il doublement à la réalité québécoise filtrée par le discours social immédiat. (195)

16 For example, in Ray Conlogue's review for the *Globe and Mail* (13 June 1990) of the Toronto remount of the McCall/Lepage *Romeo and Juliette,* he writes:

> Together with the poor white trash King Lear we saw a couple of months ago (from the New York company, Mabou Mines), this show is convincing evidence of the need for an Esthetic Police. It should be against the law to people an aristocratic play with mouth-breathing dimwits. / Consider, fellow sufferers. *How* is it that this collection of yahooing, obnoxious, drunken, inbred corn-borers open their mouths and say things like, "What light through yonder window breaks"?

17 See Marianne Novy, ed., *Cross-Cultural Performances, passim,* and especially Diana Brydon, "Sister Letters: Miranda's *Tempest* in Canada" [165]–84; Helen Peters; and Alden T. Vaughan and Virginia Mason Vaughan, *passim.*

18 See my article, "Body-Politics."

19 I am grateful here to ideas about Method acting expressed by W. B. Worthen 454–5 and by Richard Paul Knowles, "Frankie Goes to Hollywood (North)" 6.

REFERENCES

Barton, John. *Playing Shakespeare.* London and New York: Methuen, 1984.

Brisset, Annie. *Sociocritique de la traduction: Théâtre et altérité au Québec (1968–1988).* Longueuil: Les Éditions du Préambule, 1990.

Les cahiers de théâtre Jeu 48 (1988), "échos Shakespeariens".

Campbell, Wilfred. "Shakespeare and the Latter-Day Drama." *Canadian Magazine* 30:1 (November 1907): 14–18.

Cohen, Nathan. "Stratford After Fifteen Years." *Queen's Quarterly* 75:1 (Spring 1968): [35]–61.

—— "Theatre Today: English Canada." *Tamarack Review* 13 (Autumn 1959): 24–37.

Conlogue, Ray. "A Case for the Esthetic Police." *Globe and Mail,* 13 June 1990. A13.

Corbeil, Carole. "It's Very Strange to be Back" [Interview with Michael Langham]. *Globe and Mail* 24 July 1982. E1.

Garneau, Michel. *Macbeth de William Shakespeare.* Montréal: VLB Éditeur, 1978.

Godin, Jean Cléo. "Héros ambigus, rois sans royaumes." *Small is Beautiful.* Ed. Claude Schumacher and Derek Fogg. Glasgow: Theatre Studies Publications in association with IFTR/FIRT, 1991. 243–50.

Gurik, Robert. *Hamlet, prince du Québec.* Montréal: Les Éditions De L'Homme, 1968.

Guthrie, Tyrone. "First Shakespeare Festival at Stratford, Ontario." *Renown at Stratford: A Record of the Shakespeare Festival in Canada 1953.* Tyrone Guthrie and Robertson Davies. Toronto: Clarke, Irwin, 1953. [1]–33.

Hodgdon, Barbara. "Splish Splash and The Other: Lepage's Intercultural *Dream* Machine." *Essays in Theatre/Études théâtrales* 12:1 (November 1993): [29]–40.

Kennedy, Dennis. *Looking at Shakespeare.* Cambridge: Cambridge University Press, 1993.

Knowles, Richard Paul. "Frankie Goes to Hollywood (North); or, The Trials of the Oppositional Director." *Canadian Theatre Review* 76 (Fall 1993): 4–7.

—— "Shakespeare at Stratford: The Legacy of the Festival Stage." *Canadian Theatre Review* 54 (Spring 1988): 39–45.

——, ed. "Interrogating Theatrical Practice." *Canadian Theatre Review* 71 (Summer 1992).

Kott, Jan. *Shakespeare Our Contemporary.* Trans. Boleslaw Taborski. London: Methuen, 1965.

Lacey, Liam. "All the Road's a Stage for Shakespeare with a Twist." *Globe and Mail* 7 July 1989. A11.

Nelson, Ian C. and Curt Wittlin. "'What has he done?' – 'Me que c'est qu'y'a don faite?': Observations on Garneau's *Macbeth* in Québécois." *Canadian Drama/ L'Art dramatique canadien* 12:2 (1986): 351–9.

Novy, Marianne, ed. *Cross-Cultural Performances: Differences in Women's Re-Visions of Shakespeare.* Urbana and Chicago: University of Illinois Press, 1993.

Peters, Helen. "The Aboriginal Presence in Canadian Theatre and the Evolution of Being Canadian." *Theatre Research International* 18:3 (Autumn 1993): [197]–205.

Pettigrew, John and Jamie Portman. *Stratford: The First Thirty Years,* 2 vols. Toronto: Macmillan of Canada, 1985.

Reis, Kurt. "Montreal: Defending NTS." *Canadian Theatre Review* 74 (Spring 1993): 81–4.

Ricoeur, Paul. *Freud and Philosophy.* Trans. Denis Savage. New Haven and London: Yale University Press, 1970.

Salter, Denis. "Body-Politics: English-Canadian Acting at National Theatre School." *Canadian Theatre Review* 71 (Summer 1992): 4–14.

—— "Borderlines: An Interview with Robert Lepage and Le Théâtre Repère." *Theatre* 24:3 (1993): 71–9.

—— "The Idea of a National Theatre." *Canadian Canons: Essays in Literary Value.* Ed. Robert Lecker. Toronto: University of Toronto Press, 1991. [71]–90.

—— Interview with Robert Lepage in Montréal, 26 May 1993, unpublished.

Shand, G. B. Written report on Salter, "Actorly Reading in Postcolonial Space," prepared for the SAA seminar, "Actorly Reading," in Atlanta, Georgia, 1 April 1993.

Thomson, R. H. "Standing in the Slipstream: Acting in English Canada." *Contemporary Canadian Theatre: New World Visions.* Ed. Anton Wagner. Toronto: Simon & Pierre, 1985. 293–9.

Vaughan, Alden T. and Virginia Mason Vaughan. *Shakespeare's Caliban: A Cultural History.* Cambridge: Cambridge University Press, 1991.

Vigeant, Louise. "Aventure du côté du carnaval: *Vie et mort du Roi Boiteux.*" *Theatre Research International* 17:3 (Autumn 1992): special Canadian issue, eds. Jean Cléo Godin and Denis Salter: [203]–16.

Whittaker, Herbert, Introduction to *The Stratford Festival 1953–1957.* Toronto: Clarke, Irwin, 1958. ix–xxix.

—— *Whittaker's Theatre.* Ed. Ronald Bryden with Boyd Neil. Greenbank, Ontario: The Whittaker Project, 1985.

Wilson, Ann. "Staging Shakespeare." *Canadian Theatre Review* 75 (Summer 1993): 19–24.
Worthen, W. B. "Deeper Meanings and Theatrical Technique: The Rhetoric of Performance Criticism." *Shakespeare Quarterly* 40:4 (Winter 1989): [441]–55.

8

SHAKESPEARE WITHOUT HIS LANGUAGE

Dennis Kennedy

> There is a typical Hungarian story, about the very well-known Hungarian theatre director, Arthur Bardos, who left Hungary in 1949 to direct *Hamlet* in England; and he was asked by the BBC what it was like to do so. Mr Bardos answered: "Of course, it is a great honour and a challenge, but to tell you the truth, it's strange to hear the text in English because I am used to the original version, translated by Janos Arany."[1]

My subject is "foreign" Shakespeare: how Shakespeare has operated on the stage and in the mind outside English-speaking environments. This approach implies a perspective on Shakespeare's stature, and on his place in world culture, which is normally obscured in the academic and theatrical enterprises that have adopted his name. It's both natural and logical that Shakespearean studies and theatrical production have been Anglo-centered: Shakespeare was an English writer, after all, and since the eighteenth century the understanding and formal assessment of his work have been in the hands of critics and editors with profound allegiances to English literature. These days the situation is more secure than ever, for the great majority of Shakespearean commentators are professional interpreters connected to university departments of English in English-speaking countries. In many cases the officials connected to placing his work on stage have had parallel backgrounds: the leading directors and administrators of the Royal Shakespeare Company for its first two decades, for instance, read English at Cambridge under the influence of F. R. Leavis. Both the teaching and the acting of Shakespeare in English customarily start with a deep study of the linguistic clues in the text, and most English-speakers initially encounter Shakespeare as a literary creator, the champion example of a distinctive and abiding literary tradition.

Though the condition of Shakespearean studies is natural, it has been unfortunate in at least one regard, for it has tended to cloak Shakespeare's vast importance in the theatre in languages other than English. A simple test will demonstrate my point: look at the stage histories that are usually included in introductions to the numerous single-play editions of Shakespeare. Almost none will mention performances outside of the Anglo-American theatre. Three British publishers now offer series of performance histories, also in single-play formats; their record is no better.[2] Yet Shakespeare, by far the most popular playwright in England and North America, is actually the most performed playwright in the world at large. He regularly crosses national and linguistic boundaries with apparent ease. Does he cross into Poland or China as the same dramatist who is played at Stratford?

It would fit the notion of Shakespeare as the transcendent humanist to answer yes, but the truth is more complex. In fact, the performance history of Shakespeare's plays abroad suggests the opposite, and also suggests a reason why commentators normally pass over the subject. The cultural attitudes that inhere in the work, and that the Anglo-centered approach has until recently assumed to be the common heritage of Shakespeare's art, require not only linguistic translation but also cultural adaptation when they are transferred to a foreign environment. While Anglophone critics have not ignored the alternative traditions, they have tended to look upon Shakespeare's popularity in other countries as an example of his comprehensive appeal. Rather than seeing the use of Shakespeare's texts in foreign languages as a phenomenon separate from their use in English, they have normally chosen to see it as further vindication of the importance of their subject, and, by implication, of the superiority of English as the medium for Shakespearean cognition. They have constructed a universal Shakespeare based on the value of his original language.

Yet almost from the start of his importance as the idealized English dramatist there have been other Shakespeares, Shakespeares not dependent upon English and often at odds with it. The English Comedians may have played Shakespeare in the German lands in the sixteenth century, and English sailors may have played *Othello* on the African coast in the seventeenth century – the evidence is uncertain. If such performances did occur, they would have been based primarily upon gesture and extremely impoverished speech. Tantalizing as these possibilities are as early global exportations of Shakespeare, it's obvious that their actors could not have been presenting the dramatist as a literary artist or his plays as subtle verbal creations. The almost absurd conditions under which the English Comedians first worked – as troupes of actors without German, attempting to present Elizabethan plays for audiences with little or no theatrical tradition, rendering the plays essentially as dumb shows – emphatically point to the problematics of foreign Shakespeare.[3] The connections and cultural connotations that derive from playing Shakespeare in his own land in his own tongue are simply not applicable in another country and in another language. Whereas Shakespeare has been a given in English for some centuries, readers and audiences in linguistically foreign environments have had to *find* a desire for him.

The first major example of finding that desire outside of English occurred in German 200 years ago. The roughness and relatively sprawling nature of the plays, as well as their political stories, made them felicitous cultural material for an embryonic nationalist movement. Schiller's well-known project, to create a German literature and a German theatre that would transcend the petty principalities of the Holy Roman Empire and define the essence of a people, hoped to unite *das deutsche Volk* in a common, utopian resolve. Because Shakespeare was not French, and because his work violated neoclassic (i.e., aristocratic) principles, he became a rallying point for the new spirit of romantic democracy. It was, ironically, his very foreignness that made him useful as a model for the Germanic future: "*unser* Shakespeare" was an outright appropriation, dependent upon the absence of an existing tradition. Shakespeare could be made to signify what no familiar literature could signify, and simultaneously serve to validate Schiller's own dramaturgy.

In central and eastern Europe the same condition obtained in the mid-nineteenth century. In lands under the Austrian hegemony, Shakespeare's plays became part of the movement for a national literature and a bourgeois theatre separate from the court stages of the Hapsburgs. Similarly, the first translations of Shakespeare in Poland were part of a nascent opposition to foreign cultural domination. This oppositional use of Shakespeare has received an intriguing variation more recently, when the plays were used in post-war eastern Europe and the Soviet Union as dissident texts. If new plays and films critical of a repressive regime are regularly censored, producers are sometimes tempted to make the classics into coded messages about the present: Shakespeare thus became a secret agent under deep cover.

Such a catalogue, however brief, serves as a reminder that Shakespeare's work has never stood above or outside history in Europe. Shakespeare is of course part of history in Great Britain and Ireland and North America and Australia too, and has often been made part of larger political and philosophic currents. But elsewhere the absence of immersed linguistic and cultural connections to Shakespeare has meant that this appropriation has been more overt, and has met less official resistance from advocates of high culture than in the home countries. *Hamlet*, for example, has long been read in England and America inside the romantic tradition, as the outcry of an individual tortured soul, focusing on the poetic insights of the central character. This reading has been reinforced by the tendency to use the text as a star vehicle for an ardent and youthful actor. It's interesting to note how many Anglo-American productions in the past have been insensible of the fact that the play contains three rebellions – Claudius's against old Hamlet, Laertes's against Claudius, and young Hamlet's against Claudius –

and that the ending shows a belligerent outsider taking over the Danish throne. In fact, a long theatrical tradition in England cuts Fortinbras entirely, preferring to conclude with the personalized, anguished overtones of Hamlet's death rather than its political implications.

But if to the liberal West *Hamlet* is an expression of the individual spirit, to a censor in a more repressive land it is a threat. The militaristic government of Japan in 1938, for example, certainly felt threatened: the production by the New Tsukiji Theatre was required by the Tokyo censor to remove all textual references to royalty, and in Osaka it was banned entirely because "depravity was shown within the imperial chambers."[4] In eastern Europe the play has frequently received frank political readings at odds with the standard romantic interpretation. At various times in the nineteenth century the Czarist regime banned performances in Warsaw out of fear of encouraging rebellion. Most notoriously, Stalin banned *Hamlet* during the war in the USSR, its political allusions too sensitive for a supreme dictator and its hero too tentative for the nation's militant cause.

This tradition has continued to the present. In 1989, just before the collapse of the Stalinist government of the German Democratic Republic, I saw Siegfried Höchst's production at the Volksbühne in East Berlin, which treated Denmark as a literal prison from which almost everybody was trying to escape, just as almost everybody was trying to escape at that moment from East Germany. The stage was enclosed with three rows of wire fencing, and when Laertes was given permission to return to France in the second scene, he was handed a green document that looked suspiciously like the passports issued by West Germany. The audience howled in delight (Kennedy, "Berliner" 11–15). In these examples, thinking about Shakespeare has been influenced by circumstances entirely foreign to those that apply in the Anglo-American tradition, where greater political stability has robbed Shakespeare of some of the danger and force that other countries have (re)discovered in his texts. It is worth remembering that there is no phrase in English equivalent to *coup d'état.*

English-speakers are apt to assume that foreign-language productions necessarily lose an essential element of Shakespeare in the process of linguistic and cultural transfer, and of course this is true. But it is also true that some foreign performances may have a more direct access to the power of the plays. In this respect the modernity of translation is crucial. Shakespeare's poetry may be one of the glories of human life, but the archaism and remoteness of his language create enormous difficulties for audiences in the late twentieth century. The fact is, harsh as it may sound to some teachers of English, we do not speak the same language as Shakespeare: at best we speak a remote dialect of it. A foreign language, while missing the full value of the verse, can be said to have an advantage of great significance in the theatre. Even the oldest of the translations of Shakespeare in regular use today, the Schlegel-Tieck versions, are infinitely closer to the language spoken on the street in Berlin or Zurich or Vienna than Shakespeare's language is to that of London or Los Angeles or Melbourne. It is common practice in the contemporary theatre to commission new translations for new productions, so that the language not only is colloquial but also becomes tied to the interpretation and the mise en scène of the particular performance. As a result many foreign performances of Shakespeare sound similar to performances of new plays – just as performances in English of Molière or Schiller can do.

The idea of translating the plays into contemporary English is anathema to most Anglophone Shakespeareans, and probably to most Anglophone audiences. The reasons for this protectionism, however, may not be as obvious as they seem, especially when we remember that it was almost universal practice to adapt the language in the English theatre from the Restoration to the mid-nineteenth century. The reasons have as much to do with the traditions of modernist high culture and the entrenched position of the Shakespeare industry as with the inherent superiority of the originals. It's not necessary to argue the issue here; I only need to note that what is anathema in English is a fact of life elsewhere.

The differences that derive from performing in languages other than English have led to major differences in performance strategies. They are especially noticeable in the visual aspects of production: unable to place the same emphasis on Shakespeare's verbal resourcefulness, foreign performances have explored scenographic and physical modes more openly than their Anglophone counterparts, often redefining the meaning of the plays in the process. Though of course there have been, and continue to be, innovative and highly influential productions in English, the authoritative and thorough-going rethinkings of the plays we associate with Leopold Jessner or Giorgio Strehler or Ariane Mnouchkine have not occurred to the same degree in the home countries. Even Peter Brook, reinventing the plays in English since 1945, has done his most radical work on Shakespeare in French. Those differences in performance traditions tell a complicated story about the interrelationships between an English dramatist, his performance in English, and his performance outside English. To begin to understand the importance of foreign productions, and to put them in the context of Anglophone Shakespeare, it will be useful here to look at the general history of Shakespeare performance since the Second World War.

International Shakespearean representation in our time has gone through many changes, and has not proceeded in anything so convenient as a straight line. But the dominant uses and styles of Shakespeare on the stage from about 1950 to about 1980 were established by a combination of two overriding forces: the open-stage movement, and the movement to contemporize the meanings of the plays. Though it had predecessors in Germany in the nineteenth century, the open-stage movement was essentially English in theory and Anglo-Canadian in practice. Its chief object was to demystify the dramatic event by stressing its non-illusionist nature. Tyrone Guthrie, modifying the urges of William Poel and Harley Granville Barker, demonstrated that a revised architectural structure would significantly alter how Shakespeare was received in the theatre, bringing the plays closer to their audiences in both the literal and the figurative sense. The Festival Theatre in Stratford, Ontario, designed by Tanya Moiseiwitsch and Guthrie, opened in 1953, the stage initially covered by a tent; the theatre combined Elizabethan attributes with audience arrangements similar to those at the ancient theatre at Epidauros, overtly welcoming spectators as mutual creators of the dramatic fiction. New playhouses soon followed in Minneapolis, New York, Los Angeles, Chichester, Sheffield, and around the world. Some of the discoveries of the open-stage movement were widely adapted elsewhere, even modifying the interior architecture of proscenium theatres (like the Royal Shakespeare Theatre in Stratford, which resolutely divides actors from spectators), and greatly increased the ease and the speed of performance. His producers at last seemed to free Shakespeare from nineteenth-century notions of Realism.

Though the movement claimed an authenticity deriving from Elizabethan stage practice, it affected Anglophone production so deeply in the 1950s and 1960s partly because it fit inside the dominant, modernist interpretation of Shakespeare that stressed the centrality of his subtle and imagistic poetry to his meaning. The linguistic text became even more consequential to Shakespearean enactment by situating the actor on a (relatively) bare stage in a (relatively) Elizabethan mode, placing the main force of interpretation on the (relatively) unencumbered word. The movement, though not much analyzed, was so taken for granted that when J. L. Styan published *The Shakespeare Revolution* in 1977 his premise went unquestioned. Shakespeare wrote for the non-illusionist stage, Styan emphasized, and the production modalities of the twentieth century have been moving to recuperate Shakespeare's Elizabethan assumptions through a combination of architectural and performance tactics.

The second major post-war force in Shakespeare performance, the movement to contemporize the plays, was foreign in origin, though it was seized almost immediately by the Royal Shakespeare Company. This movement had two separate European parts, both thoroughly conditioned by the war: one derived from Marxist theory and Bertolt Brecht, the other from Existentialist philosophy and Jan Kott. Brecht's effect was achieved partly through his writing but more directly through the work of the Berliner Ensemble, probably the most influential theatre company in the world in the third quarter of the century. This troupe, subsidized by the government of East Germany, stressed the combined responsibility of actors, directors, designers, playwrights, and audiences to the social and political issues that lay beyond the entertainment value or the high-art virtues of attending plays. Kott, on the other hand, wished to stress the relevance and immediacy of Shakespeare's texts to the excruciations of the post-war world, and asked for theatrical representations that would reveal what he saw as the underlying cruelty of Shakespeare's fables, a cruelty not limited by political issues.

Peter Hall, greatly impressed by the visit of the Berliner Ensemble to London in August of 1956 (the very month of Brecht's death), set out to capture its organizational structure and its social commitment for the Royal Shakespeare Company, founded in 1960–1. At the same time Hall and his colleagues like Peter Brook wanted to make British Shakespeare production relevant to the modern condition, firmly moving it away from the rather operatic, high-culture-is-good-for-you posture that had generally characterized it since the Victorian era (see both Addenbrooke and Beauman). The new mode of the RSC converged with European trends in the 1960s: at Stratford, in a variety of European cities from Moscow to Milan, and eventually even in North America, some of the chief directors and designers of the age began to accent the historical messages of Shakespeare's plays for the present, often in a committed or engaged context, and in simple scenographic environments deriving from Elizabethan practice.

These tendencies of post-war Shakespearean performance received substantial theoretical support. Though the procedures of the RSC and of other major companies were frequently attacked by traditional scholars, a number of critics and theatre historians in the 1960s and 1970s provided research and commentary that endorsed radical experimentation. The two most important of these for theatre, interestingly enough, were foreign. Both wrote under socialist regimes in central and eastern Europe. Kott spoke for himself; the Brechtian strategies were best fortified by the scholarship of Robert Weimann.

Kott's *Shakespeare Our Contemporary* (published in Polish and French in 1962 and in English in 1964), probably the most widely read book of Shakespearean criticism since A. C. Bradley's *Shakespearean Tragedy* (1904), overtly annexed the Elizabethan dramatist to the absurdist environment of post-war Europe. Kott wrote in implicit opposition to the Stalinist government of Poland, a nation whose identity had been forcibly redefined, and whose freedom had been savagely abridged, first by German and then by Soviet annexation. Kott read Shakespeare, as it were, by the searchlights of a police state. In the histories he saw the "Grand Mechanism" of implacable human corruption, in the comedies a dark and bestial vision of sexuality, in the tragedies a kindred comic grimace reminiscent of Samuel Beckett. As Peter Brook said, "Kott is undoubtedly the only writer on Elizabethan matters who assumes without question that every one of his readers will at some point or other have been woken by the police in the middle of the night" (*Shifting Point* 44).[5] It was through Brook, in fact, that Kott affected the theatre most directly, especially through Brook's (in)famous RSC productions of *King Lear* in 1962 and *A Midsummer Night's Dream* in 1970.

It's hard to pinpoint how Kott altered performance traditions, since Shakespeare had normally been subject to contemporary revision and revaluation anyway. In the modernist period, however, critics were strongly inclined to see Shakespeare as somehow existing outside of time, a refuge of immutability secure from the insistent intrusions of the twentieth century, as Hugh Grady notes. Kott gave to the theatre of the 1960s and 1970s a theoretically backed fortitude to admit that Shakespeare, despite the cultural accretions that inevitably cling to the work, exists on stage in the present tense, and that representation of Shakespeare can exhibit powerful and intellectually provocative visions of the present. What was particularly new was Kott's injunction that Shakespeare should be read as a dramatist of pain. By drawing analogies to the apocalyptic nightmares of the European aburdists, he deprived Shakespeare of his comfortable status as a tamed classic. Of course many commentators and some audiences found Kott's ideas excessive or inappropriate; on the other side, by 1980 these ideas had themselves become a new kind of theatrical orthodoxy. But there can be no doubt that *Shakespeare Our Contemporary* broke down a number of artificial, Anglo-centric values that had dogged Shakespearean criticism and production into the post-war era.

Kott's working assumption was that human nature is unchanging and essentially comic in its absurdity. While he stressed the particularity of the post-war condition, he seemed to ratify a determinate universe in which human fate remained inscrutable, the black void our only end. The circus and the theatre, where human beings grapple with extreme issues that change nothing in the outer world, became for him the pertinent metaphors for life, and Beckett's plays the characteristic comic expression of the era. Thus thinking about Gloucester's clownish leap from Dover Cliff in *Lear,* Kott is immediately reminded of Didi and Gogo's clownish attempt to hang themselves in *Waiting for Godot*:

> Gloucester did fall, and he got up again. He made his suicide attempt, but he failed to shake the world. Nothing changed. . . . If there are no gods, suicide makes no sense. Death exists in any case. Suicide cannot alter human fate, but only accelerate it. It ceases to be a protest. It is a surrender. It becomes the acceptance of world's greatest cruelty – death.
> (Kott 151)

Obviously indebted to Sartre and Camus, the passage also reflects a view of the world, congenial to liberal western democracies, that privileges the anguish of the individual over the destiny of the social group. For Shakespeare the world was a cruel place, for us it is still a cruel place. We cannot affect our fates, only hasten them: personal survival and stoic perseverance are solemn protests against the cosmic odds, hugely stacked against us.

This kind of Kottian fatalism regularly appeared in productions of the comedies during this period that liked to suggest that human beings were caught in a trap of their own making. Konrad Swinarski's *Midsummer Night's Dream* (Krakow, 1970) is an interesting example: a round of sinister sexuality was treated with nightmare intensity, with two secret policemen silently observing throughout; political power and sexual power were intertwined. In the histories and tragedies, productions under Kott's influence often suggested that evil was an unending, cyclical force. Borrowing a favorite dramaturgical structure from Beckett, directors sometimes added *da capo* endings to plays like *Lear* and *Macbeth*, codas that saw the same cycle of destruction replaying itself. Perhaps the most widely seen example of the *da capo* approach was in a version of *Macbeth* by another Polish director, Roman Polanski's 1972 film (in English): after Shakespeare's final scene, the camera shows Donalbain as a disenfranchised younger brother climbing through a storm to seek out the witches, and hearing the same music Macbeth heard at the beginning of the play.

While Kott's influence was vast and international in scope, his book spoke with the greatest immediacy to eastern Europe, as my examples tend to suggest. Just as his notion of the "contemporary" requires historicizing, his synchronic approach to Shakespeare was itself part of cold-war history. Brook noticed this phenomenon with his 1962 *King Lear*, a production that many English-speaking commentators thought too "European" (i.e., foreign) anyway, which traveled both east and west over the next two years. On tour in the U.S., the director observed that it failed to connect with audiences rather remote from its themes of absence and loss; in eastern Europe, however, it found its true home. "The best performances," Brook wrote, "lay between Budapest and Moscow" (*Empty Space* 21–3).

Robert Weimann's effect on international Shakespeare has been less obvious, though the issues he set out have been equally powerful tools in the theatre. If Kott saw the world as cruel and unmitigated middle-earth, Weimann saw it as a space to be changed. Marxist in thought and historical in method, Weimann was especially interested in how the theatre could recover in Shakespeare a popular tradition, empowering general spectators with the status the playwright and his stage had given them in the sixteenth century. Weimann's major work, published in East Berlin in 1967 as *Shakespeare und die Tradition des Volkstheaters*, was translated and updated in 1978 as *Shakespeare and the Popular Tradition in the Theater*. It asked for a "unity of history and criticism by which the past significance and the present meaning of Shakespeare's theater" could be explained with reference to its "structural quality" and its "social function." Two overriding historical facts must condition everything we think about Shakespeare:

> On the one hand, Shakespeare's theater is irremediably a thing of the past; on the other, his plays have survived the conditions from which

> they originated and are continually revitalized on the modern stage. . . . The tension between what is past and what lives for us today is obvious; and yet, from the point of view of the function of literary scholarship, it seems impossible to relegate the pastness of Shakespeare's theater to the "pure" historian and its contemporaneousness to the "pure" critic or modern producer.
>
> (Weimann, *Popular Tradition* xiii)

Accepting Marx's premise that art is "one of the special modes of production," Weimann insisted that we cannot sever Shakespeare's plays from the social and historical conditions of their original performance (as literary critics as diverse as Bradley and Kott have tended to do). At the same time, when we fail to "separate pastness from what is alive, history from interpretation," we only compound the confusion by failing to distinguish between "the history of a work's origins in the past and the story of its effects in the present." As he put it in a separate essay, "today *any* Shakespeare staging has to come to terms with the tension between Renaissance values and modern evaluations" (Weimann, "Past Significance" 115; also see Taylor 301–2).

In dedicating the book to Manfred Wekwerth and Benno Besson – "my friends in the theater who have come closest to a modern Shakespeare in the popular tradition" – Weimann showed his colors most clearly. Wekwerth and Besson, who at various times worked at and were the managers of the three major theatres in East Berlin, the Deutsches Theatre, the Volksbühne, and the Berliner Ensemble, were the leading Brechtian directors of Shakespeare in the 1960s and 1970s. Indeed, Wekwerth directed (with the collaboration of Joachim Tenschert, in 1964) Brecht's own adaptation of *Coriolanus*, one of the defining productions of the Berliner Ensemble. Thus for Weimann and for his friends, *die Tradition des Volkstheaters* meant more than the words *the Popular Tradition in Theater* convey in English: Weimann's title referred not only to Shakespeare's popular audience but also to the Marxist-Brechtian blueprint for theatrical production which privileged reception over intention, the minds of the spectators over the personalities and aspirations of the artists.

In the West, "Brechtian" has become a description of style. The term is often detached from the social and political commitment that underlay the comprehensive system of theatrical writing and performance that Brecht and his associates worked out in Berlin after the war. This is especially true with Shakespeare, and even became true at the RSC in the late 1960s, despite Peter Hall's early leftist leanings. But in the GDR, and on other important stages in Europe, Brechtian Shakespeare remained revolutionary. As Weimann counseled, its method of production emphasized the pastness of the texts and thus found itself free to redefine their meanings for the present. Populist directors like Roger Planchon in Lyon, Leopold

Lindtberg in Vienna, and Giorgio Strehler in Milan, as well as Wekwerth, Besson, and Friedo Solter in Berlin, struck a bargain with Shakespeare: he delivered a Renaissance classic text, they overlaid it with a post-war social text. By stressing class distinctions among the characters, the recessive political tensions in the fable, or the complicity between terror and power, for example, they offered visions of Shakespeare that seemed to straddle the past and the present.

Unlike the Kottian method, which tended to suggest the unchanging nature of a cosmos ruled by cruel but invisible forces, Brechtian productions wished to suggest that human beings could control and thus change their own fates. Attempting to alienate the spectator from the purely emotive aspects of the drama, these productions hoped to prompt a new ideological awareness of the spectator's position within the political and economic construct. An audience would be most connected to Shakespeare when it was distanced from him, when it ceased merely spectating and started acting, or at least thinking.

Thus Shakespearean performance after the war, whether influenced by Kott or by Brecht or by a mixture of the two, discovered contemporary themes and stressed the spectator's inclusion in those themes. Not all productions, of course, demonstrated the same inclinations. In Ontario, for example, the Stratford Festival Theatre was the architectural model for audience incorporation but, perhaps because of Guthrie's own apolitical (or politically conservative) stance, seemed devoid of social commentary. On the other hand, the New York Shakespeare Festival in Central Park worked hard (though not always successfully) to find a progressive American expression equal to the excitement generated by the European theatre thinkers. In general terms, by the mid-1960s Shakespeare performance, both Anglophone and foreign, sought a message in the play; whatever the message might be, the production almost always achieved its utterance by limiting the manifold possibilities of the raw text.

This method of handling classic texts, common in the twentieth century, has been greatly facilitated by the enormous growth in authority of the stage director. There are many things to say about the advent of the director as the chief artistic force in the theatrical enterprise, but one thing that perhaps hasn't been said enough is that the director's rise is intimately tied to theatrical modernism. The modernist ideal – planted by Appia and Craig and much cultivated in the early century by directors like Reinhardt and Meyerhold – encouraged the director to fuse the elements of scenography, acting style, and intellectual theme into a single aesthetic experience. The mediation of the theatre was channeled through the mediation of the director, and justified on the grounds that for complex dramas an audience wants a single concept or point of view provided. Needless to say this paradigm still has numerous adherents in the theatre, and is often the working assumption even in training programs. For modernist

Shakespearean performance the director was a godsend: he became a manager of the formidable possibilities of a text otherwise too distant in time, language, and thought. (The gendered pronoun is deliberate; until quite recently the vast majority of directors were male.) Despite their substantial differences, both Brecht and Kott countenanced the modernist inclination for Shakespeare in that they proposed that the director control and shape theatrical meaning.

But starting in the mid-1970s the modernist ideal of unified production began to break down. For Shakespeare, a number of European directors and companies that had earlier subscribed to the Brechtian and Kottian modes started to experiment with expressions of diverse savor, particularly in the visual realm. As Europe moved out of the period dominated by the effects of the war, Shakespearean representation began to reflect a new set of concerns, often affected by a new internationalism and by the global effects of multinational capitalism. The burgeoning wealth of the west and Japan, encouraging vast tourism as well as an international consumer economy, moved Shakespeare, along with culture in general, from the stern faces of socialism and absurdism. The work of directors like Planchon, Strehler, and Brook no longer seemed restrained by the distressed clothing and distressed ideas familiar from *Mother Courage* and *Waiting for Godot*, the two plays that defined the post-war era.

Peter Zadek's travesty versions, seen in West Germany starting in the 1960s, were pertinent transitions to an iconoclastic but less ideological Shakespeare. Meanwhile younger directors like Peter Stein and Ariane Mnouchkine, originally affected by Brecht and by Marxist dialectics, began to sketch the outlines of a self-consciously postmodern Shakespeare. As Kott himself noted, the contemporary distrust of politics in the west has caused theatre artists to substitute a "new visual expression" for Shakespeare in place of the rough-edged emphasis on intellectual meaning of the post-war avant-garde, whose workers were, in any event, "restricted to the limited resources of the small stage" (Marowitz 100).

Postmodern experiments with Shakespeare were held in check in Great Britain and North America until quite recently by the powerful routines of the RSC and Ontario, which continued to assert the centrality of the text and of traditional acting based upon textual analysis. There is little doubt that the Elizabethan English language played a large part in this state of affairs. Peter Hall, for example, said in 1988 that out of his career as a director of about twenty-five Shakespeare productions, only one was not located by a Renaissance reference: "unless what's on the stage looks like the language, I simply don't believe it" (Berry 209). In Europe and Asia, however, partly because of the freedom from an accustomed linguistic approach to Shakespeare, no such control existed, and the postmodern delight in eclectic transtemporality has been given free rein. As a result, some of the most innovative and exciting productions of Shakespeare in the past twenty years have come not from the RSC but from Europe, east, west, and central; from Soviet Georgia; and from Japan. These productions often made it their business to register the cultural differences between the original texts and the target audiences, going directly against Hall's precept. In other words, Shakespeare was again being presented for his foreignness rather than for his familiarity, as he had been in German in the eighteenth century. Just at the time that the number of Shakespeare performances around the globe has vastly increased, the deviations between Anglophone and foreign performances have been heightened.

And yet post-war performance of Shakespeare has often demonstrated a fruitful tension between the foreign and the native. The pervasive internationalism of film has been crucial here, particularly the influential work of Grigori Kozintsev and of Akira Kurosawa, both of whom adapted Shakespeare's tragedies by a process of cultural transfer. The apparent ease by which these master filmmakers brought new meanings to old drama has in turn affected a number of stage directors. Brook, for example, was much struck by how Kurosawa's *Throne of Blood* (1957) recast the *Macbeth* story in cinematic images of a cross-cultural nature. From Kurosawa's samurai tale, Brook learned to leap over the archaism of the text by concentrating on fable and theme, and his Shakespeare work in Paris since 1974 has tended to pull away from the textual responsibility he had felt in his earlier productions at Stratford (David Williams 42). He told his translator, Jean-Claude Carrière, that the major danger of linguistic conversion was translationese, what Carrière refers to as a language of "traduit de." The ideal performance script for Paris, Brook said, would be one that appeared to be "a new play, written in French, and written by Shakespeare."[6] The cross-cultural method reached a peak of sorts with Brook's production of *The Tempest* in 1990, in which an interracial troupe of actors combined an African modality with performance tactics borrowed from Brook's version of *The Mahabharata,* which was also written by Carrière.

The internationalism of film, which depends only on a distribution system that is part of the normal procedures of capitalist commerce, has been paralleled in recent years by a more complicated theatrical internationalism. The rapidity and ease of jet transport has allowed touring by theatre companies on a large scale, just as it has done for professional sports teams, and has simultaneously brought spectators from all over the globe to theatrical centers like Tokyo, New York, Stratford, Paris, and Berlin. The Channel-hopping spectator of the past has been replaced by the ocean-hopping spectator and the ocean-hopping company, equally at home in Los Angeles or London, Toronto or Milan, Sydney or Prague – or, in keeping with contemporary aesthetics, equally *not* at home. For Shakespeare, this postmodern condition of nearly borderless theatre, exaggerated even further by the collapse of the Soviet empire, has created great curiosities of playgoing: Korean spectators at Stratford laughing at three-and-a-half hour performances of comedies in an ancient language they do not understand; the critic of *The Guardian* using "Euro-Shakespeare" to castigate British theatres for their lack of multiracial casting; a Japanese company bringing a violently beautiful and thoroughly foreign *Macbeth* to Scotland.[7]

There is no one conclusion to draw from all of this, except that foreign Shakespeare is more present than ever before, interrogating the idea that Shakespeare can be contained by a single tradition or by a single culture or by a single language. Perhaps the native familiarity that English-speakers assume for Shakespeare is part of a larger illusion, which might be called the myth of cultural ownership. In the end Shakespeare doesn't belong to any nation or anybody: Shakespeare is foreign to all of us. In the theatre we will continue to see a range of attitudes to the ownership of the plays, just as we see in contemporary Shakespearean scholarship. Some productions will want to point up the otherness of the texts, others will continue to want to possess or absorb them.

Either way, the texts themselves remain both distant and elusive. The span is enormous between the original conditions of the texts and their performances today, and will grow greater. In Weimann's terms, the situation of the plays is completely gone; what we have left are the traces. These traces, of course, fascinate us, disturb our dreams, and make us knock on the door through which they came. In general, foreign productions of Shakespeare, freed from the burden imposed by centuries of admiring his language, have been more ready to admit that the door to the past is locked.

In English the language will always be important to our appreciation, yet our ability to reach the plays directly in their original language lessens year by year. Our own English continues to change, and eventually only specialists will be able to read the texts, much less listen to them comfortably in the theatre. This may well happen within the next fifty years. In fact, some of us teaching Shakespeare believe that it is happening now, at an accelerated pace. Reflecting on performances outside of English, we can see more clearly how Shakespeare is alien, as well as what we continue to find indigenous or domestic about him. What is it that endures when he is deprived of his tongue? It's a question that will haunt the future.

NOTES

1 Anna Földes, in a panel discussion transcribed in Elsom (94). The present essay is a revised version of the introduction to my edition called *Foreign Shakespeare*, a collection of papers about Shakespeare in the non-English-speaking theatre (© Dennis Kennedy 1993. Reprinted with the permission of Cambridge University Press). The essay was first presented in a slightly different form for a seminar on performance history, organized by James C. Bulman, at the International Shakespeare Conference in Stratford in 1992.

2 The three series are "Text and Performance" (Macmillan), "Shakespeare in Performance" (Manchester University Press), and "Plays in Performance" (Bristol Classical Press; future titles to be published by Cambridge University Press). Of the numerous Shakespeare volumes now available, only David Hirst's *The Tempest* (Text and Performance, London, 1984) uses a major foreign example (Giorgio Strehler's 1978 production in Milan). Two volumes on *King Lear* treat Grigori Kozintsev's Russian film version of 1970: Alexander Leggatt's (Shakespeare in Performance, Manchester, 1991) and Gamini Salgado's (Text and Performance, London, 1984). Bernice Kliman's *Macbeth* (Shakespeare in Performance, Manchester, 1992) devotes two pages to Ninagawa's Japanese production.

3 Simon Williams (32–3) notes that the early English Comedians were more admired for musical and acrobatic qualities than for dramatic ones, and provides a detailed account of the formal arrival of Shakespeare in German in the eighteenth and nineteenth centuries. Limon treats the early playing conditions in detail.

4 The quotation is from the collected writings of Koreya Senda, who played *Hamlet* in the production, in Senda's *Engeki hyôron shû* (Tokyo: Miraisha, 1980), 5: 287. See Kennedy and Rimer.

5 Brook read Kott's essay "King Lear or Endgame" (which is the centerpiece of *Shakespeare Our Contemporary*) in French prior to its publication. But the influence went both ways: Kott saw Brook's production of *Titus Andronicus* (Stratford, 1955) on tour in Warsaw in 1957. "*Titus Andronicus* has revealed to me a Shakespeare I dreamed of but have never before seen on the stage," Kott wrote in his review (reprinted in *Shakespeare Our Contemporary* 353). See Kennedy, *Looking at Shakespeare*, chapter 6.

6 Reported by Jean-Claude Carrière, in a talk in Los Angeles in 1991. I discuss the issue of cultural imperialism raised by Brook's work, along with the political implications of the orientalism of Ariane Mnouchkine and the "occidentalism" of Yukio Ninagawa, in "Shakespeare and the Global Spectator." See also "Shakespearean Orientalism," my Afterword to *Foreign Shakespeare*; and Patrice Pavis, "Wilson, Brook, Zadek: An Intercultural Encounter?", in the same volume.

7 The critic was Michael Billington, "From the Stage of the Globe," *Guardian Weekly* 5 May 1991: 22. The Japanese production was Yukio Ninagawa's *Macbeth* at the Edinburgh Festival in 1985.

REFERENCES

Addenbrooke, David. *The Royal Shakespeare Company: The Peter Hall Years.* London: Kimber, 1974.

Beauman, Sally. *The Royal Shakespeare Company: A History of Ten Decades.* Oxford: Oxford University Press, 1982.

Berry, Ralph, ed. *On Directing Shakespeare*, 2nd edn. London: Hamish Hamilton, 1989.

Brook, Peter. *The Empty Space.* New York: Atheneum, 1968.

—— *The Shifting Point, 1946–1987.* New York: Harper & Row, 1987.

Elsom, John, ed. *Is Shakespeare Still Our Contemporary?* London: Routledge, 1989.

Grady, Hugh. *The Modernist Shakespeare: Critical Texts in a Material World.* Oxford: Clarendon Press, 1991.

Kennedy, Dennis, ed. *Foreign Shakespeare: Contemporary Performance.* Cambridge: Cambridge University Press, 1993.

Kennedy, Dennis. "Ich Bin ein (Ost) Berliner: *Hamlet* at the Volksbühne." *Western European Stages* 2 (1990): 11–15.

—— *Looking at Shakespeare: A Visual History of Twentieth-Century Performance.* Cambridge: Cambridge University Press, 1993.

—— "Shakespeare and the Global Spectator." *Shakespeare Jahrbuch* 131 (1995): 50–64.

Kennedy, Dennis and J. Thomas Rimer. "Koreya Senda and Political Shakespeare." *Shakespeare on the Japanese Stage.* Ed. Takashi Sasayama, Ronnie Mulryne, and Margaret Shewring. Cambridge: Cambridge University Press, forthcoming.

Kott, Jan. *Shakespeare Our Contemporary.* Trans. Boleslaw Taborski. New York: Anchor Books, 1966.

Limon, Jerzy. *Gentlemen of a Company: English Players in Central and Eastern Europe, 1590–1660.* Cambridge: Cambridge University Press, 1985.

Marowitz, Charles. "Kott, Our Contemporary." *American Theatre* (October 1988): 100.

Taylor, Gary. *Reinventing Shakespeare: A Cultural History, from the Restoration to the Present.* New York: Oxford University Press, 1989.

Weimann, Robert. *Shakespeare and the Popular Tradition in the Theater: Studies in the Social Dimension of Dramatic Form and Function.* Trans. and ed. Robert Schwartz. Baltimore: Johns Hopkins University Press, 1978.

—— "Shakespeare on the Modern Stage: Past Significance and Present Meaning." *Shakespeare Survey* 20 (1967): 113–20.

Williams, David. "'A Place Marked by Life': Brook at the Bouffes du Nord." *New Theatre Quarterly* 1 (1985): 39–74.

Williams, Simon. *Shakespeare on the German Stage, 1586–1914.* Cambridge: Cambridge University Press, 1990.

9

HISTORICIZING ALAN DESSEN

Scholarship, stagecraft, and the "Shakespeare revolution"

Cary M. Mazer

While we are engaged in the process of theorizing Shakespeare in performance, it might be useful to recall that there was once a time, fairly recently, when, unlike now, stage-centered Shakespeare scholars and theatrical practitioners could actually talk to one another.

A two-way on-going conversation, a reciprocally beneficial exchange between scholars and practitioners, is not, evidently, the goal of our current process of theorizing. Our scholarly interest in performance today seems to be primarily descriptive and analytical. Armed with new and sophisticated theoretical apparatuses and historical methodologies, stage-centered scholars (on the evidence of other essays in this volume) seek a vocabulary and a method to describe what happens on the stage in a performance of one of Shakespeare's plays: what was going on theatrically, 400 years ago, in the cultural and historical moment of the play's original performance; and what is going on now, in the phenomenology of actor, audience, playhouse, and script, according to the very different theatrical aesthetics operating in today's theatre. Both the aesthetic practices encoded within the playscript and the aesthetic practices at work in a modern performance are viewed as forms of cultural production, which can be understood only in relation to other social and cultural formations. Our reading of a performance, whether historical or contemporary, is an act of contextualizing, of *historicizing*, the performance in its cultural moment.

This enterprise is admirable, especially when it is descriptive. It runs into problems, though – and it actively inhibits a dialogue between scholars and theatrical practitioners – when it becomes prescriptive. A theorized and historicized description of an aspect of the playscript in performance runs the risk of becoming not merely a description of the ways a script has worked, or how it might work, in performance, but a prescription for how it *must* work; at worst, it becomes not only an analysis of *how* the performance signifies, but a set of instructions for *what* the performance must signify, an assertion of what the play can and must, effectively, *mean*.

Even when such scholarship is not prescriptive, it is unclear how interested theatrical practitioners really are in what performance-historians and performance-theorists have to tell them. For the most part, directors and their collaborators do not theorize or historicize their own work, nor are they necessarily interested in ways that scholars theorize or historicize their work for them. Moreover, directors for the most part do not view the performance they create as a "realization" of the "score" of the playscript, which would benefit from the participation of a scholarly "score-reader" who could identify for them what is theatrically nascent in the script waiting to be "realized." Rather, directors and their collaborators create performances out of the theatrical raw materials at their disposal, materials which include (but are not limited to) the playscript; they seek to "tell" the "story" that they perceive is in the script, and to find theatrical means of telling this story, according to the particular material conditions in which they are working. If, and only if, what they read of contemporary scholarship matches their sense of the story they wish to tell, will scholarship be of any use to them at all.

There was a time, though, when scholars were hopeful that what they had to offer was actually of interest to actors and directors, and when scholars believed that contemporary and historical performances of the plays had something to teach them in turn. This era of optimism crested in 1977 with the publication of *The Shakespeare Revolution*, J. L. Styan's book-length celebration of the interconnectedness of stage and study. *The Shakespeare Revolution* has three interrelated theses. First, Shakespearean performance in this century, Styan argues, has come increasingly close to the conventions and aesthetics of the theatre for which the plays were originally written, discarding the distinctly non-Shakespearean pictorial illusionism of Irving and Tree in favor of the open stage and "non-illusionistic" modes of theatrical representation. Second, Shakespearean scholarship has become increasingly sensitive to the way the plays work in performance, moving away from an emphasis on language and anachronistically novelistic definitions of character and narrative structure, and moving towards a "stage-centered" appreciation of Elizabethan theatrical conditions and conventions, and the open-ended interpretive possibilities of performance (the term "stage-centered" is Styan's coinage). Third, these two developments – each tantamount to a revolution – have led to a fruitful collaboration between practitioners and scholars, resulting in criticism by and about contemporary performance, and productions which draw directly upon the findings of contemporary scholarship.

From the perspective of the past two decades, there are many reasons to challenge both Styan's premises and his conclusions. Indeed, there were effective challenges to Styan's glorification of stage-centered scholarship and scholarship-centered performance even as Styan was writing in the 1970s. At the same time that Styan was praising the innovative directors of the twentieth century for their fresh readings of the plays in performance and praising contemporary scholarship for its newly sensitized theatrical consciousness, John Russell Brown, a pioneering stage-centered scholar in his own right, was arguing that the symbiosis between performance and scholarship worked to the detriment of both; that both the "Director's Theatre" and the scholarly Shakespeare industry were narrow-minded, reductionist, and authoritarian; and that scholarship and the Director's Theatre together threatened the most vital component of the performance event, the actor.

Although the validity of Styan's main theses was arguably untrue even as he was writing *The Shakespeare Revolution*, the book stands as an extraordinary document of its own time. For *The Shakespeare Revolution* succeeded in articulating the great creation myth of its era. According to Styan, stage-centered scholarship and scholarly performance represent the culmination of a historical process, the result of inexorable progress and evolutionary inevitability, the fruits of a movement of history that had begun with William Poel and Granville Barker at the beginning of the century and had come into full flower with Peter Brook's *A Midsummer Night's Dream* for the Royal Shakespeare Company in 1970.

From the perspective of the 1990s, it is now more important for us to understand how Styan understood his own historical moment – how he positioned himself and his fellow stage-centered scholars as the culmination of a historical process – than it is for us to assess whether or not he understood it correctly. For *The Shakespeare Revolution* is as much a product of its time as it is a history of the times that preceded it. The dialogue between stage and study that Styan and others claimed was occurring in the 1970s needed an antecedent history to give it legitimacy and inevitability, and Styan's book, with its elaborate historical throughlines and causal relations, did just that.

From our point of view, then, it might be sufficient for us to say that the dialogue took place, and not, as Styan suggests, to claim that it was the end-product of an evolutionary process. Or we might go one step further: it could be argued that the celebrated dialogue (which Styan calls salutary and Brown considers pernicious) might not have taken place at all; that the participants merely wished to believe that a dialogue was taking place; and that they were able to create the illusion of a dialogue because stage-centered scholars and theatre practitioners each had a causally independent but complementary sense of how the dramatic script worked. Scholars and practitioners, I would argue, each had their own understandings of what a dramatic "text" is, their own sense of how it is organized, and their own appreciation of a text's intrinsic organic "unity." And they each believed that the unity of the artistic product was the result not only of these unifying organizing principles, but of the presence of a unitary organizing artistic authority behind it. For one brief moment, scholars and practitioners were speaking in the same ways about the texts they were working with in their respective, highly specialized, arenas. And because they each were speaking a similar language amongst themselves, they could imagine that they were speaking to one another.

It behooves us, then, to situate stage-centered scholarship and the putative "Shakespeare Revolution" in the shared assumptions about organic form and artistic authority that prevailed in both scholarship and theatrical practice in the 1970s. We must, in short, historicize our own enterprise of Shakespearean performance theory and criticism. And we can begin by historicizing the nature of our enterprise in the 1970s, the era which invented the Shakespeare Revolution as a means of describing and legitimizing itself.

* * *

I propose to do so by taking a closer look at the scholarship of Alan C. Dessen. As a scholar, Dessen is the heir to the tradition exemplified by Richard Southern, Bernard Beckerman, Glynne Wickham, and Andrew Gurr, among others. Like these scholars, Dessen seeks to extrapolate a set of aesthetic theatrical principles from the "external" evidence of theatre architecture and the "internal" evidence of the surviving playscripts.[1] In the decades since Dessen's work on the subject began to appear in the 1970s, his reading of Elizabethan stagecraft has become even more rigorously grounded in empirical evidence and has been even more willing to debate the nature of evidence itself.

Moreover, Dessen has, in the past two decades, actively engaged in the dialogue between study and stage so lauded by Styan. He has not, to my knowledge, served as a production dramaturg, nor has he served as an official observer during an extended rehearsal period. But ever since his days working in the educational programs at the Ashland Shakespeare Festival in the late 1960s and early 1970s, he has taken advantage of opportunities to see individual productions repeatedly, as they develop over the length of a run, playing before different audiences and in different venues. No other scholar I know has so ably learned how to cultivate professional friendships with working actors and directors as Dessen has at Ashland, the Canadian Stratford, the ACTER tours, Santa Cruz, and the Royal Shakespeare Company, or has so effectively drawn out theatre people about their working methods and interpretive conclusions.[2]

There is, furthermore, an integral and sophisticated connection between Dessen's scholarship on Elizabethan stage conventions and his scholarly reviews of contemporary Shakespeare productions. And it is in the complementarity of these two scholarly activities – historical research, and scholarly analysis of contemporary production – that Dessen articulates a view of history and the nature of performance that allows us to historicize the nature of Dessen's scholarly enterprise most clearly.

At first glance, there would appear to be an irreconcilable conflict between these two activities. Reviews of contemporary performances are usually based on the premise that the range of interpretation to be discovered through performance is effectively unlimited, and that a scholarly review should record those interpretive choices which add to the aggregate of our knowledge of how a play works in performance, creating, as it were, a collective theatrical variorum edition of each play. Dessen's books and essays on Elizabethan theatrical practice are, as we shall see, based on a very different premise: that there were distinct systems of meaning embedded within the plays in performance, communicated via a system of visual patterns and associations, which are perceivable only when we learn the Elizabethan theatrical conventions of time and place, properties and space, light and darkness, actions and activities, physical realities and implied fictions; and that these theatrical conventions are fundamentally different from the "realistic" conventions of the twentieth century.[3]

Dessen, in his precisely articulated guidelines for reviewing contemporary Shakespeare productions "for the record," sees no contradiction between these activities. While he does not endorse an unlimited range of potential interpretations for any given script, he does not condemn a production for creating a set of effects or generating a set of associations or meanings through means which were unavailable to Shakespeare in his own theatre; nor does he condemn a production for creating meanings which are patently alien to the play's possible original meanings. What Dessen values most is when a production teaches him something. Sometimes this occurs when the production shows him things about the play he didn't know were there; more often, it occurs when the production shows him what's in the play precisely because it isn't there in the production.

Dessen pays particular attention to such instances, which he calls "trade-offs," or "the road not taken." Such moments clarify how things work; Dessen's practice of recording "what was *not* done or *could* have been done" ("Reviewing" 607, Dessen's emphases) is equivalent to Brecht's principle of "not this but that." A production's cuts, for example, can reveal with some clarity the previously unimagined function of the passage in the original script: "Premature surgery to remove a supposed wart may leave a scar, an emptiness, a diminished thing" ("Shakespeare's Scripts and the Modern Director" 59). Most often, Dessen will use a perceived "trade-off" not to criticize the contemporary production nor to praise the Shakespearean original, but to note the difference between the two artistic sensibilities, aesthetic systems, and theatrical conventions at work: the Elizabethan stagecraft encoded in the original script versus the theatrical practices of the present day. For example, after describing a 1978 production of *The Winter's Tale* in Ontario, which chose to show Paulina explicitly not consenting to a marriage with Camillo at the end of the play, Dessen observes that "the interpretive choices in the Ontario production therefore highlight a revealing gap between modern psychological or cultural reasoning and the interpretive logic of Shakespeare and his audience" ("Modern Productions" 221).

Measuring the breadth of this "revealing gap," understanding "significant differences between then and now" (215), is the goal of much of Dessen's writing about contemporary performance. Moreover, it is the key to Dessen's historical scholarship on the theatrical conventions of Shakespeare's stage. We read Shakespeare today, Dessen writes, borrowing an image from Bernard Beckerman, wearing a pair of spectacles. In this case, the pair of spectacles is our modern notions of theatrical realism, psychology, motivation, etc. We must, Dessen argues, "shed the spectacles of realism" (*Viewer's Eye* 109) and recognize the presence in Shakespeare's scripts of an aesthetic system that employs a distinct set of aesthetic principles and that yields a distinct set of theatrical meanings. Dessen asks us to understand the mechanics of the system of theatrical conventions, "the terms upon which the original dramatists, actors, and spectators agreed to meet," and to recognize them as distinct from the terms upon which dramatists, actors, and spectators meet in today's theatre; "to recognize the original conventions," Dessen observes, "is often to discover distinctive Shakespearean metaphors and meanings" ("Shakespeare and the Theatrical Conventions of his Time" 98).

In identifying the differences between Elizabethan "patterned action" and modern "psychological realism" ("Modern Productions" 214), Dessen's project is essentially historicist: it locates a work of art's meanings, its strategies for creating meanings, and its larger function within the formation of culture, in its historical moment, as distinct from the way culture is formed and meanings are generated in other historical periods, including the present. Dessen articulates his historicist principles most clearly and directly in the introductory chapter (characteristically titled "The Problem of Evidence") in *Shakespeare and the Late Moral Plays*, the 1986 book which is the least explicitly stage-centered of his works since the early 1970s. The "moral play" tradition of the late-Tudor period, Dessen argues, holds out yet another set of codes tacitly comprehensible to an Elizabethan audience and yet not widely understood or perceived today. Dessen justifies his reconsideration of a tradition that had been written about at considerable length by older generations of literary historians by citing the reception theories of H. R. Jauss and Raymond Williams's notion of "the selective tradition," the way in which a contemporary reader will select from the recorded culture of an historical period (itself a small segment of the culture as it was actually lived) only those features which correspond to the contemporary systems of interests and values. In order to get beyond the "selective tradition" to a more comprehensive understanding of the culture of the historical period, the scholar must steer between the "twin pitfalls" of what Paul Zumthor calls "naive historicism" and "blind modernism." "We inevitably see the past," Dessen observes, repeating his favorite metaphor, "through lenses compacted of our own assumptions and interests" (*Late Moral Plays* 5).

In his writings about historical performance conditions, as in his analyses of the late moral plays, Dessen equips us to see the past without spectacles – or, more accurately, to see the past through new spectacles ground according to Dessen's own specifications. But what are Dessen's own spectacles? To what extent does he inescapably view the past through lenses compacted of his own assumptions and interests? Dessen's spectacles, as salutarily prescribed as the lenses may be, and as clearly as we can now read the fine print of history by looking through them, are themselves focussed and cut and ground according to his own tacit historical assumptions. The time has come, then, to "historicize Alan Dessen," to understand in historical terms what Dessen and some of his precursors understand about theatre and theatrical practice, and to account for why they understand what they do.

The key to Dessen's thinking about theatrical signification and theatrical significance lies in the actual theatrical work of the 1970s. And the best place to look is in the work of the Royal Shakespeare Company, not because it was better or more important, but because the work was more visible and accessible and subject to wider scholarly scrutiny. There is a special irony in using contemporary performance to describe Dessen's understanding of historical performance, especially since, as we have seen, Dessen spends much of his theatrical reviews and almost all of his historical scholarship delineating differences between the aesthetics of contemporary theatre and the aesthetics of Shakespeare's theatre. Furthermore, Dessen did not actually *see* any of the RSC's work, he tells me, until well into the 1970s. Our goal, though, is not to seek causal relationships between theatrical and scholarly practice, any more than it is to confirm Styan's contention that an active dialogue was taking place; rather, our goal is to identify ways of thinking about the nature of the text, performance, the theatre event itself, and the nature of the artistic act that goes into its creation, that were tacitly shared by stage-centered scholars of the 1970s and active theatre practitioners on the international scene. Dessen acquired his understanding of Shakespeare's theatre from the same larger cultural practices that shaped the thinking of the theatre directors of his day. Even when Dessen suggests that there is a "revealing gap" between Elizabethan stage conventions and contemporary theatrical practice, his understanding of historical stage conventions is itself conditioned by the discourse surrounding contemporary theatre and theatrical language. The spectacles through which Dessen sees the Elizabethan theatre were the same spectacles worn by directors and theatregoers in the 1970s, ground and fitted at the Royal Shakespeare Theatre, the Aldwych, and the Other Place.

* * *

The kinship that Dessen's way of thinking has with the Shakespearean performance sensibilities of the 1970s has less to do with theatrical meaning than it does with the ways that meaning is created in the theatre. And so we must look beyond Dessen's interpretations of theatrical signals – the most exasperating aspect of his work – to his discussion of the sign systems themselves. We therefore need not concern ourselves with whether the presence of a non-speaking "gentle Astringer" in *All's Well that Ends Well* signifies a metaphorical blindness, or whether Gertrude's seeing, or not seeing, the Ghost is "a means to italicize Hamlet's tragic blindness" (*Modern Interpreters* 155). Dessen confesses that he cannot "prove" his interpretations; "but to screen out such possibilities is to limit our perspectives, narrow our range of vision, and leave us, as modern readers of Shakespeare, dangerously close to Gertrude who insists that she see 'nothing at all' but still claims confidently: 'yet all that is I see'" (*Modern Interpreters* 155). Similarly, Dessen describes, at the end of his book on *Titus Andronicus*, the way different recent productions treat the ending of the play, and in particular the potent image of Aaron's child, which can be silently nurtured or savagely murdered in the play's final moments. Dessen does not favor one option over another; but he draws attention to the fact that, within the Elizabethan stage conventions encoded in the script, the opportunity for a potent image nevertheless exists. The fact that the play encodes a means of signifying is more noteworthy than the specific meaning signified.

The means of signification available on the Elizabethan stage are catalogued in Dessen's two books on the subject, and in his exemplary essay in the *Cambridge Companion to Shakespeare Studies*. These means include: "symbolic actions," such as the linked images of downwards sword thrusts in *Hamlet*; "obvious fictions," which increase the audience's awareness of the significance of an event by placing the action in "theatrical italics"; the "stage psychomachia," which personifies aspects of a character's personality by physicalizing distinct choices or courses of action; actions or stage emblems underscored by the verbal or gestural references to "this"; significant moments of stage violence; and patterns of light and darkness created through the theatrical conventions of the day-lit stage, along with corresponding patterns of characters "seeing and not-seeing." "Fictional" details are indicated by "theatrical" means: locality and activity are signaled by props (e.g. candles and torches signifying darkness), costume (boots signifying haste), people (a jailer with keys signifying a prison), etc. These theatrical objects, set-pieces, and activities, along with significant gestures and stage groupings, are organized by the playwright into patterns which accumulate meaning through repetition, according to a principle that Dessen calls "linking analogues." The flexible conventions of localization (which allow Orlando and Old Adam to appear starving on one side of the stage while a banquet is prepared on the other, or Edgar and Kent to appear simultaneously as though in different locales discussing their respective nothingness), and the patterns created by overlapping scene endings and beginnings, allow images and emblems to be meaningfully juxtaposed. The playwright uses these juxtapositions and linking analogues to generate patterns of images and emblems that accumulate significance throughout the play, whether it is Hamlet's metaphorical blindness mirrored by Gertrude's failure to see the Ghost, or the sequence of hands and body parts marking their presence or absence in *Titus Andronicus.*

* * *

Now consider the theatrical strategies of John Barton's 1973 production of *Richard II* for the RSC. This production received much scholarly attention in its time on both sides of the Atlantic, and the minor scholarly industry that sprang up around the production is itself revealing: the production evidently spoke a theatrical language that stage-centered scholars were equipped to read.

Far down stage center on the apron is a small round dish of earth. This is not linked to any one specific location, but it serves physically or symbolically in a variety of scenes and in a variety of functions. John of Gaunt kneels and gestures to it as he talks of "This earth of majesty" being "leas'd out," emphasizing, almost gesturally, the word "this" in each phrase of the speech; Richard, returning from Ireland, leans down and touches it, saying "Dear earth, I do salute thee with my hand." And after the Queen reprimands the Gardener, he plants a sprig of rue in it: "Here did she fall; here in this place / I'll set a bank of rue." Similarly, Gaunt refers to a large bound volume when he speaks of the "inky blots and rotten parchment bonds"; from this same book Northumberland asks Richard to read aloud "These accusations and these grievous crimes / Committed by your person and your followers / Against the state and profit of this land"; and Richard carries the volume with him as a burden to his prison. When making plans to confiscate Gaunt's property to finance the Irish wars, Richard tries on a plumed helmet and looks at himself in a mirror; this same mirror is brought on and smashed in the deposition scene, and Richard wears the oval frame around his neck for the rest of the play. The Duchess of Gloucester appears in a trap door down center; later, the body of Gaunt will be lowered into this same trap. The bench on which Gaunt sits in his death-bed scene opens up as a chest containing his confiscated possessions, and then serves as his coffin (in an interpolated funeral scene); at the end of the play, Exton brings on the same box as though it contained the truncated corpse of the deposed King.

Barton's *Richard II* was noted for its severe formal symmetries, and these symmetries also formed recurrent patterns: the Queen with her two ladies, the three lords plotting the return of Bolingbroke over the grave of Gaunt, and the Gardener and his two monk-like assistants, all mirror one another. Bolingbroke furtively returns from banishment walking alongside Northumberland's black hobby horse; Richard returns from Ireland on a free-standing white horse symmetrically flanked by his followers; and Richard is taken off to prison tethered between two symmetrical hobby horses.

I have purposefully not talked about many of the stylistic excesses and overstated metaphors of the production that so excited and angered many scholarly theatregoers of the time: the Duchess of Gloucester's resemblance to a Noh-theatre ghost, the masks (in the first few performances, at least) worn by the Queen's ladies, the Welsh Captain's report spoken antiphonally like a Greek chorus, or Northumberland's appearances late in the play as a giant black bird of prey on stilts. I have not mentioned the all-too-literal pair of staircases flanking the set, on which a hydraulic bridge rose and fell with the King's fortunes, most notably as Richard descended Phaeton-like into the base court, his pleated circular metallic-gold robe glistening in an amber spotlight like the sun. Nor have I said anything about the play's central meta-theatrical Player-King metaphor, which was established in the opening pantomime, in which an actor dressed as Shakespeare and carrying the First Folio (the same book later used by Gaunt and Richard) stands between Richard Pasco and Ian Richardson and decides who will play the king that night. The metaphor reaches a climax in the moment when the Groom pulls off his hood and reveals himself to be Bolingbroke (or an image of him), and looks at Richard through the empty frame (that prop again!) as though they were mirror-images of one another; and it is rounded off in the closing pantomime, in which the two actors flank a crowned figure of death.

The most interesting thing about Barton's production, for our purposes here at least, is not what the director was trying to say about the play in his production, but the system of aesthetic conventions he employed to say it. The conventions were no doubt devised to serve a specific thematic reading of the play: Barton ritualized his stage images in order to emphasize the ceremonial theatricality of kingship and the play-acting inherent in the king's two bodies. The choric effects and rigid symmetries, which helped to create a sense of a complex ritual of kingship, stripped down the physical action to a set of clear and direct visual signs. For all of the visual embellishment, the production actually pared things away. York brought on news of Bolingbroke's invasion wearing an incongruous metal neckpiece over his white gown, as the Queen describes him entering "With signs of war about his aged neck"; Ross and Willoughby enter booted when they are described as "Bloody from spurring, fiery-red with haste." This economy of means is, of course, typical of the Elizabethan theatre, and proved wonderfully suited to the play: after all, when York and his Duchess quarrel about whether York should go to King Henry and reveal Aumerle's treachery, they fight with a servant over a pair of boots.

Barton's *Richard II* is not necessarily typical of the productions of the RSC of the period. Indeed, it is not possible to characterize a company style or aesthetic in a decade that included the stripped-down white gymnasium of Peter Brook's *A Midsummer Night's Dream* (1970); the hydraulic neo-Gordon Craig stage machinery for Trevor Nunn's Roman season (1972);

Terry Hands's kettle-drum and follow-spot productions of *Henry IV*, *Henry V* (1976), *Henry VI* (1977), and *Coriolanus* (1977); the timber unit-setting shared by *King Lear*, *Much Ado About Nothing*, and *Troilus and Cressida* in 1976; Buzz Goodbody's *Hamlet* (1975), Trevor Nunn's *Macbeth* (1976), and John Barton's *Merchant of Venice* (1978) at the Other Place; and Michael Bogdonov's modern-dress *Taming of the Shrew* (1978), to name only a few of the more prominent examples. These and many other productions had widely differing approaches to cutting and transposing the text; to the interpolation of pageantry and processions; to Elizabethan, period, contemporary, or "neutral" sets and costumes; to pictorial or spatial composition; and to the relative prominence of an overriding interpretation.

But Barton's extravagant and highly-conceptualized *Richard II* is indicative of a way of thinking about the aesthetic conventions governing the plays which potentially can describe the larger body of the company's work during the period. This way of thinking began in the late 1960s, when the young Trevor Nunn succeeded Peter Hall as artistic director; and it arguably peaked and began to decline at the beginning of the 1980s.

Sally Beauman marks the transition in the 1960s when she describes the "Moss on the Tomb" scandal attending the final rehearsals of Nunn's production of *The Revenger's Tragedy* at Stratford in 1966. Hall had left for London, leaving Barton in charge of operations. Barton and Hall at that time were committed to the gritty "Berliner Ensemble naturalism" which had characterized the Hall/Barton *The War of the Roses* (1963): "if a messenger came on from a presumed journey then he must have conspicuous mud on his boots" (Beauman 292, quoting Terry Hands). For three days (until he finally relented), Barton quarreled with Nunn and his designer, Christopher Morley, insisting that the tomb have a layer of moss on it.

This in-house controversy exemplifies a fundamental shift in understanding about the way that theatrical signs are read by an audience: a shift from the notion of decor as a verisimilar indicator of fictional context (a tomb with moss on it), to one in which each element of decor, and each prop, entrance, stage grouping, or piece of business, is a single element in a larger poetic pattern of signification (the tomb in relation to other tombs, other horizontal objects, other actions of burying, etc.).[4] Perhaps the most aggressive statement of this newer aesthetic was Brook's *A Midsummer Night's Dream*, not, as Styan argues in *The Shakespeare Revolution*, because it represented the crowning achievement of the revolution in non-illusionism which began with William Poel and Granville Barker, but because the production was all foreground and no background. The white walls of Sally Jacobs's box is a frame without a picture, a context which provides no context at all, a space which is emptied of information so that it can be filled with the information provided by the theatre event itself. The issue is not a matter of illusionism or non-illusionism, but of figure and ground.

The RSC did not develop a single means of emphasizing figure over ground. But every time they experimented with a technological or grandly conceptual solution, they almost immediately pulled back from the experiment: the hydraulic lifts installed for the Roman plays in 1972 were not replicated at the Aldwych in 1973, where the productions were restaged with simpler units and elements; Barton's *Richard II* was remounted in 1974 without the staircases or the bridge, with the pedestal for the throne serving as the only fixed scenic element; the 1976 experiment at Stratford with a fixed Elizabethan-style gallery behind the stage was not repeated. In each case, the directors and the designers invented a mechanism for foregrounding the actor, the object, and the gesture; and every time they did so, they ultimately discovered that they could still convey the foreground without using the new mechanism. This tendency ultimately led directors away from the mainstages of the Royal Shakespeare Theatre and the Aldwych to the neutral, non-frontal spaces of the Other Place and the Warehouse; and it ultimately led to the construction of the aggressively non-frontal Elizabethan-inspired Swan Theatre.

This emphasis on signifying objects in space corresponded to a freshly articulated understanding of the relation of these objects to one another. Actors in Barton's 1978 *Merchant of Venice*, speaking at the Shakespeare Institute conference that year, told of the director rehearsing the series of scenes leading up to Jessica's elopement as a single unit, in order to emphasize musical modulations in tone and rhythm. Terry Hands began to refer to the plays as "poems," because of their visual and theatrical organization of images. He writes in his introduction to Sally Beauman's volume documenting his 1976 *Henry V*:

> We talk so much about Shakespeare's poetry that I feel we often forget how limited our real view of that poetry is. There are endless discussions about metre, and stopped lines, parenthesis, colour. Yet all those discussions seem to remain at one level, that of the line itself. . . . But surely this is not the case. He creates people, talking really, *within* a poem. There is poetry in structure, in juxtaposition, in rhythm. A poem is communication through image – and it is an ambiguous communication at that. Each individual image defies analysis, and together they add up, not to a thesis but to an experience. The ambiguity is intentional. The less it is explained by decor and costume, the greater is its richness. Whatever else we attempted or achieved in the production of *Henry V*, everything – rehearsals, staging, performance – was aimed at communicating its poetry. Not just the spoken line, but the real poetry of the whole. The golden armour of the French, Henry's armour for his coronation in *Part Two*, the follow spots, Farrah's canopies, Guy's music, the empty stage, the

> actors' changing styles and utterance, all were images within the overall poem.
>
> (26–7, Hands's emphasis)

The director's role in identifying the images, and in shaping the "poem," is not passive: the other interviews in Beauman's volume testify to Hands's willingness to adapt and transform the shape of the text and the play's visual imagery to suit his own purposes, and the company's shared sense that they not infrequently knew better than Shakespeare how to create poetic juxtapositions and relationships. By the time the same creative team came together for the uncut *Henry VI* trilogy, Hands had refined his notion of a play's inherent poetic organization in performance. He chose "not to do even our own usual reshaping of a few corners and reorganizing the occasional speech," but "just to put it all very crudely, very naively down on the stage – everything that was there, warts and all, in the hope that one or two of them would turn out to be beauty spots." Dessen quotes this passage (from an interview with Homer Swander in *Shakespeare Quarterly*) repeatedly (see "Shakespeare and the Modern Director" 59), as evidence of a praiseworthy new trust in the uncut texts and the artistry of the dramatist. But whether the director theatrically manipulates the imagery of an overly familiar script or chooses to follow blindly the theatrical imagery of a relatively virginal text (though the director's hand was by no means absent in the *Henry VI* stagings), both approaches equally document a new sense of a play as an organic whole, organized around stage images composed of objects, gestures, groupings, props, and set-pieces, orchestrated in time and space.

The poetic organization of visual elements that characterized Barton's ritualized, formal, quasi-Greek, and pseudo-Asian *Richard II* was evident in many other RSC productions of the period which operated within different, aesthetically distinct production styles and concepts. The architectural styles of the overall structures which directors built from the playscripts were different, but the directors shared a sense of the basic building blocks and how they could be used. These basic building blocks included, for example, objects or set pieces which doubled or trebled their specific localized use: witness the chest, the mirror, and the book in Barton's *Richard II*, or the plinth which serves as both Juliet's bed and the tomb in Hands's 1973 *Romeo and Juliet*. Scenes could be overlapped or played simultaneously, sharing images or objects: in the Hands *Romeo and Juliet*, for example, Romeo appeared in Mantua above, and Balthazar spoke his description of Juliet's funeral, while attendants below transformed Juliet's bed into a bier. Directors learned new ways of exploiting the juxtaposition of verbal and visual imagery from the end of one scene to the beginning of the next: at the end of the Harfleur sequence in Hands's *Henry V*, the raked panel in the stage, which had served as the breach at

Harfleur, slowly sank back into the stage while Henry, weary from the siege, stood before it; Katherine, with her attendant Alice, standing behind the sinking panel, slowly came into view "like a Venus, rising from the waves," as though she was an image of the France that Henry hoped to conquer, or a reminder "of the curiously blank area in Hal/Henry's life through the three plays" (Beauman, *Henry V* 153). Directors learned to use the ensemble of actors, in and out of the characters they were playing, to similar effect: in Hands's *Henry VI, Part One*, when the fiends summoned by Joan abandon her, the company of actors, dimly visible in the darkness behind a downstage light-curtain, silently walked into the wings.

There was no clear RSC house "style" in the 1970s. But there was certainly a basic vocabulary of effects, a repertoire of theatrical elements from which a play could be built, a variety of ways that meaning could be generated on the stage, and a shared sense of how the overall meaning of a play in performance ultimately resided in the accumulated theatrical meanings of its individual parts.

* * *

> The modern director can learn from the scholar or critic a different, perhaps a neo-Elizabethan, habit of mind, a way of seeing the personae and events of a Shakespearean play not only as an exposition of character but also as an unfolding of a larger pattern that can be enhanced and driven home by action, staging and gesture. In such a pattern, units or sequences of plays have their own intrinsic interest yet can echo or prefigure each other, thereby yielding a complex multiple unity not apparent to the casual reader or to many an actor or director bound by his own sense of theater. Conversely, the excitement that a director gains by reshaping, cutting, or expanding an Elizabethan play may be at the expense of another kind of excitement present in the original that grows out of the divergent parts coalescing into a larger whole before the eyes of the audience.
>
> (*Viewer's Eye* 29–30)

Here, in 1977, the same year that *The Shakespeare Revolution* appeared, Alan Dessen argues for a "multiple unity" (a term he borrows from Madeleine Doran, who in turn borrowed it from art historians), and suggests that scholars can teach practicing theatre people to acquire a "neo-Elizabethan habit of mind." But it is clear that theatre people, at least at the RSC, had already acquired such a habit of mind, had already learned to look beyond the mere exposition of character to a larger pattern of action enhanced by stage imagery. And the images they had discovered in the scripts were created from patterns of props, set pieces, groupings, gestures, and symbolic actions, analogously linked in performance; from associations created by the juxtaposition of images from one scene to another, of words and images from adjoining scenes; and from the interplay of scenes taking place simultaneously, as though in two locations, on the same stage. Directors had discovered precisely those theatrical signals identified by Dessen as being characteristically Elizabethan.

How is it that Dessen and the principal RSC directors had acquired these same habits of mind? Styan would argue it was a result of a spirit of communication between scholar and practitioner, and a shared respect for the plays as scripts. Others might argue that, as a result of a steady evolutionary progression which started at the beginning of the century, the RSC directors and Alan Dessen had finally, simply, and inevitably, discovered the truth.

I would suggest instead that Dessen and the directors of the 1970s share much more than their coincidental discovery of certain Elizabethan staging principles. Their habits of mind lie much deeper, in a shared faith in the play script as an organic entity, with its own unity and integrity, an appreciation at least partially traceable (as Barbara Hodgdon argues) to F. R. Leavis, the influential scholar who was, it should be noted, Peter Hall's and John Barton's teacher at Cambridge. But what stage-centered scholars and theatre practitioners share goes even further. For if the script is a unified and integral work of art, then there must be, behind it, an authority: the artist, with a single artistic mind and imagination, who gives the work organization, unity, and integrity, who makes the play, in theatrical parlance, *work*.

For Dessen, this artistic authority is the playwright. Shakespeare "works" within a set of cultural codes and uses a set of aesthetic conventions that we do not necessarily understand and cannot necessarily recapture. Tamper with the theatrical fabric of the organic work of art; cut, delete, or transpose the text; impose a directorial interpretation or overriding metaphor, and you interfere with the integrity of the work, throw the ecosystem out of balance, unravel the fabric of the whole. If, on the other hand, you return to the original scripts, and return to the original stage directions, you can begin to understand how these stage directions, and the images they created, worked in the theatre. And by these means you can recreate in the theatre a work of art that is as organic and integral as was the lost original. Even if you cannot know the author's intentions, you can still see the patterns that the author's intentions shaped. Recreate the patterns in a way that your audience can understand, teach your audience to recognize these patterns, or at least condition your audiences to be subliminally affected by them, and you've recreated the play the author created.

Dessen titles his chapter on Deborah Warner's 1987 *Titus Andronicus* "Trusting the Script," and by this he means both trusting the uncut and unedited text (including, for example, the full length of Marcus's speech on discovering the mutilated Lavinia), and trusting the stage directions (such as "Enter Titus as a Cook"). *Titus Andronicus* is Dessen's ultimate test case, because directors have failed for so long to see that there was an effective, organic play encoded within the script; and because, once recognized, that original organic work of art is so hard to recapture. Indeed, Dessen finally doubts whether the original work of art can be captured at all. The "price tag" for creating an effective theatre piece out of *Titus*, Dessen writes,

> involves some form of "translation" wherein some significant features of the original script . . . are metamorphosed into images and effects deemed suitable or safe for today's audience. Like Philomela who is so much a part of this story, *Titus* can live on, even take wing in our theatres but, apparently, only at the cost of subtle or, in some cases, radical changes in its original script. (115)

Titus Andronicus, then, is the limiting case, the instance that defines the extent to which the past – the author's effects, through the author's means – can ever be recaptured.

The directors of the 1970s shared the scholar's sense of the play in performance as an organically unified entity created by an artistic authority; only they didn't always agree with critics, scholars, or even with one another, about who that authority is. The debates at the time about the Director's Theatre and the extent of a director's interpretive license, about Shakespeare "straight and crooked," questioned where authority in the theatre lay; but it didn't challenge the notion of authority itself.[5] Sometimes directors are willing to cede authority to the playwright; sometimes they claim that authority for themselves. One year, Terry Hands and his actors, rehearsing *Henry V*, may condescend towards what they perceive as Shakespeare's lapses; two years later, preparing the *Henry VI* plays, they speak of their implicit faith in Shakespeare's theatrical skills, even if they don't always understand the playwright's purposes in the effects they are recreating. John Barton directs a radically "crooked," but still recognizably Shakespearean, *Richard II* one year; and then he virtually rewrites Shakespeare for a disastrous *King John* the next.

The director, Peter Brook explains, uncovers the "hidden" play, something that's there in the play waiting to be found, but which remains hidden if the director isn't there to find it. To directors who claim that they only want to let the play speak for itself, Brook warns, "If you just let a play speak, it may not make a sound. If what you want is for the play to be heard, then you must conjure sound from it" (38). Whether directors define themselves as interpreters or as independent creators, as advocates or appropriators, as facilitators or repairmen, they are investing themselves, in the playwright's name or in their own, with authority, with the power to create a theatrical work in which the parts are carefully devised and precisely calculated to come together to form a lively, organic whole in performance.[6] For one brief period of time, in the mid-twentieth century, directors *did* define the script as a "score" waiting to be "realized"; no wonder that scholarly score-readers felt that they could finally communicate with them.

Stage-centered criticism of Shakespeare shares this sense of an organically unified work of art created by an author. The work of art resides, stage-centered scholars hasten to point out, not in the words of the script, but in the performance that can be built from it; and other artists, they acknowledge, are involved in the process of creating that performance. But, they argue, the work of art – the performance – is still shaped by the dramatist who originally created it, who encoded the performance he intended into the words and stage directions of the script; we only need to train ourselves to read them properly. Shakespeare, as a craftsman in the theatre, knew how to use the resources of his theatre to create his work of art. By understanding his theatre, we can be confident of knowing, if not what Shakespeare *meant*, then at least how he put his work of art together. Stage-centered scholarship is, therefore, perhaps the only branch of literary study where one can still practice the intentional fallacy with impunity.[7]

It is not surprising, then, that stage-centered Shakespeare scholarship spread its wings and gave itself a name in the 1970s, when Shakespearean directors were debating their own authority and devising new ways of orchestrating the experience of the overall work of art in performance. Nor is it surprising that Alan Dessen and the RSC would both be engaged in the activity of articulating the theatrical means by which Shakespeare put his work of art together, both in the mechanics of the theatrical parts and in the way the parts come together to form the whole.

Nor, finally, is it surprising that J. L. Styan should celebrate, in 1977, the twin triumphs of enlightened Shakespeare in the theatre and theatrical Shakespeare in the study. For the true "Shakespeare Revolution" of the day was neither scholarship, nor performance, nor the interplay between them, but a definition, historically specific to the 1970s, shared by both scholarship and performance, of what Shakespeare *is*.[8]

NOTES

1 The terms are Beckerman's.

2 Dessen's recent book on *Titus Andronicus* for Manchester University Press's "Shakespeare in Performance" series is dedicated "To Deborah, Brian, Donald, Estelle, and Sonia," the director (Warner), Titus (Cox), Marcus (Sumpter), Tamora (Kohler), and Lavinia (Ritter), respectively, of the 1987–8 RSC production of the play, which occupies the center of Dessen's study. The influence evidently flows in both directions: Patrick Stewart, in his chapter in *Players of Shakespeare* on preparing the role of Shylock for John Barton's 1978 production of *The Merchant of Venice*, acknowledges his debt to an earlier essay by Dessen on the Elizabethan stage Jew. Stewart's citation of Dessen, though, is not untypical of the way theatre practitioners read scholarship. Dessen writes about the dramaturgical function of an Elizabethan stage type, about character as a theatrical signifier; Stewart, an actor trying to inhabit a character's presumed

psychological interiority, reads Dessen's essay to justify his choice of an emotional action. Dessen writes about how a character functions; Stewart talks about what a person does.

3 I follow Dessen's telling practice, in his *Titus Andronicus* study, of using inverted commas when describing theatrical signs which we take to be real, e.g. "real," as opposed to abstracted or formalized, stage blood.

4 Trevor Nunn confirms that the RSC was developing a coherent performance aesthetic, and notes that this aesthetic preceded Brook's *A Midsummer Night's Dream*, in a series of interviews with Mary Judith Dunbar about his 1969 production of *The Winter's Tale*, quoted in her forthcoming book on *The Winter's Tale* for Manchester University Press's "Shakespeare in Performance" series.

5 The terms "straight" and "crooked" come from a review essay by Peter Thomson in *Shakespeare Survey*, in which he attempts to come to terms with the Barton *Richard II*.

6 Even John Russell Brown, in seeking to "free" Shakespeare from directors and scholars alike, is merely investing a different set of artists – the actors – with the power of creating an organic work in performance.

7 The new stage-centered textual scholarship of Steven Urkowitz and others is likewise based on this notion of the author's theatrical authority: each published text represents a distinct performance script; when the playwright revised the script, he revised not only the individual parts, but the way the parts fit together to form an organic whole in performance.

8 Alan Dessen, Barbara Hodgdon, Dennis Kennedy, and Phyllis Rackin shared their responses to an earlier version of this essay, and made valuable suggestions about revisions.

RERERENCES

Beauman, Sally. *The Royal Shakespeare Company: A History of Ten Decades.* Oxford: Oxford University Press, 1982.

—— ed. *The Royal Shakespeare Company's Production of Henry V for the Centenary Season at the Royal Shakespeare Theatre.* Oxford: Pergamon, 1976.

Brockbank, Philip, ed. *Players of Shakespeare 1: Essays in Shakespearean Performance by Twelve Players with the Royal Shakespeare Company.* Cambridge: Cambridge University Press, 1985.

Brook, Peter. *The Empty Space.* New York: Atheneum, 1968.

Brown, John Russell. *Free Shakespeare.* London: Heinemann, 1974.

Dessen, Alan C. *Elizabethan Drama and the Viewer's Eye.* Chapel Hill: University of North Carolina Press, 1977.

—— *Elizabethan Stage Conventions and Modern Interpreters.* Cambridge: Cambridge University Press, 1984.

—— "Modern Productions and the Elizabethan Scholar." *Renaissance Drama* 18 (1987): 205–23.

—— "Reviewing Shakespeare for the Record." *Shakespeare Quarterly* 36 (1985): 602–8.

—— *Shakespeare and the Late Moral Plays.* Lincoln: University of Nebraska Press, 1986.

—— "Shakespeare and the Theatrical Conventions of his Time." *The Cambridge Companion to Shakespeare Studies.* Ed. Stanley Wells. Cambridge: Cambridge University Press, 1986.

——"Shakespeare's Scripts and the Modern Director." *Shakespeare Survey* 36 (1985): 57–64.

—— *Titus Andronicus.* Shakespeare in Performance. Manchester: Manchester University Press, 1989.

Greenwald, Michael L. *Directions by Indirections: John Barton and the Royal Shakespeare Company.* Newark: University of Delaware Press, 1985.

Hodgdon, Barbara. "The Critic, the Poor Player, Prince Hamlet, and the Lady in the Dark." *Shakespeare Re-Read: The Text in New Contexts.* Ed. Russ McDonald. Ithaca, NY: Cornell University Press, 1994.

Sinfield, Alan. "Royal Shakespeare: Theatre and the Making of Ideology." *Political Shakespeare: New Essays in Cultural Materialism.* Eds. Jonathan Dollimore and Alan Sinfield. Ithaca, NY: Cornell University Press, 1985.

Styan, J. L. *The Shakespeare Revolution.* Cambridge: Cambridge University Press, 1977.

Taylor, Gary. *Reinventing Shakespeare: A Cultural History, from the Restoration to the Present.* Oxford: Oxford University Press, 1989.

Thomson, Peter. "Shakespeare Straight and Crooked: A Review of the 1973 Season at Stratford." *Shakespeare Survey* 27 (1974): 143–54.

Wells, Stanley. *Royal Shakespeare: Four Major Productions at Stratford-upon-Avon.* Manchester: Manchester University Press, 1976.

10

RETHINKING THE PERFORMANCE EDITIONS

Theatrical and textual productions of Shakespeare

Laurie E. Osborne

When actors and directors undertake to produce a Shakespearean play, they start from a text. They base their choices in staging, inflection, and motion on one of the myriad textual reproductions available, assuming its accuracy, its authenticity, and its originality as the backdrop of their specific production. In the case of productions of *King Lear*, those assumptions have been radically questioned by textual bibliographers who point out that most *Lear* texts offer a conflation of Folio and quarto materials which ultimately is neither authentic nor accurate in its representation of the "original" texts.[1] Now those who produce *Lear* on stage must face the question of which of its multiple texts to use.

I wish to extend the issue of textual multiplicity and its relationship with performance in rethinking the often-overlooked performance editions of the eighteenth and nineteenth centuries. These texts bear elaborate titles like "The Tempest, A play; by William Shakspeare. With prefatory remarks. The only edition existing which is faithfully marked with the stage business, and stage directions, as it is performed at the Theatres Royal. By Wm. Oxberry, Comedian," or more succinct claims like "Shakspeare's Two Gentlemen of Verona, A Comedy; revised by J. P. Kemble; and now published as it is performed at the Theatres Royal." Positioned by their aggressively theatrical titles, these editions are all but invisible to textual bibliographers and those who study the histories of textual editing. They are perceived as profoundly tainted in their relationship to the protean theatre because they frequently offer rearrangements of scenes, added dialogues and characters, and extensive cutting which revise in radical ways Shakespeare's "original" texts. They are equally suspect in the eyes of performance scholars who regard promptbooks and their notations as more useful and accurate in their representation of performance. However, performance editions are a significant site where textual studies and performance theory intersect.[2] It is my contention that the new work in textual bibliography opens up alternate editorial traditions, including editing which is grounded in performance. Just as important, the ongoing efforts in performance theory to explore the historical specificity of the theatrical reproductions of Shakespeare's works offer insight into the historicity of these texts.

The new textual bibliographers who acknowledge multiple texts validate textual alternatives beyond a new acceptance of both quartos and Folios. When textual studies reveal that we have only edited copies of Shakespeare's works and ask us to accept a range of copies as authentic texts, they open up not just plays like *Lear* to new consideration but also the rest of Shakespeare's works.[3] All Shakespearean editions are copies; there is no recoverable original, even for those plays like *All's Well that Ends Well* for which bibliographers suggest that the edited text was taken from Shakespeare's foul papers. In fact, the more vigorously textual bibliographers search for some singular, original authorizing text, the more obvious it becomes that there is no original to be found.[4]

The attempt to valorize the original is evident from the principles laid down for traditional bibliographic research. Fredson Bowers explicitly insists that determining the original source of an edition, Folio or quarto, is essential to establishing the editorial procedures used in approaching that material (*On Editing* 4). He also argues that the material practices in Jaggard's printshop obscure the text and suggests that "Ultimately we shall know more about the characteristics of these compositors so that something may be attempted in the way of lifting the veil of print that hides the underlying copy" ("Search for Authority" 32). More recent textual critics have urged a return to the earliest texts in order to study "not the author's 'original' perhaps, but what he hath left us" (Warren 35). Even Grace Ioppolo, who argues that Shakespeare's texts are inherently multiple because of his own revising, begins and ends her claim with the Folios and quartos. The aims here are admirable, and the rewards in terms of illuminating the text(s) are correspondingly valuable.

However, the very procedures these critics promote involve comparing copies, either to discover the origins for the early texts or to affirm their originality. Warren, Taylor, and others compare Folios and quartos to assert the original validity of both *Lears*. Ioppolo approaches Shakespeare in part by comparing Folios and quartos but also by extending her examination to the manuscript texts of other playwrights in the period to discover patterns of revision. Her work reveals that sixteenth-century written texts were constantly emended and altered in ways which typesetters often did not register as alternate versions. The concept of the "original" remains, but Shakespearean textual bibliography, old and new, derives from the fact that only copies exist. It is comparison, not origins, which authorizes any text.

In effect, seeking to unveil some original text or even treating Folios and quartos as the originals comes inevitably to implicate these readers in a comparison of copies, whether they recognize it as such or not. Even in the case of a single early text like the Folio *Twelfth Night* or *Macbeth*, there are implicit copies, versions suited to the abilities of different actors like a Viola who could not sing, cleansed of references to God in order to accommodate the Licensing Act, or revised with the inclusion of materials written by other playwrights (Ioppolo 80–4). However valuable such comparisons are in exploring Shakespeare's plays as they were published and circulated in the sixteenth century, they also implicitly confine the play historically to the presumed period of conception and initial publication.

This bibliographical research reinforces what performance critics have long maintained: there is no perfect, authorially sanctioned text of a script for performance. The productions of Shakespeare's plays reveal the flaw in imagining a fixed and immutable canon of his work, since every presentation, whether in text or performance, represents a version of the play, not the play itself. With this in mind, I shall apply to Shakespeare's plays the interrelationships between three ways of conceiving literary creations which textual critic Jerome McGann posits: the actual physical texts; the play whose features provide the site for producing those texts; and the work, identified as the "global set" of the texts and plays arising in the history of producing Shakespeare's plays, both on stage and in print.[5] I suspect, however, that my interest in the "global set" of all texts and plays extends beyond McGann's practical attentions as an editor to all texts which he perceives as contributing to the "literary" production of the work. Nevertheless, his insistence on the necessarily collaborative nature of texts and the "immutable law" (9) of change in the textual condition contributes valuably to my argument that textual theory and performance theory can and should be mutually illuminating.

Moreover, my approach to Shakespeare's texts deliberately complicates McGann's partially metaphoric decision to treat "every text . . . not as an object but as an action" (183). He makes the equation in order to insist on the historical specificity of particular texts – that is, their physical features and the historically contingent factors which have enabled and resisted the production of the poem or play as a physical, lexical object. Since a play is most often produced doubly as text and performance, the playtext is even more obviously identified as an action. In using McGann's formulation, I see the edited texts of the plays as more closely akin to performance than one normally would.[6] The multiple Shakespearean texts as well as the individual productions of the plays participate in their immediate context of enactment; both contribute to the work by positioning the play as a site of material reproduction.[7] This conjunction is displayed with particular effectiveness in the eighteenth and nineteenth centuries when performances and performance editions burgeoned simultaneously.

Long after the quartos or Folio of any Shakespearean play, editions appeared which register the theatrical alterations in his works. These performance editions are not authoritative in any sense that the textual bibliographers would accept – even their contemporaries deplored editions like Bell's for their editing practices as J. P. Genest's comments attest:

> In 1773 and 1774 Bell, a bookseller in the Strand, published an edition of Shakspeare in numbers, each number containing a play – this has been censured as the worst edition of Shakspeare ever published; which *strictly* speaking is true, as it presents the plays in a mutilated state. (439)

However, despite Genest's obvious disapproval, even he was willing to concede one area of importance: "in another point of view, this edition is very useful, as it is copied from the Prompter's book, and gives the names of the performers who acted the characters, as near the time of publication as Bell could procure them." As these comments suggest, the authority of these texts – like that of the Folio and quartos – lies in their position within a series of editions whose origins are self-consciously designated as the stage.

Precisely because of their status as secondary and ephemeral, in opposition to the scholarly enterprise of recuperating *the* Shakespearean text, these texts reveal most pointedly the ways in which playtexts, like other texts and performances, are always embedded in time. Performance editions both generate and display the multiplicity of the play's material existence in an historical continuum.[8] The editors continually negotiate the links between their texts and performances, striving to ally their product to the theatrical product and in consequence, paradoxically, producing elaborated coded texts. The resulting proximity of text and performance produces a distinctive editorial anxiety, as the text claims the primacy of the theatre to justify its textual variations and competes with the theatre by presenting itself as an alternative reproduction of the Shakespearean play.

This participation in reproducing Shakespeare's plays as *works*, in McGann's sense, forms the basis for the two major ways I will position the performance editions at the conjunction of text and performance. First, the complex strategies of self-representation in these texts produce bibliographic codes which link text to performance and simultaneously reveal the ambiguity of that linkage. Both the strategies and the editorial anxiety position the performance editions in a common editorial tradition with the Folio, for it, too, displays these features. Second, because of their alliance with theatre, these texts register more vividly than do scholarly editions the ideological pressures of the historical moment which positions both text and performance. As a result, I would argue against reducing these texts to statistical data and ignoring their additions and rewritings of the Shakespearean text as Halstead's very useful compilation implicitly does.[9] Indeed, their radical divergences from the scholarly norm are the features which are most useful.

The many performance editions of Shakespeare produced in the late 1700s and 1800s were inspired in large measure by the renewed attention to

Shakespeare in the theatre. When Garrick undertook his revivals of Shakespeare on the stage, an unprecedented flood of performance editions followed almost immediately, in part because of rapidly accelerated printing practices. From the Restoration onwards, most plays that were performed, even if only once, were published. This wholesale publication of plays, however briefly they appeared on stage, explains to some degree the many individual editions of less popular plays which were available. For example, *Oxberry's New English Drama* published *Two Gentlemen of Verona* in 1823 even though its own introduction to the comedy acknowledges that "the popularity or neglect of a dramatic piece is no unfair criterion of its value" and implies that the comedy "is constantly ill received in the Theatre." Despite its relative unpopularity, there were seven separate performance editions of the comedy published between 1774 and 1850.[10]

One reason for this increasing publication of performance editions was the Copyright Act of 1710 which gave playwrights ownership of their own works, at least for fourteen years. As a consequence, plays were more often sold by their authors than pirated, as some have speculated was the case with many of the quartos. Since the authors often insisted that the whole of their play be published, most performance texts published prior to Bell's did not follow the stage's alterations to the playtext. As Shirley Strum Kenny describes the publication of playtexts from 1660 to 1800: "Commonly printer's copy, while doubtless closely resembling the script sent to the play house, did not reflect the cuts and revisions made during the rehearsals in the early runs" (316). The speed of publication was one factor as playwrights whose works had been purchased by publishers sometimes sent their texts to the booksellers even before rehearsals had started.

Shakespeare's plays, however, represented an unusual case in this history of performance editions. Since he was not a living author, his copyright, according to the Act, was to remain with its current owner, Jacob Tonson. Once Tonson's rights were auctioned off in 1772, performance editions of Shakespeare's works began to proliferate, entering the marketplace with Bell who inaugurated a new approach to publishing such texts (Taylor, *Reinventing* 69–70). Bell paid closer attention to the stage production, including cast lists and cuts from performance; his editions (1773 and 1774), like the *New English Theatre* texts associated with Oxberry, offered "innovative popular editions which, for the most part, tried to reproduce both the reading and the acting texts, at least as far as stage cuts were concerned" (Kenny 327). In the case of Shakespeare, performance editors were unhampered by any authorial insistence that the whole text be preserved. Logically, then, it would seem that Shakespeare's performance editions could come closer to the theatrical production than other playtexts whose living authors might demand that the whole text be printed.

Although much more numerous than the available sixteenth-century Shakespearean texts, these editions relied on an appeal to the theatre audience comparable to the appeal which the quartos apparently had and which the Folio hints at when Heminge and Condell claim: "So much were your L L. likings of the severall parts, when they were acted, as before they were published, the Volume ask'd to be yours" ("Epistle Dedicatorie"). Even though some of the texts may derive from so-called foul papers, the Folio acknowledged that the source of interest for the text, like that for these later editions, lay in the performances which preceded the publication.

The strategies nineteenth-century performance editions used to ally themselves with the theatre, as well as the resulting editorial ambiguities, connect them with the Folio. The proximity these texts claim to performance is evident in the way Shakespearean performance editions, along with others, exploit the appeal of the theatre. The nineteenth-century foregrounding of current theatrical figures exceeds that of the Folio and quartos since most performance editions include the names of other authorities prominently in their titles or front pages. Whether through editorial acknowledgements as in *Bell's Shakspeare* (1774) and *Select British Theatre* (1815) or through overt recognition in the title of the volumes as in the cases of *Inchbald's British Theatre* (1808) and *Oxberry's New English Drama* (1823), including contemporary theatrical personnel in the editing process serves two distinct purposes. First, name dropping is one of the strategies which these editions use to draw their texts closer to the theatre and theatrical practice. Second, the prominent mention of theatrical personnel further confuses the issue of who was ultimately responsible for editing the individual text.

As an open gesture of acknowledgment to the theatre – however much (or little) actual theatrical promptbooks or personnel may have contributed to the edition – the association with contemporary theatrical production presumably helped to market the edition. Similarly, the preface of the Folio augments Shakespeare's name and texts by offering Heminge and Condell, familiar figures from the King's Men and Shakespeare's fellow shareholders, who present themselves as mere gatherers of Shakespeare's texts. Their posture effectively masks Jaggard's enormous responsibility in editing the texts. Since the attention paid to the Folio has unveiled Jaggard's role, the strategy implied in their introduction is less obvious than the use which later editions make of actors and other theatrical personnel. After all, the Folio editors had no need to convince their readers that their text was close to performance: that relationship was self-evident, as they acknowledge from the outset. The self-conscious positioning of later performance editions asserts a connection to the theatre which is largely understood in the Folio. The theatrical authorities invoked on their title pages assure their purchasers that they are buying a copy of the play as performed *now*, different from earlier performance editions and responsive to a specific, and transitory, historical moment.

In effect, however, these invocations of theatrical personnel are as suspect and complex as Heminge and Condell's simple gathering of papers has turned out to be. In the nineteenth-century performance editions, references to a variety of well-known people of the theatre were complicated by the fact that they actually participated in the preparation of the volume to widely varying degrees. Mrs. Inchbald, for example, was limited entirely to writing introductions to the plays:

> "One of the points of my agreement was, that I should have no control over the time or the order in which the prefaces were to be printed, but that I should merely present them as they were called for and resign all other interference to the proprietor or editor of the work."
>
> (As quoted in Manvell 128)

In fact, she did not even have any say in which works were to be included in edition:

> it cannot be too strongly emphasized that the plays were not chosen by her, and that, in many cases, one has only to turn to the prefaces to find out that, had she had her own way, this or that "lamentable tragedy" would certainly not have found a place among the candidates for classical honours.
>
> (Littlewood 104)

Given the limitations of Mrs. Inchbald's participation in preparing the volumes which bear her name, the question remains of who actually edited these texts.

Compare the "hands-off" editing of Mrs. Inchbald with the way the publishers of *Select British Theatre* acknowledge Kemble's involvement: "When the Publisher undertook the present work, he determined that every care should be taken to render it perfect: but he confesses that the task would have been beyond his means, but for the able and most friendly aid of Mr. Kemble. The unwearying attention of that Gentleman to these volumes while they were passing through the press has given the confidence of presenting a Correct Work to the Public" (*Select* I: viii). Kemble was apparently very much involved in preparing the texts for publication. Yet Kemble's texts in the *Select British Theatre*'s bound volumes show signs of being taken from his earlier, individually published copies of the plays rather than from any carefully gathered new collations. Kemble's biographer, James Boaden, does not even mention Kemble's editorial work for *Select British Theatre*, though he offers this description of Kemble's treatment of the plays he chose for performance:

> Now this, in Mr. Kemble's notion of the business, was, not to order the prompter to write out the parts of some old mutilated prompt-copy lingering on his shelves, but himself to consider it attentively in

> the author's genuine book; then to examine what corrections could be properly admitted into his text; and, finally, what could be cut off in the representation, not as disputing the judgment of the author, but as suiting the time of representation to the habits of his audience, or a little favoring the power of his actors.
>
> (Boaden 2)

The implication is that Kemble's "editing" of these plays took place in preparation not for publication, but for performance. Moreover, Boaden's comments suggest that Kemble adjusted his texts to his audience's expectations and his company's skills rather than deliberately editing for readers.

Though Mrs. Inchbald's involvement in her edition did not extend beyond writing the introductions and Kemble's contribution to the *Select British Theatre* texts was apparently large, these performance editions insisted equally on associating theatrical professionals with their texts. They present the plays as at least doubly authored, by Shakespeare and by the producer of the performance. In effect, all performance editions tend to offer the plays as collaborative efforts, associated with and created by both author and theatrical companies. This tends to obscure the task of textual editing in the process of emphasizing a relationship with the theatre, and consequently to underscore the performance edition's status as but one version of the play.

Paradoxically, achieving that association with the theatre often produces an array of new textual materials. Just as the treatment of stage directions in so-called bad quartos of Shakespeare's plays is taken as strong evidence of their origin in performance, so the stage directions published in these performance editions suggest a move closer and closer to the theatrical promptbook, with its notations of actions, props, and stage positions. The Dolby *Merchant of Venice* (1824) even includes a full page for the "Position of the Characters at the Fall of the Curtain," complete with an engraving representing the curtain in the process of coming down and an array of character abbreviations placed where the actors and actresses would occupy the stage – Jes. Lor. Ner. Gra. Ant. Por. Bas. Some of the editorial additions are explicitly intended to recall particular performances – Oxberry's engraving of Maria Tree as Ariel opposite the title page in *The Tempest*; the cast lists, single and multiple, given from Kemble on; commentary on particular performances in some of the introductions, like those of Mrs. Inchbald; and ever more detailed stage directions. The increasingly elaborate prefatory materials served to orient the editions in terms of their connections to actual productions, connections which the Folio had no need to enforce since it did not compete with a tradition of scholarly editions. While the quartos more commonly approached their connections to performance by indicating a specific occasion before a specific, and always illustrious, audience, nineteenth-century performance editors concentrated on the popular theatrical figures rather than the audiences.

Still other materials added to these texts seem aimed particularly at actors and directors as potential buyers, like Lacy's inclusion of page numbers for every character's entrance. By implying the text's usefulness for actors as one of its marketable features, *Lacy's Acting Plays* extends the theatrical materials in the performance edition to reflect a varied readership beyond the playgoer. In addition to its theatrically useful notations of the pages where characters enter and its extensive costume descriptions, Lacy's 1859 edition of *The Merchant of Venice* includes alternate endings for the comedy, thus outdoing previous performance editions like Inchbald's and Oxberry's. Whereas lightly edited versions of the final Act had been authorized from Bell on, Lacy offered a revision of the end of the trial scene which concludes the play with Portia revealing her identity immediately upon her success as the lawyer. The text marks the alternative with a dividing line and comments that "As this Play is sometimes performed in four acts, Dr. Valpy's alteration is inserted here, that being usually adopted." Interestingly, the edition produces a fascinating typographical confusion in its presentation of these alternative endings: they seem to be interleaved, since the editor relegates the alternative text to the bottom half of two successive pages. This text presents its alternate endings together, thus emphasizing the multiplicity of performance to the extent that a text can.

Whenever these texts are themselves taken up by the theatre, the blurring of the boundaries between performance and text becomes even more evident. Purchased and used by actors and directors, performance editions were often transformed back to performance when they became working texts in the theatre. Most promptbooks in the nineteenth century take one of these performance editions as their base text and then add their own markings or, as in the case of Samuel Phelps, restore missing materials.[11] John Philip Kemble often used his own published performance editions, marking new stage directions, additions, and cuts which might then in turn be incorporated in his new performance editions.[12] Thus the play produced as a text from performance could in turn produce more performances, leading in turn to more texts.

However, when the markings in the play text prepared for performance were brought explicitly into the editorial project, such promptbook notations became part of the bibliographic code or the paratexts of performance editions (McGann 13–14). Thus, paradoxically, the efforts to ally text and performance yielded an elaboration of textual materials in nineteenth-century performance editions which mirrored the increasingly involved annotations and materials which appeared in successive scholarly editions, culminating in the variorums. Texts within the same editorial tradition, whether scholarly or performance-oriented, competed through bibliographic one-up-manship in the nineteenth century. As Steevens, Malone, and Furness each produced editions which encompassed and improved on the textual annotations of the previous edition, each successive performance edition sought to outperform the one before. In fact, the competition for connections with the stage resulted in some editions whose verbal texts of a given Shakespearean play were practically identical – Kemble (1815), Oxberry (1821), and Cumberland (1830). These lexical similarities may result from one editor simply marking the earlier editor's text to be typeset as his own, a strategy familiar to those who examine the genealogy of scholarly editions and still practiced today. Nevertheless the bibliographic apparatus and strategies used for invoking the stage were distinctly different. Kemble included elaborate stage directions and cast lists; Oxberry offered as well an introduction, directional signals for exits, and often a final tableau; Cumberland added to all these innovations elaborate descriptions of the costumes for each character. The choices of what extra material to include became the differentiating factor, significant because such materials were, ultimately, directed at multiple audiences.

Another obvious purpose of these elaborations lies in the competition between performance editions and scholarly texts. Sometimes a performance edition even openly declared its allegiance to performance over scholarly editing, while revealing the ambiguities of the editorial procedure which I have been analyzing. As noted, the introduction of Oxberry's 1823 Edition of *Two Gentlemen of Verona* analyzes at length the infelicities of the comedy; it then asserts, "The foregoing observations upon the character of this play, refer to the copy left us by Shakspeare, and not to the altered drama, to which some of them are not exactly applicable. The reader will find, for instance, that *Valentine's* ungallant behavior toward *Silvia* has been expunged, that *Proteus'* attempted rape has been softened down, and that some attempts have been made to amend the construction of the fifth act" (viii). This introduction, which indicts the comedy with "An invariable failure to excite any interest, [which] pretty convincingly denotes that there is some inherent defect in its construction" (iii), thus closes by asserting that the present text includes alterations introduced by Victor. Although some revisions clearly met with Oxberry's approval, Victor also "improved" Launce and Speed in ways which lead this same introduction to assert baldly that "the attempt to 'copy Shakspeare's magic' has here, as in all other instances, been utterly abortive" (viii). In *Two Gentlemen*, the pressures of performance editing display dramatically the conflict between inevitable textual and theatrical revisions and the claims that Shakespeare's "magic" resists alteration.

One important effect of exploring these editions is to align the Folio's strategies and concerns more with these texts than scholarly editions. Linking the Folio and later performance editions illuminates an editorial tradition which produces texts positioned as copies, marked and possibly tainted by their relationship with the theatre's multiple performances. As textual studies bring valuable insight into the material production and bibliographic coding of performance editions, so attention to the texts' association with performance sheds fascinating light on the hazards of this particular editorial project. The problems attendant upon performance editing in both the early and later texts arise from contradictions between, on the one hand, the necessity of claiming the source of interest in performance and, on the other hand, the threat that the self-evident multiplicity of theatrical performances will taint the text with a similar variability. These contradictions produce an editorial anxiety as evident in the Folio as it was in the two most influential performance editions of this period, *Bell's Shakspeare*, presumably based on Garrick's promptbooks, and *A Select British Theatre*, based on John Philip Kemble's versions of the plays.[13] All these texts openly affirm the theatre as their authority and source of interest. The Folio insists that "though you be a Magistrate of wit, and sit on the Stage at *Black-Friers*, or the *Cock-pit*, to arraigne Playes dailie, know, these Plaies have had their triall alreadie, and stood out all Appeales" (A3). The claims of *Bell's Shakspeare* and the *Select British Theatre* are equally forthright. Bell announces that because "The THEATRES, especially of late, have been generally right in their omissions of this author particularly, we have printed our *text* after their regulations" (Bell I: 8). The introduction to *Select British Theatre* claims the plays "are given here as they are acted, and the Work may form a rational companion to the Theatre" (*Select* I: iv). In fact this introduction praises Kemble specifically for the "truth impressed by him on dramatic performances" (vii). Such truth presumably authorizes all these editions.

Despite this apparent assurance that the theatre is the appropriate source for these plays, performance editors also insist on the purity and stability of their texts, especially in comparison with other texts which are linked to performance. The Folio, for example, affirms its text in opposition to quartos, the "diverse stolne, and surreptitious copies, maimed, and deformed by the frauds and stealthes of injurious impostors" (A3). Bell's edition of 1774 actually takes the "original" Folio as a flawed performance edition which it must cure of "those cobwebs, and that dust of depraved opinion, which Shakespeare was unfortunately forced to throw on them" (Bell I: 6). *Select British Theatre* in effect echoes the assertion of the Folio that readers have hitherto been abused with flawed copies: "Whoever has cast his eye over the pages of the plays in common use, will have seen that AUTHORITY have they none; they are printed from copies of copies, corrupted and uncorrected; or what is worse, corrected into apparent meaning, but not that of the Author" (*Select* I: iv). These other copies were versions written for the theatre and thus inaccurate, yet Kemble's text often included even greater changes to the Folio and quarto texts. Thus each successive text offers its own performance edition while claiming to correct the intrinsic flaws in previous performance editions.

Just as important, these later texts often promoted themselves as a fixed standard which could limit the dangerously multiple and varying performances. Bell's edition openly seeks to impose its text on the theatrical professionals – "We would hope, that a reasonable standard being thus laid down, professors of drama [that is, actors and directors] will not be so forward, as capriciously and arbitrarily to deviate from it" (Bell I: 7). In *Select British Theatre,* the introduction castigates the flawed copies in very revealing terms:

> Here therefore is a fertile source of error, from which we are not likely to be preserved, but by some man of letters, who has the proper veneration for the Author, to lead him to seek for purity, and that Enthusiasm for the Stage, to desire him to fix it there, when it has been ascertained. Such a man is Mr. Kemble. (I: v)

Part of the rhetoric here is that of a vendor affirming the value of a new product; but the ambivalence toward, and even the competition with, the theatre is striking, especially since the theatre is claimed as the text's source.

The paradoxical claim that these editions offer a textual stability against which the stage itself should be measured is just one example of the contradictory attitude which the performance edition adopts towards its own materials. In the Folio, this editorial double bind between acknowledging and rejecting or ignoring the theatre is explicitly framed as a paradox in the Dedication: "We are falne upon the ill fortune, to mingle two most diverse things that can bee, feare, and rashnesse; rashnesse in enterprize, and fear of the success" (A2). Rashly publishing these trifles while fearing that their trivial collection will succeed, the Folio editors must admit the humbleness of their subject matter, playtexts, at the same time that they insist on the value of publishing them.

The later editions of Bell and Kemble echo this odd conjunction of humility and hubris. In the same preface where Bell affirms that his edition purifies Shakespeare's text, he mentions "a delicate fear" raised by Garrick that "the prunings, transpositions, or other alterations, which, in his province as manager he had often found it necessary to make, or adopt, with regard to the text, for the convenience of representation, or accommodation to the powers and capacities of his performers, might be misconstrued into a critical presumption of offering to the literati a reformed and more correct edition of our author's works" (I: 8). Considering that Bell has suggested the greater purity of his text as well as its usefulness as a fixed standard against which the theatre should be judged, this retreat from competition with the scholarly "correct" editions to affirm his own as merely "a companion to the theatre" is unexpectedly self-effacing.

Select British Theatre offers its own version of the editorial contradiction in a much condensed form: "Where the play called for curtailment,

[Kemble] omitted; where additions had been approved, he adopted; – but the basis must be the Author's, and should be preserved in its original state; – he therefore accurately copied the original text" (I: vi). Somehow Kemble can accurately copy the original but still radically rework the plays. As the humble transcriber of Shakespeare's original text, he nonetheless altered the text where it "called for curtailment" or even added to it, if need be. For example, his version of *Two Gentlemen of Verona* (1815) not only cut both Proteus's declared intention to force Silvia's love and Valentine's offer to give her to his friend, but also expanded Valentine's responses as he watches Proteus and added several speeches to Silvia's role which invent her sympathy for Proteus and her promotion of his marriage with Julia at the end of the comedy. Clearly the infelicities which the Oxberry editor laments led Kemble to introduce and reproduce a wide array of changes which somehow remain authentic to the Author's intention.

Because of curtailments and additions like those to *Two Gentlemen of Verona* and *The Merchant of Venice*, performance editions establish Shakespeare's plays as sites of ongoing reproduction, revealing the global set of material practices which establish a particular play's currency as a work. One set of examples demonstrating the importance of these texts within the work is the group of Kemble's four performance editions of *Measure for Measure* (1796, 1803, 1804, and 1815). The Duke's closing speech troubled editors from Warburton on, producing by the end of the nineteenth century extensive annotations. Both Vincentio's treatment of Escalus and Isabella and Shakespeare's treatment of his source came under considerable attention here. By the time of Steevens's 1798 edition, the last speech of this comedy was treated almost line by line.

To be sure, Kemble's text did not give lengthy footnotes at the end of the comedy – after Bell very few performance editors resort to footnotes. However, he added to the Duke's closing speech in order to resolve some of the issues left hanging at the end of the play:

> For thee, sweet saint, – if, for a brother sav'd,
> From that most holy shrine thou were devote to,
> Thou deign to spare some portion of thy love,
> Thy duke, thy friar, tempts thee from thy vow;
> In its right orb, let thy true spirit shine,
> Blessing both prince, and people: – thus we'll reign
> Rich in possession of their hearts, and, warn'd
> By the abuse of delegated trust,
> Engrave this royal maxim on the mind,
> To rule ourselves, before we rule mankind.
>
> (Kemble [1803] 68)

These lines re-establish the Duke's authority and, more important, render his courtship of Isabella much less peremptory in tone, expanding his courtship and justifying her agreement. Although the ten added lines appeared in italics in the 1803 performance edition, when they first appeared in Kemble's 1796 performance edition there were *no* indications that they differed from the rest of the Duke's speech.[14] Not only did Kemble add his own final lines and include various new cuts and re-arrangements, he consequently returned *Measure for Measure* to the stage successfully from 1794 through the mid-nineteenth century. Even Rosemary Miles, editor of the facsimile of his 1796 performance edition, while deploring the rampant changes which Kemble enacts in the playtext, acknowledges in her introduction that "to Kemble, as adaptor if not actor, remains much of the credit for helping this play out of the partial oblivion in which he found it" (iv). As the repeated performances and texts which inspired Kemble's attest, it is the combined influence of performance and performance edition which revive *Measure for Measure* by revising it and recreating it as a work.

Given the importance of rethinking performance editions both in terms of their relationship to the Folio and in relationship to each other, we tend to dismiss them too readily. Performance editing often radically shifts the sense of the play and, considered in relation to other editions, can offer fascinating revelations about the nature of such editions, including the Folio. Because of their marginal status, these performance editions respond more noticeably to the ideological pressures which also affect other, more scholarly productions of Shakespeare's texts.[15] Several of the examples I have already cited demonstrate how performance editions respond more emphatically to issues which concern scholarly editions as well.

Whereas scholarly editors wrestle with explaining the "indelicate" suggestions made by Julia in *Two Gentlemen of Verona* and Portia in *Merchant of Venice* as they adopt their crossdressed disguises, performance editions often cut outright these troublesome references to codpieces and crude masculine behaviors. Lacy's recorded alternative ending to *Merchant* completely eliminates Portia's sexual teasing about the possession and use of her "ring." Scholarly editors may analyze the infelicitous structure of the final scene of *Two Gentlemen of Verona*, but performance editions provide an alternative ending which reflects nineteenth-century ideologies of female chastity and masculine protection by cutting Proteus's offer to rape Silvia and supplying Silvia herself with a much more substantial response than the silence recorded in the early texts. This revised ending, like that offered in Lacy's alternate ending for *Merchant*, resolves conflicts between the sexualized representations of Shakespearean heroines and nineteenth-century ideological constructions of feminine virtue. Its reworking of Silvia's and Valentine's interactions in the final scene also resembles Kemble's revised final speech in *Measure for Measure*, as both emphasize how implicated masculine behaviors are in nineteenth-century models of proper female behavior. Taking such textual changes seriously is a crucial step toward uncovering how producing and reworking Shakespeare's plays not only extends them as works, in McGann's sense, but also registers historically specific ideological pressures like those operating in the developing construction of early Victorian femininity.

Just as important, attending to these texts exposes the significant interplay between material enactments on stage and on the page. This flexible interaction between material versions of the plays persists even in our current performance editions, the mechanically reproduced multiplicity of Shakespearean films available on tape and laserdisk. Like the performance editions of earlier centuries, ours join Shakespeare's name with those of current acting and directing talents. Even more vividly than the nineteenth-century editions, these video editions record performance choices, reproducing them as an integral part of what Shakespeare's works are now. The video editions even occasionally seem to share the ambiguous claim to be the authoritative version of a particular play, especially for many students who take the version they have seen as the play in its fixed form (especially in the case of the omnipresent BBC video editions). Nevertheless, their sheer reproducibility – demonstrated in the many available versions of single plays – insure that these, too, are only some of the multiple productions constituting the work. That such versions continue to move back and forth in different material forms is equally clear now when BBC television productions, among others, are reproduced again in textual form as screenplay texts.

I would like to close by considering briefly how film further inflects the dynamic interactions of the work, revealing the play not as a unitary object, but a site of reproductions. The play I have in mind, *Much Ado about Nothing*, is not one widely read in secondary schools and did not, until recently, possess the "name recognition" of *Hamlet* or *A Midsummer Night's Dream.* Until last year, I could be relatively sure that few students enrolling in my Shakespeare course would have heard of the comedy before. Kenneth Branagh's *Much Ado about Nothing*, produced in 1993, expanded the global set of the play's enactments to include its unexpected appearance as a feature film. This material reproduction in one of our most popular entertainment forms raised *Much Ado*'s cultural currency dramatically. The film, now available on videotape and widely marketed to academics from the beginning, serves as one striking example of this new form of performance edition.

Once more in this case, the performance edition challenges and tests the boundaries between text and performance. In fact, the videotape arrived in the stores only shortly after its screenplay, accompanied by stills from the film, appeared in bookstores under the title, *Much Ado about Nothing, By William Shakespeare: Screenplay, Introduction, and Notes on the Making of the Movie by Kenneth Branagh.* Branagh gives "film directions" not only for settings, film cuts, and expressions, but also for specialized camera manoeuvers. The paratextual materials beyond these markings within the screenplay include an introduction, a synopsis, a cast list in photographs, and two brief essays entitled "The Film" and "The Shoot." As in earlier editions, the efforts to authenticate this material reproduction as close to performance, paradoxically, produce multiple textual strategies and audiences. After Branagh details the changes he has made from the original texts, he makes a claim in his introduction which will sound familiar: "The adaptation was at the service of our attempt to find the essence in the piece, to find the spirit of the play itself" (xvi). The performance on film, which is obviously not identical to the text, belies this claim of a unitary spirit of the play. The very doubleness of these reproductions refutes the singularity assumed by "the spirit of the play itself."

Furthermore, although some would suggest that the film (or videotape) is the performance and the book I have just described is the performance edition, the two are actually so complexly interwoven that they both combine performance and edition. The filmed performance – in its film editing, its reproductions, and its marketing as a material product – binds together the supposedly ephemeral and historically grounded performance with the supposedly fixed, repeatable, and transcendent text. Far from securing the textual form as the performance edition, the similar marketing, sale, and treatment of the videotaped and textual reproductions locate both as performance editions: together they reveal their mutual participation in the work, *Much Ado about Nothing*.

Theorizing the performance editions does not seek to bridge some imagined gap between text and performance; instead, it underscores the crucial relationships between historically grounded, materially reproduced versions of the plays. Produced on stage, on paper, or on film and videotape, multiple productions reveal the play as a set of possibilities for material realization. Only exploring the interrelationships of the versions – the work in its range of enactments – can clarify how a given play is constituted as a site for meaning at a given time. Whether the time which interests us is the sixteenth century, the nineteenth century, or the last ten years, performance editions are a crucial component of our investigation into both text and performance.

NOTES

1 Randall McLeod, in "UnEditing Shakespeare" offers numerous examples of how the editorial treatment of *Lear* in particular revises the *Lear* texts without leaving any sign of the alterations imposed on the Folio text. Michael Warren eloquently calls for a return to the Folio in "Textual Problems, Editorial Assertions in Editions of Shakespeare." See also the important collection addressing *Lear, The Division of the Kingdom: Shakespeare's Two Versions of Lear*, ed. Gary Taylor and Michael Warren.

2 For this reason, I am also renaming these texts. Although they have commonly been labeled "acting editions," that appellation does not convey the collision/

collusion between the totality of performance and the entirety of text which "performance edition" conveys.

3 Jonathan Goldberg's essay, "Textual Properties," calls strongly for such a consideration of this new work in bibliography, but does not sufficiently explore the theatrical element which his title could also suggest.

4 Peter Stallybrass and Margreta de Grazia make similar arguments against the concept of the original in "The Materiality of Shakespearean Text."

5 As McGann frames these in *The Textual Condition*: "The 'text' is the literary product conceived as a purely lexical event; the 'poem' is the locus of a specific process of production (or reproduction) and consumption; and the 'work' comprehends the global set of all the texts and poems which have emerged in the literary production and reproduction processes" (31–2).

6 Harry Berger explores this proximity in terms of the creation of the reader as imaginary and imagining audience in *Imaginary Audition.*

7 The most thorough exploration of the play as a site for the material reproductions which make up the work requires the sustained examination of a particular play as in my book, *The Textual Erotics of Twelfth Night.*

8 The multiplicity I am suggesting differs from Ioppolo's multiplicity of revision principally in that I am unwilling to cleave to the author as the only legitimate source of revision. For me, as for McGann, time is the greatest reviser of all.

9 William P. Halstead in *Shakespeare as Spoken.* His work collates the cuts and other alterations in more than 5,000 promptbooks for Shakespeare's plays. Much of my information has been cross-referenced with his collations, though Halstead does not really distinguish between printed editions, which are my focus, and marked promptbooks and typescripts.

10 These are listed in Halstead: Bell (1774); Butters (1800); two Kemble editions (1808 and 1815); Oxberry (1823); Cumberland (1830); and French (1845).

11 Samuel Phelps, in his 1840 promptbook of *Twelfth Night* which uses the Kemble text, restores much of the Folio text that was commonly cut from the performance editions and in general aims to return the text to its Folio version.

12 For evidence of Kemble's re-marking of his own texts as promptbooks, please see Charles Shattuck's *John Philip Kemble Promptbooks.* My own essay, "Antonio's Pardon," traces the relationship between promptbook markings, including Kemble's, and the editorial addition to Orsino's speech at the end of *Twelfth Night,* pardoning Antonio.

13 For a discussion of these conflicts, particularly as they affect the texts of *Twelfth Night,* please see my essay, "The Texts of *Twelfth Night.*"

14 *Measure for Measure, 1796,* adapted by J. P. Kemble, facsimile edition.

15 For an excellent analysis of the ways performance texts reveal ideological pressures evident in other editions of a play, see Michael Neill's "Unproper Beds." He does not confine himself to editions and so treats promptbook evidence as well, but his discussion of how the prejudices evident in performance texts relate to those of critics and editors of the play suggests that these editions can be a rich source for understanding the ideological pressures on other editorial endeavors.

REFERENCES

Berger, Harry. *Imaginary Audition: Shakespeare on Stage and Page.* Berkeley and Los Angeles: University of California Press, 1989.

Boaden, James. *Memoirs of the Life of John Philip Kemble, Esq.* Vol. II. London, 1825.

Bowers, Fredson. "A Search for Authority: The Investigation of Shakespeare's

Printed Texts." *Print and Culture in the Renaissance.* Ed. Gerald P. Tyson and Sylvia Wagonheim. Newark: University of Delaware Press, 1986.
—— *On Editing Shakespeare.* Charlottesville: University of Virginia Press, 1966.
Genest, John P. *Some Account of the English Stage from the Restoration in 1660 to 1830.* Vol. 6. Bath: 1832.
Goldberg, Jonathan. "Textual Properties." *Shakespeare Quarterly* 37 (1986): 213–17.
Halstead, William P. *Shakespeare as Spoken.* Ann Arbor: University of Michigan Press, 1979.
Holderness, Graham. "Radical Potentiality and Institutional Closure: Shakespeare in Film and Television." *Political Shakespeare: New Essays in Cultural Materialism.* Ed. Jonathan Dollimore and Alan Sinfield. Ithaca, NY: Cornell University Press, 1985.
Ioppolo, Grace. *Revising Shakespeare.* Cambridge, Mass.: Harvard University Press, 1991.
Kenny, Shirley Strum. "The Publication of Plays." *The London Theatre World: 1660–1800.* Ed. Robert D. Hume. Carbondale, IL: Southern Illinois University Press, 1980.
Littlewood, S. R. *Elizabeth Inchbald and Her Circle: The Life Story of a Charming Woman (1733–1821).* London: Daniel O'Connor, 1921.
Manvell, Roger. *Elizabeth Inchbald: England's Principal Woman Dramatist and Independent Woman of Letters in the 18th Century England: A Biographical Study.* Lanham, MD: University Press of America, 1987.
McGann, Jerome. *The Textual Condition.* Princeton: Princeton University Press, 1991.
McLeod, Randall. "UnEditing Shakespeare." *SubStance* 33–4 (1982): 26–55.
Neill, Michael. "Unproper Beds: Race, Adultery and the Hideous in *Othello.*" *Shakespeare Quarterly* 40 (1989): 383–412.
Osborne, Laurie. "The Texts of *Twelfth Night.*" *ELH* (Spring 1990): 37–61.
—— "Antonio's Pardon." *Shakespeare Quarterly* 45 (Spring 1994): 108–14.
Shattuck, Charles. *John Philip Kemble Promptbooks: The Folger Facsimiles.* Charlottesville: University Press of Virginia, 1974.
Stallybrass, Peter and Margreta de Grazia. "The Materiality of Shakespearean Text." *Shakespeare Quarterly* 44 (1993): 255–83.
Taylor, Gary. *Reinventing Shakespeare: A Cultural History from the Restoration to the Present.* Oxford: Oxford University Press, 1989.
Taylor, Gary and Michael Warren, eds. *The Division of the Kingdom: Shakespeare's Two Versions of Lear.* New York: Oxford University Press, 1983.
Warren, Michael. "Textual Problems, Editorial Assertions in Editions of Shakespeare." *Textual Criticism and Literary Interpretation.* Ed. Jerome McGann. Chicago: University of Chicago Press, 1985. 23–37.
Willis, Susan. *The BBC Shakespeare Plays: Making the Televised Canon.* Chapel Hill: University of North Carolina Press, 1991.

Performance editions of Shakespeare's plays

Bell's Shakspeare. London, 1774.
Inchbald's British Drama. London, 1808.
Lacy's Acting Plays. London, n.d.
Measure for Measure, 1796, adapted by J. P. Kemble. Ed. Rosemary Miles. London: Cornmarket Press, 1970.
The Merchant of Venice, A Comedy. Dolby's British Theatre Vol. VI. London, 1824.
The Merchant of Venice: A Comedy. Lacy's Acting Plays. Vol. 25. London, n.d.

Much Ado About Nothing, By William Shakespeare: Screenplay, Introduction, and Notes on the Making of the Movie by Kenneth Branagh. New York: W. W. Norton & Company, 1993.
Select British Theatre. London, 1815.
The Tempest. Oxberry's New English Drama. London, 1823.
Two Gentlemen of Verona. Oxberry's New English Drama. Vol. 17. London, 1823.
Two Gentlemen of Verona. Select British Theatre. Vol. I. London, 1815.

11

DROWNING THE BOOK

Prospero's Books and the textual Shakespeare

Douglas Lanier

> In one of the rooms of the Fortuny Palace there are eight books from Prospero's Library. They are magical books. In many senses all books are magical. Fortuny had a library in which many of the books were manufactured by him, for he had the engrossing and engaging habit of booking every phenomena [*sic*] – photographs, texts, postcards, ephemera, which by their juxtaposition and organization on consecutive pages of a book gave them the characteristics we expect of a book – display, sequence, order, chronology. A film has the same characteristics – display, sequence, order, chronology – but, in its linear, rolling, celluloid shape, the film may competently refer back to an earlier order of textual display that preceded the book – the scroll – a linear exhibition of facts and events. However the scroll, like the film, has a superb advantage. With a film the eye is only permitted to read one image at a time and the brain has to remember the sense of sequence. With a scroll the eye has no trouble at all in scanning the immediate past and the immediate future almost the same time as it views the present. Maybe we should re-invent the cinema as a scroll.
>
> (Greenaway, *Watching* 22–3)

For recent performance criticism, the phrase "Shakespeare wrote for the stage, not for the page" has become something of a rallying cry. Questioning our conception of Shakespearean textual authority, at least as an ideal against which Shakespearean stagings might be judged, has become an enabling ritual of performance studies. The irony is that despite the ascendancy of performance the opposition of stage and page continues to shape Shakespearean criticism, although the polarity of that opposition has been largely reversed (Worthen 445; see also Levin). Against the protocols of close reading, where from the comfort of the study a reader can tease out surpluses of textual meaning, we have learned to set the practical demands of theatrical performance, where an actor must render meaning in definite intonations and actions. Against the authority of the

Shakespearean text – particularly that editorial chimera posited by earlier generations, the single definitive copy as it issued from the author's pen – we have learned to set the historical panoply of Shakespearean performances. For those critics willing to embrace the post-modern tiger, Shakespeare has become (indeed, always was) Shakespeare*s* (see Goldberg), a series of culturally specific, multiply-mediated historical events to which any given Shakespearean text is an incomplete and certainly not a regulatory guide. In fact, the question of how to conduct Shakespearean criticism in the absence of a determinant critical object has preoccupied many in our critical generation.

Nevertheless, for all its radical implications the adage "Shakespeare wrote for the stage, not for the page" reveals, by the logic of negation, the very tenacity of the fact it seeks to efface: that Shakespeare has come to us principally as a book. Unlike Renaissance audiences, who experienced Shakespeare's work first and, for many, solely in performance, modern audiences almost invariably encounter Shakespeare first as a text or, at the very least, with an awareness that a "literary" text subtends what they see on the stage. This simple phenomenological distinction has sweeping and stubborn implications. The extraordinary authority of the Shakespearean text, at least in the eyes of most outside the academy, has tended to render modern performances of Shakespeare supplemental, fleeting theatrical variations, of varying authenticity, on a prior, originary book. Thus it is not by chance that, as Michael Bristol observes, "the historical success of textuality and of the powerful institutional apparatus that supports it coincides with the virtual collapse of theater as a strong, independent center of cultural authority" (Bristol 97; see also 91–119). We can glimpse the intimidating shadow that the Shakespearean book casts upon the stage in a notice printed in Royal Shakespeare Company programs: "*Please* would you bear in mind that following the text during the performance is very distracting to the performers especially when you are seated in rows close to the stage." This plea acknowledges, in the very high temple of Shakespearean performance, the tension between the textual and the theatrical Shakespeare. Shakespeare can take the stage only insofar as the actors are not made to stand before the judgment of his book.

For this is not *a* book: it has become *the* quintessential text, the *Ur-book*, the model for English literary textuality, not a script but secular scripture. This book has functioned historically as a crucial touchstone for editorial and interpretive procedures which, being first successfully applied to the Shakespearean text, can then be extended to literary practice in general; that function has continued, ironically enough, with poststructuralism, cultural materialism, and even performance criticism itself. Its widespread status as a cultural icon is difficult to overestimate. An edition of Shakespeare is prominently displayed as a talisman in the ready room of *Star Trek*'s Captain Jean-Luc Picard, our generation's most popular intellectual hero. The most important Shakespearean text, the First Folio, is, it is safe to say, the single most recognizable book in literary history, and its aura has come to underwrite everything from advertisements for beer and copying machines to the Folger Shakespeare Library. Even though the First Folio eschews many of the monumentalizing strategies that characterize other Renaissance folio publications, it has nevertheless become, as Ben Jonson predicted, a "moniment without a tombe." In their letter to its first readers, Heminge and Condell purposely conflate the restored textual corpus and the resurrected authorial corpse when they promise a body of works "now offer'd to your view cur'd, and perfect of their limbes . . ., absolute in their numbers, as he conceived the[m]." Even the rather plain Droeshout engraving of Shakespeare, a portrait without the typical accoutrements of laurel leaves, architectural frames, classical verses, or even a determinate background, has come to emblematize, with Shakespeare's eyes gazing out to meet ours, the book's promise to its readers: unmediated contact with its author. In short, for us Shakespeare has become his book, and in so doing has acquired the qualities of an artifact – physical presence, permanence, costliness, monumentality – qualities to be set against the ephemerality and twice-removedness of performance.

Little wonder, then, that performance criticism would cast the textual Shakespeare as its threatening *doppelganger*. One strategy for exorcizing that threat has been to co-opt the text as a theatrical document; that is, to see it as a performance score, reading it, as John Barton and Cicely Berry do, as a meticulous blueprint for its stage performance, instructive to the actor in its every detail, down to fine points of metrics, line endings and punctuation (for examples, see Barton, Berry, and Hapgood). John Barton's *Playing Shakespeare* series, shrewdly discussed by William Worthen, provides an instructive example. Barton sets his approach against that of literary critics, who tend to value sweeping pronouncements about meaning without much regard for practical matters of staging. Whereas the critic replaces the opaque text with his own commentary, standing in Shakespeare's stead, the actor, so Barton maintains, merely serves as a conduit for Shakespeare's voice encoded in the theatrical score. To demonstrate, Barton prompts David Suchet to read a high-flown critical passage about *Hamlet*'s ambiguity, then directs Michael Pennington in mock earnest, "come and follow that." This critic-bashing gesture, one which, Worthen points out, also draws upon tensions between America and Britain for cultural authority over Shakespeare, reveals Barton's need to rob the textual Shakespeare of its power as a precondition for authorizing the performative Shakespeare. As Worthen points out, Barton fails to acknowledge the extent to which his attention to "commonsense" performability masks the ideological embeddedness of modern acting. One might add that Barton also fails to acknowledge that the "score" his actors "realize" comes to us, even in its earliest forms, mediated by interests arguably unconcerned with performability: copyeditors, typesetters, booksellers, readers (see Dillon). It is, in other words, as a condition of its preservation no longer merely a "script." More to the point, Barton's strategy of recasting the text as a theatrical "score" paradoxically invests the text with even more authority, with the consequence that its every jot and tittle articulate a theatrical intent that any given enactment can only aspire to.

Another tactic for exorcizing the textual Shakespeare has been to forge an affiliation between performance criticism and textual criticism. Like many performance critics, revisionist editors have sought to show that the various textual records we have inherited from the past do not point toward some single authentic Shakespeare but are, like performances, variants without a standard. Indeed, many have gone so far as to argue that textual differences have their beginnings, or at least their analogues, in different performances before different audiences. A superb summary of this approach can be found in Stephen Orgel's two articles on Shakespearean textual authority, "What is a Text?" and "The Authentic Shakespeare." In the former Orgel stresses the lack of secure authorial imprimatur on any dramatic text we encounter from the Renaissance. By 1988, however, the terms of his argument have subtly shifted. In "The Authentic Shakespeare," Orgel argues that Shakespeare himself wrote anticipating the lack of final authorial control – wrote, in other words, assuming that his script would be cut or changed, in accordance with the conditions of Renaissance playhouse practice, "a situation he understood, expected, and helped to perpetuate":

> And it implies as well that Shakespeare habitually began with more than he needed, that his scripts offered the company a range of possibilities, and that the process of production was a collaborative one of selection as well as of realization and interpretation. (7)

Here Shakespeare's intent is extended over various performances of the script, in Orgel's words its "range of possibilities," and by making the process "collaborative" Orgel manages to retain Shakespeare the author as an integral part of the playhouse proceedings after the script left his hands. The effect of this argument is tacitly to suggest that Shakespeare anticipated and approved both textual and performative variations. Thus, in an article that outlines the problem of an authentic Shakespearean authorial imprimatur, Orgel offers a hypothesis suggesting that revisionist bibliographic and performance studies have the best claim to Shakespearean authenticity, or, more precisely, an authentically Shakespearean inauthenticity.[1]

Thus for all their desire to do so, performance criticism and its allies have not quite left behind the problem of the author and the authoritative text. The battle cry "Shakespeare wrote for the stage, not for the page" seeks to authenticate performance approaches by making them accord with Shakespeare's general (if not specific) *telos* for his work, by suggesting that since Shakespeare wrote anticipating variations we are warranted in studying them. Yet even this valorization of Shakespearean *différance* has not had the effect of dispelling the immense authority of the Shakespearean text. Quite the contrary: by refetishizing the textual archive in its every material particularity, the new New Bibliography has simply extended Shakespeare's cultural aura to ever more documents. In fact, the extraordinary attraction and authority of the "document," increasingly a feature of the construction of editorial authority in revisionist circles, itself begs to be placed in a wider cultural perspective, that of the late capitalist nostalgia for the "uniqueness" of hand-reproduced artifacts, a nostalgia particularly acute in an age of electronic reproduction. Arguably the rise of performance criticism is a recuperative response of literary institutions to the challenge of video and cinematic media as newly hegemonic bearers of cultural authority. So long as Shakespeare remains textual, his fate (and the fate of the institutional apparatus harnessed to him) is tied to a specific medium – the book – whose cultural supremacy is now under serious challenge. But once Shakespeare is (re)grafted on to performative media or textual documents (re)conceived as performative scores or unique artifacts, he and the cultural capital he represents can be uncoupled from the decline of the book in an increasingly post-literate society.

I rehearse this familiar competition between stage and page not to endorse the longstanding prejudice against the theatre chronicled by Jonas Barish or to reinstate the Shakespearean text as an essentialist or transhistorical ideal. Rather, I want to observe that the Shakespearean book is part of the historical legacy under which modern Shakespearean performance has labored. Because performance criticism has, as a gesture of self-authorization, felt the need to push away from the monumentality of the Shakespearean book, it has been slow to recognize the ways in which the burden of the text manifests itself in Shakespearean production, at least in those productions that choose to confront it directly. In many ways the cinema has more readily taken up the challenge of textual authority than has the theatre, perhaps because filming Shakespeare entails more consciously translating the work from one medium (and cultural register) to another. As early as 1916, in one of the first feature-length Shakespearean films, Edwin Thanhouser confronts the textual Shakespeare by opening his *King Lear* with the shot of acclaimed Shakespearean actor Frederick B. Warde reading a book. In close-up that book is revealed to be *King Lear*, at which, via a camera trick, Warde dissolves into the character Lear and the narrative proper begins (Rothwell and Melzer *Screen* 3; and Rothwell, "Representing" 75–7). Similarly, the burden of the book prompts a cinematic prologue for Kenneth Branagh's recent *Much Ado About Nothing*. The film opens with Emma Thompson as Beatrice reading the lines of the song "Sigh no more, ladies," as the words flash, sing-a-long style, on the darkened screen. The first shot, of an idealized watercolor landscape, is transformed with a camera's turn into a lush panorama of the real

Italian countryside. Both sequences serve the same end: to signal the subordination of a static artifact – the text, a painting – to its living enactment in the film. In both movies, the directors demonstrate, if only momentarily, the perennial struggle of Shakespearean cinema to free itself from the constraints of bookishness.

Of course, it has long been recognized that Shakespearean cinema has had to negotiate the problem of transferring stage performance into a fully cinematic vocabulary. Olivier's *Henry V*, to take a much-discussed example, addresses the issue from its very first shot of a wind-tossed playbill for the play's first performance at the Globe that emerges from a blue mist, as if blown from another time, to flatten itself against the movie screen. The image economically conflates theatre and film, Renaissance London and modern Britain,[2] and prepares the viewer for the metamorphosis from Elizabethan stage performance to cinematic epic that Olivier effects in the first reel. Unlike Branagh's *Henry V*, where the central drama is whether the callow Henry can become an adult epic hero, the dramatic focus of Olivier's movie as it opens rests not on Henry V, who is represented as psychologically complete from the first, but on Olivier the actor and whether he can inhabit the larger-than-life dramatic role of Henry. The first shot of Olivier, about to enter the stage from the tiring room, shows us an unlikely heroic figure: rouge-cheeked and beardless, effeminate in manner, offering a weak cough (see Donaldson 1–30). If there are credentials to be established in the opening scenes, in other words, they are Olivier's as a performer, not Henry's as a king, and in that regard the authority of the written text becomes a crucial foil. The bearer of that authority is the figure of the bespectacled prompter, a surrogate reader, the first of the acting company to cross the Globe's stage, bearing the script and acknowledging the viewer with a bow before seating himself stage-left. Throughout the Chorus's opening speech – indeed, throughout most of the first three scenes – we see the prompter at the edges of the frame, following the performance closely in his promptcopy. His function as a monitor of textual fidelity is confirmed when in the first scene someone misses the cue "Is it four o'clock?," and he leaves his seat to check why four bells did not sound. His omnipresence is a reminder of the textual ideal that casts its shadow over the performance we are seeing.

Thus it is relevant that the second scene is conceived as a send-up of textual authority, punctuated by Ely's strewing of documents all over the stage. As if to underline the thematic link, we see the prompter pay assiduous attention to his script as Canterbury comically explicates the documents relating to Salic law – both act as bearers of textual authority. This farcical sequence ensures that we see Henry V's claim to power transcending anything conferred upon him by Canterbury and Ely's bundle of documents. Rather, his stature as royal authority rests upon his theatrical declamations of patriotism, displayed first in the grand rebuke he wrests from the Dauphin's insulting gift of tennis balls. In Olivier's film, this sequence also addresses Olivier's relation to the authority of the Shakespearean script, for as he replies to the French ambassador, launching into the first extended demonstration of his stature as a performer, our view of the prompter and his book is, for the first time in the movie, blocked by Henry and his onstage audience. This image marks, I think, the replacement of one source of authority – the Shakespearean text, the document – by another – the theatrical virtuosity of Laurence Olivier and/as Henry V. Indeed, after this moment the break between Olivier the actor and the epic character he portrays is no longer foregrounded: royal and thespian legends have been successfully conflated. Even more significant is Olivier's exit: as he exits stage left, the prompter, who, we see, has removed his glasses and attended to the actor's performance without reference to his script, nods in deference to the actor. Olivier hardly acknowledges the gesture. This small, telling nod sets the seal of *textual* approval upon Olivier's performance, marking his fidelity not only to the classical British theatrical tradition, but also to the text the prompter holds in his hand, even as the gesture implicitly approves the replacement of that text by the movie performance we are seeing. Later, for Henry's departure from Southampton, Olivier shifts the focus of the scene from Henry's denunciation of the traitors (which he cuts entirely) to a grand declamation of his French campaign. The climax occurs when Henry moves to the foreground to set his royal seal to a document, so that instead of documents conferring authority upon him, with a marvelously theatrical flourish Olivier/Henry confers *his* authority upon *them*. On this "authentic" stage, where the authority of the original Shakespearean text over the stage is made especially visible, Olivier conspicuously establishes that the actor is king.

With the possible exception of Jean-Luc Godard's *King Lear* (see Donaldson 189–225), the most thoroughgoing attempt to confront this onus of a textual Shakespeare, and certainly the most controversial, is Peter Greenaway's *Prospero's Books*. Perhaps because he was first trained as a painter and only later ventured into film (see Rayns; see also "Peter Greenaway") and has consistently characterized himself as "still, primarily, a painter who's working in cinema" (Smith 60), Greenaway has been especially sensitive to the gap between the immaterial, transitory nature of the cinema and the monumentality of other art forms, particularly painting and, in his last several films, books. In fact, his entire cinematic canon might be fruitfully seen as an extended interrogation of those representational codes by which we make order of reality.[3] Those codes are, for him, exemplified by familiar masterworks of western art which constitute an ideal order of signification, masterworks Greenaway liberally recreates and deconstructs in his films. In *Prospero's Books* Greenaway recasts *The Tempest* within a filmic vocabulary that constantly acknowledges its competition with Shakespearean textuality while remaining faithful (or, perhaps more accurately, "faithful") to the play's received text.

Greenaway's interest in this project might be profitably seen in light of his other "high cultural" project, a video dramatization of the first eight cantos of Dante's *Inferno*, entitled *TV Dante*. Like *Prospero's Books*, this work employs images manipulated by video paintbox technology to create a kaleidoscopic visual experience filled with Greenaway's characteristically jarring images. And, as in *Prospero's Books*, John Gielgud supplies the main voiceover as Virgil. Yet unlike *Prospero's Books*, *TV Dante* seems to concede that the textual condition of the *Commedia*, as well as its cultural distance from the modern age, cannot be overcome, for throughout the stunningly illustrated episodes, Greenaway intercuts explanatory lectures by more than twenty historical and literary scholars. Essentially video footnotes, the lectures are handled seriously and not ironically, with the final effect that the images and text, work and commentary, are at war with one another. Of course, this procedure may have been partly imposed upon Greenaway by the demands of the mass-market television audience for which this work was destined, but in any case in this context *Prospero's Books* would seem to address the very disjunction that characterizes *TV Dante*, the gap between a historical text laden with cultural capital and scholarly commentary, and its modern performance or video realization. Whether Greenaway has overcome that gap in *Prospero's Books* has remained the key issue in its reception, as the terms of the film's many negative reviews reveal (for examples, see Alleva, Bernard, Brown, Nadotti, Turan, and especially Coursen).

The specific filmic vocabulary Greenaway adopts in *Prospero's Books* places the "literary" linearities of narrative and character at the service of the image, the spoken word, and the body. In many ways, *The Tempest* is an apt choice for this recasting, for its bookishness is everywhere manifest. The play occupies pride of place in the First Folio and, according to longstanding tradition, is Shakespeare's reflection upon and leave-taking of his writing career. Within the play itself, the power of books is ambivalently figured – Prospero's books give him access to powerful magic, but the seductive lure of retreat into those books also led to the loss of his dukedom, and Prospero's recognition of that temptation leads to his climactic vow to "drown my book." His ambivalence, we shall see, transfers to Greenaway's film in unexpected ways, at the most obvious level in Greenaway's insistence upon keeping books before our eyes while at the same time foregrounding the ways in which cinema as a visual and performative medium exceeds the formal capabilities of a written text. Greenaway's focus on the Shakespearean medium becomes clearer when one compares *Prospero's Books* with its avant-garde predecessor, Derek Jarman's 1979 film of *The Tempest*. Both productions share, as a reflex of their anti-realist cinematic aesthetics, an interest in the imagery of Renaissance hermeticism and a fascination with masque-like styles. Both are resolutely auteurist: Greenaway's central scenario, that Prospero imagines the events of the play, is an echo of Jarman's. One of the early scripts for Jarman's production featured Prospero as a mad Blakean magus, "recreating the performances of each of the characters while they visited him" in an asylum (Collick 99); as his film now stands, the last shot, of Prospero asleep in a chair, suggests that the entire film is his dream. In both of Jarman's scenarios, Collick argues, Prospero becomes a figure for the alienated bohemian intellectual, a reading which might easily be extended to Greenaway's treatment of Prospero. But whereas Jarman's approach critiques the politics of mainstream Shakespearean productions through camp, disrupting the play's status as an icon of straight high culture by irreverently mixing pop and high cultural references and stressing transgressive sexualities, Greenaway's attention is fixed on the question of the Shakespearean medium, experimenting with *how* the play's meaning is conveyed while essentially leaving the play's conventional heterosexual content and high cultural register intact. Jarman interrogates content, Greenaway form. Taking Prospero's books as his point of departure, Greenaway uses *The Tempest* to meditate upon the status of Shakespeare in an age of electronic performance. By problematizing the oppositions among text, performance, and film, that meditation produces a self-consciously hybrid form for Shakespearean performance and draws our attention to many of the unarticulated premises and practices of contemporary performance criticism.

Greenaway adopts several strategies in the film for addressing the burden of the Shakespearean book. First, he puts before us Prospero's act of reciting and writing down what will eventually become the text of *The Tempest,* showing us not a finished Shakespearean book but the imaginative process by which that book is produced. Until the final act, Prospero speaks all of the character's lines as part of his process of visualizing the work-in-progress. The play's action, much to the irritation of many reviewers, is radically de-narrativized, that is, handled as a series of static though visually sumptuous dumb shows that emblematize the text's imagery, rather than as the kind of drama of character familiar to twentieth-century audiences. The effect is to force a new relationship between spoken classical text and visual image: by eschewing the characterology of the realist stage and cinema, Greenaway is free to treat the text as a collection of intensely imagined verbal images that he can defamiliarize by (re)literalizing them as arresting visual tableaux.

Central to Greenaway's technique is the image of the written text, kept obsessively before the viewer. In a mise en scène littered with antique tomes, again and again the camera returns to Prospero as he scribbles out the foul papers in his study. Periodically passages of the handwritten text flash across the screen or are written on parchment as we watch. The recurring dip of Prospero's quill in watery blue ink serves as an important leitmotif, reminding viewers of the writing process that lies behind all they see. At its simplest level, this picturing of writing allows Greenaway to convert the Shakespearean text into pure cinematic image, to focus on the image rather than the meaning of the handwritten words. The script we are shown is at times elaborately ornamented with calligraphic flourishes (in a relatively authentic Italic hand). The handwriting even features visual puns – the "l" of the word "sail" is, for example, drawn as a ship's mast – all of which tend to draw attention to the text's visual look, its status as a visual object, rather than to its meaning. More important, by reframing the text in this manner, Greenaway acknowledges his desire to be faithful to it while dismantling its received monumentality and authority. The text of *The Tempest* emerges from the film less an immutable, inevitable artifact than the record of a self-directed imaginative performance that unfolds within time, open to chance and revision. In the opening sequence, Greenaway highlights this gap between monumental text and performative process by having Prospero experiment with the word "Boatswain," the first word of *The Tempest*, performing it as a kind of theatrical warm-up, savoring its sound to the delight of Ariel, and repeating it in different voices and different emotional registers. At the same time, we watch the word being written in Prospero's manuscript, and the juxtaposition draws our attention to the fact that its written form – "b-o-a-t-s-w-a-i-n" – does not capture how it is pronounced – "bo'sun" (see Barker 27 and Yacowar 694).

It might seem that the scenario of Prospero as author is designed to refashion *The Tempest* into something of an autotelic artifact, a work that leaves behind the problematic of Shakespearean authorship by, in effect, writing itself. In reality, however, this scenario simply complicates the question of authorship. Greenaway is, of course, manipulating the traditional identification of Prospero with Shakespeare, but he adds to it a third variable, our awareness of John Gielgud's stature as the last of the great triumvirate of "heroic" Shakespearean actors, one of the few capable of bringing off a performance of all the play's parts. The merging of author, character, and actor is deepened by our recognition that Gielgud, like Prospero and Shakespeare, is here giving a valedictory performance, playing a part with which his Shakespearean career has long been identified.[4] Indeed, some of Greenaway's iconographic choices seem calculated to recall past glories of Gielgud's career. Robert Tanitch notes, for example, that the *Times* critic said of Gielgud's 1930 performance as Prospero that he "looked like a Doge just stepped from the canvas of an Italian master"; that comparison is elaborated by Greenaway's allusion, through his costuming of Gielgud, to Giovanni Bellini's *Leonardo Loredan, Doge of Venice*. Similarly, Prospero's laughter in delight at his own creation early in the film recalls Gielgud's performance as the dying author Clive Langham in Alain Renais's *Providence* (1977) (Tanitch 22). By casting Gielgud as Shakespeare/Prospero and deepening the resonances of this triple identification, Greenaway manages to conflate virtuoso performing with the act of writing: at least within the fiction of *Prospero's Books*, Gielgud's performance becomes the source of *The Tempest*'s text, rather than that text the source of his performance. The overall scenario is designed, in sum, to deconstruct the text-performance nexus. It taps into the insight that performances tend to "textualize" the script, that is, fix its interpretive possibilities into one definitive shape, so that to all intents and purposes the actor becomes, for those who encounter the play first through him, the work's "author," the final arbiter of its meaning; equally, it recasts the text as a fossilized record of what amounts to a performance by the author, directed in his imagination to himself.[5]

Elaborating upon Prospero's passing references to the library allows Greenaway another means to refashion the textual Shakespeare. One by one he interjects into the narrative of *The Tempest* Prospero's library of twenty-four magical books, representing each as a source of the text we witness being written. In the film's opening sequence, for example, the Book of Water, a collection of Da Vinci's sketches of water, provides the source material for Prospero's magical tempest; Prospero's mention of his dead wife Susanna is prompted by his Alphabetical Inventory of the Dead; Gonzalo's famous set-speech outlining his ideal island commonweal, we observe, is culled from the Book of Utopias. Through such allusions Greenaway makes visible *The Tempest*'s intertextuality, its status as a collection of discourses culled from a variety of prior sources rather than a unified, freestanding artwork. This technique allows Greenaway to claim Shakespeare/Prospero as a precursor and warrant for his own postmodern bricolage aesthetic. Prospero's source texts are themselves not conventional books, but rather encyclopedic gatherings of imagery and lore on various topics, compendia of Renaissance discourses.[6] And because Prospero's books are collections primarily of images, not words, they allow Greenaway to reverse the priority of text to image he faces as a latter-day Shakespearean, confronted (as every Shakespearean director and actor are) with the task of making the text visible: in *Prospero's Books*, images, put into play in Prospero's magical imagination, are the source of the text, rather than the text the source of the image. As Prospero's books are revealed to us, they change from inert textual objects into magically animated pictures, melding the qualities of cinema and book to produce a third form. Their illustrations spring to life as we watch; the Book of Motion, literally a collection of moving pictures, will not sit still on the bookshelf, and the Book of Colours features a spectrum of shades that transmute before the eye. As if to underline this hybridity, several of the books feature moving images that allude to Muybridge's experiments with taking still photos and converting them into movies. In fact, at every opportunity Greenaway makes books move and thus transcend their status as fixed objects. The opening tempest, for instance, is imaged as a rain of pages in Prospero's library, an image that literally dismantles the book in order to make it into a cinematic metaphor for the storm. That Prospero's library numbers twenty-four volumes is itself significant, for, Greenaway helpfully glosses (Tran 24 and Turman 107), twenty-four alludes to the number of frames per second that constitute moving pictures. Prospero's "books," "textual" collections of images that become cinematically animated, provide the model for the kind of hybrid Shakespearean "text" Greenaway seeks to produce in this film. After all, the book of *The Tempest* we witness being written joins the other works in Prospero's library in the final reel, and the very process of production from Prospero's books allows filmic "texts" to become the sources for *The Tempest*, rather than the other way around.

Perhaps most important, in a number of provocative ways Greenaway stresses the "bodily" – i.e., non-textual – medium of the performance text Prospero creates. *Prospero's Books* relentlessly draws our attention to performers' bodies;[7] it converts Shakespearean narrative into non-narrative, non-verbal bodily forms, into mime, acrobatics, static live tableaux, masque-like processionals, hyper-theatrical costuming, and abstract dance movement, in what amounts to a survey of bodily performance arts. The effect is magnified by virtue of the fact that the production recasts the ratio between spoken text and visual spectacle in favor of the latter. Caliban, for example, is portrayed by avant-garde dancer Michael Clarke entirely in terms of lithe and manic dance, his carnal nature indicated by his red and grotesquely swollen phallus; Greenaway's casting of Clarke appropriates the dancer's notoriously subversive relationship to the conservative world of the Royal Ballet, where he trained ("Trying *The Tempest*"). Ariel's actions are performed by three different actors of differing ages, a gesture that draws our attention to the relationship of character to its bodily representation, an allusion and homage to a technique of avant-garde cinema (Phelan 48). Even the preposterous costumes of Alonso's royal party, with elaborate black doublets, ruffs the size of cartwheels, and corkheeled shoes with puffball tassels – costumes that severely inhibit the actors' ability to move – effectively convey their enervated overcivilization. In fact Greenaway pushes the limits of his technique by using even bodily excretions for expressive purposes. Caliban shits, pisses, and vomits on books, and the opening tempest is conjured, memorably enough, by Ariel's urinating on a model ship.

What has drawn the most critical fire has been the production's nudity, a prominent feature in Greenaway's recent work – nearly all of Prospero's army of magical spirits are unclothed, a choice that the beleaguered Greenaway has defended in interviews as a homage to the idealized nude body of Renaissance art. Yet Greenaway's own remarks about nudity suggest that more than a mere homage is at work, particularly since many of the bodies Greenaway puts on display are pointedly *un*ideal. Nudity in

Shakespearean productions, at least from a cursory survey of major productions of the last decade, has tended to be in the service of rather specific themes: sexuality (almost exclusively female sexuality), with Lady Macbeth, Cressida and Titania as prominent examples; and vulnerability, with Lady Macbeth (in her mad scene), Desdemona, Lear, the Fool, and Edgar as memorable instances. *Prospero's Books* stands as a notable exception. Its bodies are patently *not* in the service of thematics, a fact that explains why many have labeled the production's nudity gratuitous. Yet the controversy over this element of Greenaway's production reveals, I think, much about Shakespeare's status as a classic *text.* Nudity in Shakespeare, as a particularly insistent case of theatrical embodiedness, seems to many not merely a violation of decorum but an assertion of physical presence on the actor's part that can be justified only with a narrow and very special thematic warrant from the text.[8] Greenaway has pointed out that cinema (and, we might add, theatre)

> usually uses people as personalities rather than bodies. You do see a lot of naked people but usually to reveal something about sexuality . . . I want to see the physicality of an actor, the size, the bulk, the shadow they cast on the wall. (Greenaway, in Pally, "Cinema" 47)[9]

Thus his interest in nudity in this production is not thematic or prurient, but formal, that is, in the physical body as a medium: in *Prospero's Books* the nude body becomes a formal element that, by its very insistence upon the bodiliness of the performer, forcefully counters Shakespeare's textual-ness even as it transmits the text's meaning. Branagh uses brief nudity in much the same way in the opening sequence of *Much Ado,* as yet another early signal of his film's movement away from bookishness toward embodiment; it is less troubling because Branagh gives it a thin veneer of thematic motivation. In the case of *Prospero's Books,* it is noteworthy that most of the nudity is confined to Prospero's spirits, the bodily media of his art, through whom he imagines his text and performs his magic. (The exception, the brief nudity of the royal party and Ferdinand after the tempest, is deployed far more conventionally to indicate their physical vulnerability to the storm.) Like books, nude bodies are never far out of the frame, and they serve the same purpose as the often shocking images to which Greenaway gravitates: to try to give the cinematic image the physical immediacy of live theatre, to overcome the text-like two-dimensionality of the screen.

Nevertheless, even in the case of nudity, Greenaway points as much to the link between body and book as to their differences. When Prospero imagines Antonio's *coup d'état,* he sees two conjoined waves of destruction, one of bloody bodies, the other of books. Throughout the film the pages of Prospero's books are filled with images of nude bodies, hovering between two- and three-dimensionality, moving pictures and static icons. In fact the title credit for the movie is projected over a giant book out of whose pages spring real people who slide down the book's spine. By merging the qualities of texts and physical bodies, words and things, Greenaway takes every opportunity to complicate the nature of Prospero's books. As we watch the Bestiary of Past, Present and Future Animals, for example, printed images of animals become real animals; the Book of Earth associated with Caliban is, we are told, "impregnated with the minerals, acids, alkalis, gums, balms, and aphrodisiacs of the earth"; and Prospero's herbal, stuffed with actual plants, is a haven for real insects and fills the air with milkweed. This undecidability points to an ambivalence typical of Greenaway's *oeuvre.* He is, on the one hand, repulsed by the frailty of the human body and attracted to the ideal order of canonical art, its formal beauties, significance, and seeming permanence; yet, on the other hand, he is unconvinced that art offers anything more than a comforting illusion that does not correspond to an enigmatic, brutal reality. At the climax of Prospero's opening monologue, where he seems to retreat into the world of books out of grief for his wife's death, we learn of Vesalius's lost "Anatomy of Birth" whose "descriptive drawings of the human body . . . move and throb and bleed" when its pages are turned: "It is a banned book that queries the unnecessary processes of aging, bemoans the wastages associated with progeneration, condemns the pains and anxieties of childbirth, and generally questions the efficiency of God." This book, more than any other of Prospero's, seems to articulate the pathos of the evanescent human body, and Greenaway underlines that pathos with the image of Prospero's wife Susanna who, like some living version of a Renaissance anatomical drawing, peels away her skin to reveal her viscera, an image he follows with that of her face beneath a death shroud. The body's vulnerability and evanescence, Greenaway seems to suggest, demands an act of preservation that only an artistic work can provide. Yet the Shakespearean text, he suggests by his focus on the *act* of writing and imagining, is false to the very bodily processes that bring it into being. It is cinema, as an enduring record of the bodily process of creation, a hybrid of body and book, that serves as Greenaway's substitute for both.

The opening sequence of *Prospero's Books,* like that of Olivier's *Henry V,* functions as a sophisticated, if elliptical, prologue to the concerns of the work as a whole. The first image of the film, repeated several times, is a close-up of a water drop, an allusion to Harold Edgerton's famous strobe studies of water in motion (Collins and Collins 54). Throughout this opening sequence water – the basic material of the tempest – and film are metaphorically linked by virtue of the fact that both are fluid media, and in the case of water drops, ephemeral.[10] By means of overlaid images, Greenaway builds up metonymic equivalences between the cinematic medium, water, and the process of writing (linked by Prospero's watery blue ink). These links converge in the first book in Prospero's library, the Book of Water, itself an exemplar of the kind of fluid, filmic text Greenaway is laboring to create. A volume of drawings that seek to capture the motion of water in still pen and ink images, the Book of Water transforms before our eyes into a genuine moving image of water. (Indeed, the repeated command "bestir, bestir" in this opening sequence seems to address the images in the book as much as the doomed mariners.) A traveling shot reveals Prospero in a stylized bathhouse, his hand upraised to catch falling drops of water as an open book is superimposed. In a fleeting metaphor for Greenaway's own poise between text and performance, Prospero raises one hand to declaim his lines and to catch the water, while he rests his other hand on an open text. By doing so, Prospero himself becomes the medium in which text, performance, and water intersect. Prospero's experiments with "Boatswain" usher in a textual fugue on the play's opening lines, as Ariel magically invokes the storm by urinating on a model ship. Besides being an elaborate visual pun on "making water," and perhaps a comment on the almost puerile pleasure Prospero initially takes in his revenge, this pissing passage also offers wry commentary on the film's relation to Shakespearean textuality, for Ariel's water also falls on the antique text. The equation of Ariel's desecration of the book with Greenaway's as Shakespearean filmmaker becomes clearer when Greenaway flashes his directorial credit over an image of Ariel's pissing. As Ariel, so Greenaway: he embraces the violence his adaptation does to traditional textual authority as the necessary precondition for making his own cinematic "book of water."

In *The Tempest* Prospero famously vows to "drown my book" (5.1.57), an act which, unlike the breaking of his staff, most productions do not stage. Given Greenaway's interest in the Shakespearean book, it is fitting that he should elect to make Prospero's fulfillment of that promise his climax. Prospero's fifth-act revelations to Alonso and company prepare for that moment. As Prospero reveals himself, newly dressed in ruff and doublet, we hear the characters speak in their own voices for the first time, as if Prospero is also ceding his control as author by entering history, becoming one character among many. This change is marked by Gonzalo's summary of the plot in 5.1.208–13, the text scrolling across the screen in gold script as he utters the words. Certainly this image literalizes Gonzalo's wish to set down the "common joy" "With gold on lasting pillars" (5.1.208), but the gold letters are recognizably in the typeface of the First Folio: we are watching the passage of Prospero's book from a bodily process of writing into a published, public artistic monument, and with it comes Prospero's authorial (self-)dispossession. As if to underline the point, Greenaway handles the breaking of Prospero's staff as the breaking of his quill, an act accompanied by images of the closing of his books.

This sequence paves the way for Prospero's spectacular drowning of his library, each book of which is tossed into the sea which consumes it in a tempest of images. The last two volumes, revealed only in this sequence, are the most precious to those who treasure the Shakespearean text. The first is Shakespeare's First Folio, identified by the initials W. S. and the Droeshout portrait but, tellingly, not by Shakespeare's name. In an instructive bit of business, Prospero's hand lingers over Jonson's prefatory poem that asks us to "looke / Not on his Picture, but his Booke." This particular folio has only thirty-five plays, with nineteen pages left blank at the front of the book, for the inclusion of the thirty-sixth. And the second book is that thirty-sixth text, the copy of *The Tempest* we watched being written during the course of the film. That text is also, we might note, that most authoritative, desired, and unavailable of artifacts, a Shakespearean holograph, the editor's dream of an ideal text fresh from the authenticating pen of the Bard himself, unsullied by the intervening hands of actors or copysetters. Both of these books Prospero tosses into the sea – a gesture directed as much against notions of textual purity or authenticity as against Prospero's relinquishment of magic. Yet the books are not wholly lost: they are retrieved by the barbaric man-fish Caliban, here a wry surrogate for the *enfant terrible* director himself. In Greenaway's hands, Prospero's act of destroying his text only authorizes the film director's cinematic appropriation of it. "Textual" transmission, thematized early in the film by a long traveling shot of an antique tome passed hand to hand between various creatures and ending with Greenaway's directorial credit, can now pass to the creature of the water, to a desecrater of books who nevertheless saves them from oblivion.

By stuffing every frame with allusive visual references, by overlaying and recombining images using high-definition television and video paintbox technology, Greenaway offers the visual equivalent of what Harry Berger Jr. claims is our aural experience of the Shakespearean text:

> when Shakespeare is staged and you hear his language at performance tempo you are always haunted by the sense that you are receiving more information than you can process, and you wish you could slow the tempo down or have passages repeated or reach for a text.
>
> ("Bodies" 146)

The frustration of trying to take in so overwhelming an experience has shaped the film's reception. For Greenaway demonstrates that in an age of videotape, one cannot speak of any simple triumph of the performative or cinematic over Shakespearean textuality. This adaptation demands to be pored over and explicated in detail as I have just done – to be given the kind of reading, as exasperated reviewers noted, possible only with the pause and rewind buttons of a VCR (see Ebert E3). In the end, Greenaway's film is itself destined to become a cinematic "text," to be "read" according to interpretive protocols of close reading and with many of the same assumptions about "textual" monumentality. Greenaway anticipates this irony with his film's enigmatic ending. After Prospero/Gielgud begs us to set him free, the frame shrinking around him, we witness the applause of a recognizably Renaissance audience, an emblem of the historical moment of the work's "original" production. Through this audience bursts Ariel, who runs toward the viewer as if to burst through the screen into the viewer's world. Throughout the film Ariel has been the symbol and agent of Prospero's artistic process, and his sprint toward us, getting progressively younger as he runs, memorably captures the work's impulse to break free from its "original" moment of production. But Greenaway is sly in representing that impulse's ironies. As Ariel moves toward us, the screen-image flattens from three to two dimensions, and as the child Ariel seems to leap toward us, as if out of the screen and into our arms, he leaps literally upward and out of what has now become a screen-page, to leave the viewer with the final image of the film, a palimpsestic sheet of parchment, looking vaguely like a Renaissance map faded by contact with water, with just a hint of half-discernible animated graffiti. The price of surviving its historical moment is that the film must itself become a book, one from which the magical agency of Ariel, Prospero's prime image-maker and performer, has been "set free."

Greenaway's acknowledgement of his *Tempest*'s passage from performance to text points, I believe, to what performance criticism, with the important exception of Harry Berger Jr. (*Imaginary* ix–xv, 3–42), has been slow to recognize about its own practice. For performance criticism has been enabled and sustained, in ways it has not fully acknowledged, not so much by a return to the theatre as by a revolution in the Shakespearean medium. As Samuel Crowl observes, serious critical attention to performative differences, particularly in our teaching, arose at the same time as 16mm prints of Shakespearean films became available in the 1960s (3–4). The availability of videotape technology a decade later has made performance studies widely possible, even dominant within the discipline, allowing us to pore over and compare performances as never before. Yet even as these media have democratized access to performances, they have also shaped our sense of them. Video and film have encouraged us to assimilate those performances to the condition of texts, stable artifacts rather than contingent, unstable, ephemeral experiences.[11] (For all its faults, the BBC Shakespeare series was forward-looking at least in its recognition of the "canonizing" power of the videocassette; the credits that roll at the first of these videos, in Renaissance typeface with head- and tail-pieces on handmade paper, identify their "textualizing" intent, their status as substitutes for the canonical Shakespearean "text," not a challenge to the power of its textual authority.) Even as we have hailed the death of the monolithic text in favor of performative variants, the technological apparatus that has encouraged this theoretical revolution – the VCR – has been subtly re-establishing, at another level, a new monolithic and stable "text" – the ideal performance, recorded on tape, edited and reshaped in post-production, available for re-viewing. If the central insight of performance criticism is that performance is radically contingent, open to historical and material pressures that may not outlast a performance (or even an act), the stability of the records from which we work may be false to the very historicity performance criticism seeks to address. The run of a play is marked by night-to-night differences that spring from chance, design, and serendipity, differences that certainly shape reception and potentially reveal much about the performance process; yet the typical records of performance – promptbooks, set models, photographs, videotapes – tend to elide those differences, encouraging us instead to think of a given production as a self-consistent "text." Video does not capture the horizon of anxiety that live actor and audience share, the possibility that lines might be forgotten or mangled, props fall apart or become misplaced, cues missed, the anxiety that mundane material contingency may mar the performance. It thereby robs a live performance of some of its power, the sense that a potentially unpredictable situation has been made almost heroically to conform to an actor's bodily will. As the dominant medium through which we have come to study Shakespearean performance, the "videotext" may encourage us to elide the very historicity and materiality we have sought to recover with the return to performance.

Prospero's Books thus is an instance of what we might call "immanent theory," an artifact meditating on the theoretical grounds of its own existence. Greenaway himself has characterized his own work in film, painting, and literature as "an investigative procedure of approaching phenomenology on a very wide front" (Smith 55). As such, *Prospero's Books* draws our attention to the medium within which our experience of Shakespeare takes place, and the interpretive practices that medium prompts. Greenaway has been taken to task for his adaptation's lack of an explicit politics, his failure, for example, to take into account recent postcolonial critiques of *The Tempest.* It is certainly true that Greenaway's essential interest is in the relationship between the artist and his representational apparatus (Phelan 48–9). But that interest points, I think, to some of the ironies in our broadened sense of "text" in the wake of Roland Barthes, for the poststructuralist concept of "text" has enabled us to "read" "performances" but only at the expense of their phenomenological specificity. *Prospero's Books* confronts directly the issue of the Shakespearean medium, raising anew the crucial question of what forms the Shakespearean book and the cultural capital it represents can take in a post-literate age. By problematizing (though certainly not escaping from) the hegemony that Shakespearean textualism continues to hold over our critical imaginations, even in an age of electronic reproduction, Greenaway points performance criticism toward a double challenge: a fuller account of the relation of performance criticism to recording technologies, and the shaping of a practice more attentive to the mundane specificities of the media that render performance capable of study: painting, sculpture, record, tape, CD-ROM, videotape, telecast, film, stage performance, still photos, promptbooks, production notes, *and text*– the complex phenomenological palimpsest that inescapably constitutes our Shakespearean book.

NOTES

1 Orgel is, of course, not alone in construing the authorization of performative variation in this way. In his discussion of a "de-centered" performative Shakespeare, Waller notes that "today most Shakespeareans would recognize as unsatisfactory any criticism (or teaching) that dehistoricizes the Shakespearean script into a static monument," and he imagines the following scene as a kind of confirmation: "We recognize perhaps that even in his own age, each time Shakespeare himself saw one of his own plays performed, he would have seen it in a new guise, modified by factors over which he had no control" (20–1). Shakespeare's apparent lack of protest as his plays are modified in performance becomes the warrant for stage-centered criticism; the author's presence authorizes his own dispossession. And in carefully hedged terms and at the very moment she separates Shakespeare the man from "Shakespeare" the "on-going cultural activity," Marcus uses the metaphor of controlled dispersion to extend authorial intent to all manner of topical appropriations made of Shakespeare's work, particularly by dramatic companies and politically informed Renaissance readers: "Insofar as we have attempted to define the shadowy historical person behind the giant name, we have identified a playwright who used topicality not to limit, select, and shape his audiences in ideological terms but to disperse ideology prismatically so that his plays . . . would take on different colorations in different settings and times" (218).

2 Everything about this opening sequence stresses "authenticity": the playbill's typeface, layout, and (modified) old spelling, the play's extended title, the parchment paper on which it is printed, and the fact that the bill identifies the performance as *Henry V*'s 1600 premiere at the Globe. The title is clearly intended to echo the extended title of the 1600 quarto (though, for reasons of emphasis, Olivier omits the quarto's tag "Togither with Auntient/Pistoll"). Similarly "historically accurate" is the "aerial" shot following, a God's-eye view of Renaissance London reconstructed from C. J. de Visscher's 1616 engraving. Willson ("Opening" 1) argues that even the momentary dip of the camera toward the Hope before heading to the Globe alerts us that Olivier will not repeat the famous mistake of Wenceslas Hollar, who famously in his 1644 "Long View of London" engraving reverses the buildings' labels.

3 The best single discussion of Greenaway's cinematic work is Pally, "Order," though she does not discuss *Prospero's Books.* See also the defense of Greenaway's techniques and concerns by Baillon. For a useful survey of recent film adaptations of *The Tempest,* see Harlan Kennedy. His discussion of *Prospero's Books* suffers from too much reliance upon Greenaway's published screenplay, which does not coincide with the finished film, and Kennedy's misplaced emphases are picked up in Willson, "Recontextualizing." Over-reliance upon the screenplay also occasionally mars Phelan's and Yacowar's otherwise useful discussions of the film.

4 Gielgud has played Prospero in several of this century's more influential productions of *The Tempest*: Harcourt Williams's 1930 production at the Old Vic; George Devine and Marius Goring's 1940 production at the Old Vic; Peter

Brook's 1957 production at Stratford and Drury Lane; and Peter Hall's 1974 production at the National. See Gielgud 109–17.

5 The verb "textualize" is taken from Worthen 449. Set against the totality of performative possibilities offered by the written text, it is this tendency toward textualization, particularly marked in film, that troubles Belsey. For a rebuttal, compare Holderness.

6 In an interview with Pally, Greenaway claims that "works of art refer to great masses of culture, they are encyclopedic in nature . . . My movies are sections of this world encyclopedia. What I'm manipulating is our cultural illusions [*sic*] – all the very potent, meaning language of illusions [*sic*] that Western culture has" ("Cinema" 6). The "books" that constitute Prospero's library thus exemplify the "great masses of culture" to which artworks refer, and model the kind of encyclopedic density that characterizes Greenaway's own cinematic style.

7 A project shot at roughly the same time, *Les Drowned [sic] in the Seine*, takes this fascination with the body to its logical conclusion. Using detailed notes taken by morgue workers who documented drowning deaths in the Seine from 1795 to 1801, Greenaway memorializes the dead by panning repeatedly over the nude bodies of corpses (played by live actors) as a voiceover details the circumstances of their deaths. The film is nothing other than lavishly photographed dead bodies, and as the details of their lives and deaths are narrated, the facticity of the bodies comes increasingly to exceed the mass of detail marshaled to "explain" them. This ironizing technique, and the focus on the gap between rationally compiled "facts" and an uncanny bodily reality that eludes full explanation, is typical of Greenaway's earlier short films.

8 As Schechner suggests, in many ways nudity is the quintessence of theatre: "Although performing is not exhibitionism *per se*, there is in the theatre a strong will to display and to see: A show is, among everything else, a showing of the body" (91). For several of these points I am indebted to a lively discussion of these issues on the SHAKSPER discussion group on the INTERNET, from Thursday, 2 June 1994 to Saturday, 19 June 1994.

9 See also Turman 107. Greenaway's notoriety for nudity in his films began with the X rating awarded by the MPAA for *The Cook, The Thief, His Wife, and Her Lover*. The uproar created by that rating, along with a ratings controversy for *Henry and June*, eventually led to the creation of a new rating, NC-17. As if to test the limits, in *Prospero's Books* Greenaway insisted upon the nudity of the island spirits, nearly every member of the cast. Ironically, the extensive nudity led Greenaway's post-producing editing of the film in Japan at NHK studios to be done behind strictly closed doors: Japanese authorities regarded the film as pornographic (see Rodman). For a general discussion of the body-text opposition, see Berger, "Bodies."

10 When asked in an interview about water symbolism in his films, Greenaway commented, "on a practical level, water is fantastically photogenic" (Rodgers 15). In his notes for an exhibition entitled "Watching Water" mounted in Venice not long after *Prospero's Books* opened, Greenaway meditates at some length on water as a symbol in his work, often linking it with the very cinematic lighting effects he uses in the exhibition (an exhibition that, ironically enough, includes books from the movie). Indeed, by lighting the exhibition in such a way as to frustrate conventional ways of seeing the artifacts, by, for example, exhibiting artifacts under lights that flash off before the viewer has had a chance to fully peruse the work on display, Greenaway foregrounds how our expectations about the permanence and monumentality of artifacts are created by conventions of museum lighting. He interrogates those expectations by subjecting the viewer to what amounts to a fleeting cinematic experience of the

works on display, assimilating cinematic experience to exhibition experience. It is in that sense that the exhibition's title, "Watching Water," takes on special resonance. See Greenaway *Watching Water* 15 and 17.

11 The ways in which the physical records of performances shape our notions of performances and performance criticism has been cogently addressed by, for example, Dennis Kennedy 5–23; de Marinis; and the essayists collected in the opening section of *Shakespeare on Television.*

REFERENCES

Alleva, Richard. Review of *Prospero's Books. Commonweal* 119 (31 January 1991): 25–6.

Baillon, Jean-François. "Peter Greenaway: cinéma contre nature." *Études britanniques contemporaines* (April 1992): 75–87.

Barish, Jonas. *The Anti-Theatrical Prejudice.* Berkeley and Los Angeles: University of California Press, 1981.

Barker, Adam. "A Tale of Two Magicians." *Sight and Sound* ns 1 (May 1991): 26–30.

Barton, John. *Playing Shakespeare.* London: Methuen, 1984.

Belsey, Catherine. "Shakespeare and Film: A Question of Perspective." *Literature/Film Quarterly* 11: 3 (1983): 152–8.

Berger, Harry, Jr. "Bodies and Texts." *Representations* 17 (Winter 1987): 144–66.

—— *Imaginary Audition: Shakespeare on Stage and Page.* Berkeley and Los Angeles: University of California Press, 1989.

Bernard, Jami. Review of *Prospero's Books. New York Post* 15 November 1991: 31.

Berry, Cicely. *The Actor and His Text.* New York: Scribner's, 1987.

Branagh, Kenneth, dir. *Henry V.* Samuel Goldwyn and Renaissance Films, 1989; Videocassette, CBS/Fox Video, 1990.

—— *Much Ado About Nothing.* Samuel Goldwyn and Renaissance Films, 1993; Videocassette, Columbia Tristar Home Video, 1993.

Bristol, Michael. "Editing the Text: The Deuteronomic Reconstruction of Authority." *Shakespeare's America/America's Shakespeare.* New York: Routledge, 1990. 91–119.

Brown, Georgia. Review of *Prospero's Books. Village Voice* 16 November 1991: 61.

Collick, John. *Shakespeare, Cinema and Society.* Manchester: Manchester University Press, 1989.

Collins, Amy Fine and Brad Collins. "Drowning the Text." *Art in America* 80 (June 1992): 53–5.

Coursen, H. R. "'Tis Nudity': Peter Greenaway's *Prospero's Books.*" *Watching Shakespeare on Television.* Rutherford, NJ: Fairleigh Dickinson University Press, 1993. 163–76.

Crowl, Samuel. *Shakespeare Observed: Studies in Performance on Stage and Screen.* Athens: Ohio University Press, 1992.

de Marinis, Marco. "'A Faithful Betrayal of Performance': Notes on the Use of Video in Theatre." *New Theatre Quarterly* 1 (1985): 383–9.

Dillon, Janette. "Is There a Performance in this Text?" *Shakespeare Quarterly* 45 (Spring 1994): 74–86.

Donaldson, Peter S. *Shakespearean Films / Shakespearean Directors.* Boston: Unwin Hyman, 1990.

Ebert, Roger. "Director Works 'Magick' with Bard in 'Books.'" Review of *Prospero's Books. Chicago Sun-Times* 24 November 1991: E3.

Gielgud, John, with John Miller. *Acting Shakespeare.* New York: Scribner's, 1991.

Goldberg, Jonathan. "Textual Properties." *Shakespeare Quarterly* 37 (Summer 1986): 213–17.

Greenaway, Peter, dir. *Prospero's Books.* Miramax Films, 1991.
—— *Prospero's Books: A Film of Shakespeare's The Tempest.* New York: Four Walls Eight Windows, 1991.
—— *Watching Water.* Catalogue for the exhibition "Watching Water," a special project for the Venice Biennale 48th International Exhibition of Art. Milano, Italy: Electa, 1993.
Hapgood, Robert. *Shakespeare the Theatre-Poet.* Oxford: Clarendon Press, 1988.
Holderness, Graham. "Radical Potentiality and Institutional Closure: Shakespeare in Film and Television." *Political Shakespeare: New Essays in Cultural Materialism.* Ed. Jonathan Dollimore and Alan Sinfield. Ithaca, NY: Cornell University Press, 1985. 182–201.
Jarman, Derek, dir. *The Tempest.* British Film Institute/Boyd's Company, 1980.
Kennedy, Dennis. *Looking at Shakespeare: A Visual History of Twentieth-Century Performance.* Cambridge: Cambridge University Press, 1993.
Kennedy, Harlan. "Prospero's Flicks." *Film Comment* 28: 1 (January–February 1992): 45–9.
Levin, Richard. "Performance-Critics *vs.* Close Readers in the Study of English Renaissance Drama." *Modern Language Review* 81 (1986): 545–59.
Marcus, Leah S. *Puzzling Shakespeare: Local Reading and Its Discontents.* Berkeley and Los Angeles: University of California Press, 1988.
Nadotti, Maria. "Exits and Entrances: On Two Tempests." *Artforum* 30 (December 1991): 20–1.
Olivier, Laurence, dir. *Henry V.* Two Cities, 1944; Videocassette, Tamarelle's International Films, 1980.
Orgel, Stephen. "The Authentic Shakespeare." *Representations* 21 (1988): 5–25.
—— "What is a Text?" *Research Opportunities in Renaissance Drama* 24 (1981): 3–6. Rpt. *Staging the Renaissance: Reinterpretations of Elizabethan and Jacobean Drama.* Ed. David Scott Kastan and Peter Stallybrass. New York: Routledge, 1991. 83–7.
Pally, Marcia. "Cinema as a Total Art Form: An Interview with Peter Greenaway." *Cineaste* 18: 3 (1991): 6–11.
—— "Order versus Chaos: The Films of Peter Greenaway." *Cineaste* 18: 3 (1991): 3–5, 37.
"Peter Greenaway." *Current Biography Yearbook* 52 (1991): 253–8.
Phelan, Peggy. "Numbering Prospero's Books." *Performance Arts Journal* 41 (1992): 43–9.
Rayns, Tony. "Peter Greenaway." *American Cinematographer* 64 (September 1983): 46.
Rodgers, Marlene. "*Prospero's Books* – Word and Spectacle: An Interview with Peter Greenaway." *Film Quarterly* 45 (Winter 1991–2): 11–19.
Rodman, Howard A. "Anatomy of a Wizard." *American Film* 16 (November/December 1991): 34–9.
Rothwell, Kenneth S. and Annabelle Henkin Melzer. "Representing *King Lear* on Screen: From Metatheatre to 'Meta-cinema.'" *Shakespeare Survey* 39 (1987): 75–90.
—— *Shakespeare on Screen: An International Filmography and Videography.* New York: Neal-Schuman Publishers, 1990.
Schechner, Richard. "Nakedness." *Environmental Theater.* New York: Hawthorn Books, 1973.
Shakespeare on Television. Ed. J. C. Bulman and H. R. Coursen. Hanover: University Press of New England, 1988.
Smith, Gavin. "Food for Thought." *Film Comment* 26 (1990): 54–6.
Tanitch, Robert. "Look on Prospero." *Plays and Players* 453 (November 1991): 22–3.
Tran, Dylan. "The Book, the Theater, the Film and Peter Greenaway: An Interview." *High Performance* 14 (Winter 1991): 22–5.

"Trying *The Tempest.*" *New Dance Review* 4: 2 (October 1991): 20–1.

Turan, Kenneth. Review of *Prospero's Books. Los Angeles Times* 27 November 1991: Calendar 1.

Turman, Suzanna. "Peter Greenaway." *Films in Review* 43 (March/April 1992): 104–8.

Waller, Gary. "Decentering the Bard: The BBC-TV Shakespeare and Some Implications for Criticism and Teaching." *Shakespeare on Television.* Ed. J. C. Bulman and H. R. Coursen. Hanover: University Press of New England, 1988.18–30.

Willson, Robert F., Jr. "The Opening of *Henry V*: Olivier's Visual Pun." *Shakespeare on Film Newsletter* 5: 2 (May 1981): 1–2.

—— "Recontextualizing Shakespeare on Film: *My Private Idaho, Men of Respect, Prospero's Books.*" *Shakespeare Bulletin* 10: 5 (Summer 1992): 34–7.

Worthen, William. "Deeper Meanings and Theatrical Technique: The Rhetoric of Performance Criticism." *Shakespeare Quarterly* 40 (1989): 441–55.

Yacowar, Maurice "Negotiating Culture: Greenaway's *Tempest.*" *Queen's Quarterly* 99: 3 (Fall 1992): 689–96.

NOTES ON CONTRIBUTORS

James C. Bulman is Professor of English and Dean of the College at Allegheny College, Pennsylvania. General editor of the Shakespeare in Performance series for Manchester University Press, he has written books on the stage history of *The Merchant of Venice* (1991) and *The Heroic Idiom of Shakespearean Tragedy* (1985), and co-edited volumes on *Comedy from Shakespeare to Sheridan* (1986) and *Shakespeare on Television* (1988). He is currently editing *Henry IV, Part Two* for the new Arden Shakespeare (Routledge).

Anthony B. Dawson, Professor of English and Theatre at the University of British Columbia, has written three books: *Indirections: Shakespeare and the Art of Illusion* (1978), *Watching Shakespeare* (1988), and, most recently, *Hamlet* (1995) for the Manchester Shakespeare in Performance series. He has also published a number of articles relating to Shakespeare and literary and performance theory, and is currently preparing the New Mermaid edition of Marlowe's *Tamburlaine I and II.*

Juliet Dusinberre is a Fellow of Girton College, Cambridge. Her book on *Shakespeare and the Nature of Women* (1975), which initiated debates on the boy actor and gender in Shakespeare's theatre, appears in 1995 in a new edition, alongside a Japanese-language edition. She has published essays on different aspects of Shakespeare and performance in *Shakespeare Survey* and *Studies in the Literary Imagination,* and is currently editing *As You Like It* for the new Arden Shakespeare (Routledge).

Barbara Hodgdon, Ellis and Nelle Levitt Professor of English at Drake University, Iowa, is the author of *The End Crowns All: Closure and Contradiction in Shakespeare's History* (1991) and *Henry IV, Part Two* (1993) for the Manchester Shakespeare in Performance series. She is currently completing a book on performances called *Restaging Shakespeare's Cultural Capital: Women, Queens, Spectatorship*, and, in addition, is editing *The Taming of the Shrew* for the new Arden Shakespeare (Routledge).

Dennis Kennedy moved in 1995 from the University of Pittsburgh to Trinity College, Dublin, where he occupies the Samuel Beckett Chair of Drama and Theatre Studies. His books include *Looking at Shakespeare: A Visual History of Twentieth-Century Performance* (1993), *Foreign Shakespeare* (1993), and *Granville Barker and the Dream of Theatre* (1985), which won the George Freedley Award for theatre history. General editor of Pittsburgh Studies in Theatre and Culture, he is also a playwright and professional dramaturg.

Richard Paul Knowles is Chair of the Drama Department at the University of Guelph, Ontario. He has published essays on Shakespeare and on Canadian theatre in a variety of books and periodicals, and he writes and directs for the professional theatre in Canada. Currently he is at work on a book entitled *The Theatre of Form and the Production of Meaning: Contemporary Canadian Dramaturgies.*

Douglas Lanier, Associate Professor of English at the University of New Hampshire, has published articles on Shakespeare, Marston, Jonson, and Milton, and has recently completed a book entitled *"Better Markes": Ben Jonson and the Institution of Authorship.* In addition to a book-length study of literary pleasure in the Renaissance, he is currently writing about representations of Shakespeare and Shakespeareana in contemporary popular culture.

Cary M. Mazer is Associate Professor of English and Chair of the Theatre Arts Program at the University of Pennsylvania. He is author of *Shakespeare Refashioned: Elizabethan Plays on Edwardian Stages* (1981), and various articles on Shakespeare in performance, Shakespearean production history, and Victorian and Edwardian theatre. A former officer of the American Society for Theatre Research, he is also a theatre critic and dramaturg.

Laurie E. Osborne, Associate Professor of English at Colby College, Maine, has published *Twelfe Night, or what you will (F 1623)* for the Shakespearean Originals series (Harvester 1995), and her book on *The Textual Erotics of "Twelfth Night": Cultural History and the Performance Edition* is forthcoming from the University of Iowa Press in the series on Theatre History and Culture. She has also published essays on Shakespearean film and the Renaissance female audience.

Denis Salter, Associate Professor in English and Theatre at McGill University, has published widely on Canadian/Québécois theatre, Victorian theatre history, Shakespeare in performance, and postcolonial history. A past president of the Association for Canadian Theatre History/Association d'histoire théâtre au Canada, he is currently researching key words in Canadian theatre historiography, with an emphasis on Shakespeare and the idea of nation.

W. B. Worthen, Professor of English and Theatre at Northwestern University, is the author of *The Idea of the Actor: Drama and the Ethics of*

Performance (1984), *Modern Drama and the Rhetoric of Theatre* (1992), and a variety of articles on modern drama, dramatic and performance theory, and Shakespearean performance. The editor of two drama anthologies for Harcourt Brace and past editor of *Theatre Journal*, he is currently writing a book with the tentative title *Shakespeare, Authority, and Performance.*

INDEX